THE AA GUIDE TO

The Cotswolds

WITH OXFORD
& STRATFORD-UPON-AVON

About the author

Damian Hall is a freelance outdoor journalist who grew up in the hilly mill town of Nailsworth. He went to school in Stroud and Gloucester, and as a student sold ice creams on Minchinhampton Common. But he didn't think much to the Cotswolds when young because they didn't have any good football teams and Radiohead never played there.

He went travelling and lived in a much hotter country long enough to earn a passport. Yet when time came to settle down the hillbilly came back to the Cotswolds, where he now lives with his wife, daughter, a small soft spot for Forest Green Rovers and a large gooey spot for blustery walks along the glorious limestone Edge.

He contributes regularly to *Country Walking* and *Outdoor Fitness*, and his books include *Walking In The Cotswolds*, *Somerset Coast Path* and the official *Pennine Way* National Trail guide. Anyone interested in guided walks should get in touch via www.damianhall.info.

Published by AA Publishing (a trading name of AA Media Limited, whose registered office is Fanum House, Basing View, Basingstoke, Hampshire RG21 4EA; registered number 06112600)

First published 2014
Second edition 2016

Maps contain data from openstreetmap.org

A CIP catalogue record for this book is available from the British Library.

ISBN: 978-0-7495-7760-5
ISBN (SS): 978-0-7495-7631-8

Cartography provided by the Mapping Services Department of AA Publishing.

Printed and bound in Italy by Printer Trento Srl.

A05342

THE AA GUIDE TO

The Cotswolds

WITH OXFORD
& STRATFORD-UPON-AVON

YOUR TRUSTED GUIDE

CONTENTS

- USING THIS GUIDE 6
- INTRODUCTION 8
- TOP ATTRACTIONS 12
- HISTORY OF THE COTSWOLDS 16
- BACK TO NATURE 22
- LORE OF THE LAND 27
- WALKING IN THE COTSWOLDS 31
- LAURIE LEE: LOTHARIO, BARFLY, AUTHOR 35

- THE COTSWOLDS AT WAR 39
- LOCAL SPECIALITIES 44
- BEFORE YOU GO 47
- FESTIVALS & EVENTS 54
- CAMPSITES 56
- A–Z OF THE COTSWOLDS 58
- ATLAS 256
- INDEX 264

USING THIS GUIDE

Introduction – has plenty of fascinating background reading, including articles on the landscape and local mythology.

Top attractions – pick out the very best places to visit in the area. You'll spot these later in the A–Z by the flashes of yellow.

Before you go – tells you the things to read, watch, know and pack to get the most from your trip.

Campsites – recommends a number of caravan sites and campsites, which carry the AA's Pennant rating, with the very best receiving the coveted gold Pennant award. Visit theAA.com/self-catering-and-campsites and theAA.com/bed-and-breakfast-and-hotel for more places to stay.

A–Z of The Cotswolds – lists all the best of the region, with recommended attractions, activities and places to eat or drink. Places Nearby lists more to see and do.

Eat and drink – contains restaurants that carry an AA Rosette rating, which acknowledges the very best in cooking. Pubs have been selected for their great atmosphere and good food. Visit theAA.com/restaurant-and-pub for more food and drink suggestions.

Index – gives you the option to search by theme, grouping the same type of place together, or alphabetically.

Atlas – will help you find your way around, as every main location has a map reference, as will the town plans throughout the book.

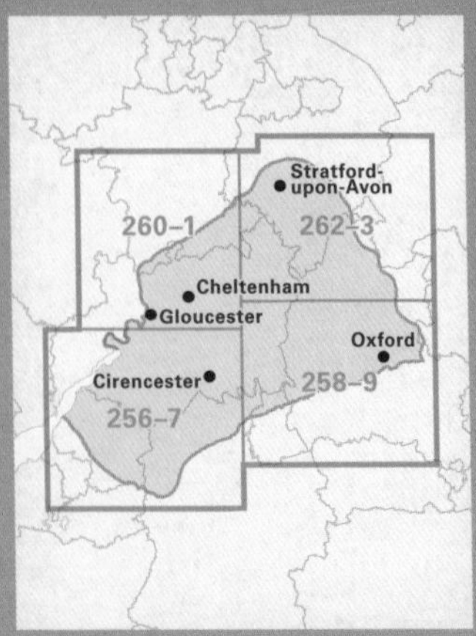

STAFFORDSHIRE
STAFFORD
BURTON UPON TRENT
Loughborough
Newport
Rugeley
CANNOCK
M6 Toll
Lichfield
TELFORD
M54
LEICESTER
TAMWORTH
WOLVERHAMPTON
WALSALL
Bridgnorth
NUNEATON
DUDLEY
SHROPSHIRE
BIRMINGHAM
COVENTRY
KIDDERMINSTER
RUGBY
Bromsgrove
ROYAL LEAMINGTON SPA
WORCESTERSHIRE
REDDITCH
Warwick
Daventry
Stratford-upon-Avon
WORCESTER
WARWICKSHIRE
NHANTS
Great Malvern
HEREFORDSHIRE
Evesham
Banbury
Brackley
Ledbury
Tewkesbury
Stow-on-the-Wold
Chipping Norton
GLOUCESTERSHIRE
CHELTENHAM
Bicester
Ross-on-Wye
GLOUCESTER
OXFORDSHIRE
COTSWOLDS
Witney
Burford
Stroud
OXFORD
Cirencester
Abingdon-on-Thames
Chepstow
Wantage
SWINDON
BRISTOL
Chippenham
WEST BERKSHIRE
Marlborough
Newbury
BATH
Devizes
Trowbridge
Frome
WILTSHIRE
BASINGSTOKE
Andover
Warminster
SOMERSET
HAMPSHIRE
Winchester
Wincanton
Salisbury
Romsey
Shaftesbury
EASTLEIGH
Yeovil
DORSET
SOUTHAMPTON
Blandford Forum
0 10 miles
0 10 20 kilometres

INTRODUCTION

You'll like the Cotswolds. Almost everyone does. If the region was an animal, it would be a plump, fluffy cat, purring contentedly by a pub fireplace. Despite the Cotswolds being the UK's second largest protected landscape (after the Lake District) and the largest Area of Outstanding Natural Beauty in England and Wales, so much of it feels cosy, comfortable, contented and just sort of...right.

There's something implicitly reassuring and irresistibly pleasing about the unapologetic idyll of syrupy villages tucked into lush curvy combes. Influential 20th-century novelist J B Priestley called the region 'the most English of all our countrysides'. A visit to the Cotswolds is likely to leave you feeling that everything is comfortingly right with the world (although you may feel the need to go to the gym after over-indulging on all that lip-smackingly fantastic nosh. Ignore it).

Most people come to the Cotswolds to experience the chocolate-box pretty villages: the centuries-old churches, cute cottages and dry-stone walls made of that oolitic limestone that glows so warmly in the sunshine, especially on a late

winter afternoon. And there are plenty of places to taste all that – both with and without the crowds. As a rule of thumb, if it begins with B it's probably very handsome but very popular.

However, if you concentrate only on that idea of the Cotswolds, you're missing out on what really makes the region special. Sure, rush around the manor houses, consume an infinite number of cream teas and 'accidentally' push other tourists into the river in order to take unobscured photos of Bourton-on-the-Water's five bridges. All that's well known and still worth experiencing. But make sure you leave time for what day-tours from London don't capture about the Cotswolds. The region's lesser-known corners offer a different sort of pleasure, should you make the effort to seek them out (see 10 hidden gems, page 67).

By that we mean the soaring views from the dramatic limestone Cotswold Edge that unravel for over 60 miles, into the moody mountains of Wales; the ruins of Roman villas with their extensive, intricate mosaics; all that fresh, healthy, locally produced, organic food enlivening the farmers' markets and local restaurants alike; ancient beech woodlands ablaze in autumn, or carpets of snowdrops in winter and bluebells in spring; thriving arts and crafts such as silversmithery and glass-making, folk music and storytelling; theatrically situated hill forts – the Cotswolds alone has 35 of them – Jurassic grasslands splashed with wildflowers, vivid orchids and flickering butterflies; that sense of timelessness found in villages that have remained much the same for centuries; real ale in cosy pubs; leisurely wanders in handsome historical towns and cities such as Oxford, Cheltenham, Cirencester and Stratford-upon-Avon; extraordinary abbeys, cathedrals and 'wool' churches; enigmatic stone circles, neolithic long barrows, round barrows, castles, shams, follies, manor houses and stately homes with blooming kaleidoscopic gardens that turn you into Alice in Wonderland; and the region's many ghost stories (or are they stories?). And let's not forget the Cotswolds' brilliant, idiosyncratic festivals, some of which include sports outrageously overlooked by the Olympics: chasing a cheese down a vertiginous hill, river football and, naturally, welly wanging.

The people here have a quirky sense of humour. But compellingly original events such as these say something vital about the Cotswolds – something that doesn't tend to make it into the tourist brochures. The region has a distinctive spirit that can be traced through the centuries. It's an ethos of seeing things through, of working hard to get things right, that plays out in a venerable craft tradition.

The skill of dry-stone walling, for example, has been kept alive in the Cotswolds for at least 5,500 years. The same technique found in the area's neolithic long barrows is still practised (and taught: see cotswoldsruralskills.org.uk) in the Cotswolds today. The region keeps its crafts alive in an era when so many other useful rural and wilderness skills have been lost to us.

When the Cotwolds' centuries-old wool industry finally declined, cloth production took its place – a genuine homespun – pun intended – industry based on local skills, ingenuity and an understanding of the natural world. Artist and social theorist William Morris moved the base of his Arts and Crafts Movement here in the 19th century, and that same philosophy is still flourishing today. It's no coincidence that the wonderful resurgence of farmers' markets is so strong here too, along with folk arts and other traditional aspects of British culture, such as storytelling. (And, yes, that includes Morris dancing, for better or worse.) Crucially all this is a celebration of local people supporting each other, of the old-fashioned concept of community lost elsewhere in the country, without it ever getting too *League Of Gentlemen*.

The Cotswolds isn't just a backdrop for tourist photos and faux-celebrity photoshoots. It's a real place, with real people, doing real things. And hopefully you'll see, enjoy and contribute to that too.

There's no firm agreement on the exact boundaries of the Cotswolds, but for this book we're reaching out to Oxford in the east, Gloucester in the west, Stratford-upon-Avon in the north and stopping just outside Bath in the south.

◀ Bliss Tweed Mill (previous page) ▼ Arlington Row, Bibury

TOP ATTRACTIONS

▲ Anne Hathaway's Cottage & Shakespeare's Birthplace

Shakespeare's wife once lived in a pretty thatched cottage on the very edge of Stratford (see page 204), and it stayed in the Hathaway family until the 19th century. Much of the original family furniture remains. About a mile and a half away is the house where the world's most famous playwright was born and grew up (see page 203). You might see a live performance in the back garden.

▼ Royal Shakespeare Company

Stratford's Royal Shakespeare Company (see page 207) is probably the best classical theatre company in the world. Since its foundation in 1879 pretty much every serious British actor has trod the boards in an RSC production. It's not just Shakespeare either; works by O'Neill, Hugo, Stoppard and more have been seen. You can book a tour round the theatres or do your best to get a ticket to a production; both worth thinking about ahead of time, obviously.

◂ Hidcote Manor Garden

Hidcote (see page 135) was created in the early 20th century, and is home to plants that were collected by the owner Lawrence Johnston from the Alps, Kenya, South Africa and others. There are plenty of varieties from the UK as well, so you'll get a comforting but disconcerting feeling of familiarity and the exotic.

▸ Cotswold Wildlife Park and Gardens

160 acres of landscaped zoological park, surrounding a Gothic-style manor house, with more than 260 different animal species (see page 81). Lions, leopards, white rhinos, red pandas, sloths, lemurs and giraffes are among the fun fauna in residence. If all the animal activity gets too much, there are also gardens with floral displays all year round.

◂ Pitt Rivers Museum

Don't miss eccentric, eclectic Pitt Rivers Museum (see page 168). Essentially one big room full of display cases, most artefacts have hand-written labels and are of an amazing range of both subject and ethnic origin. The shrunken heads are infamous, but there are also toys, canoes, religious items, weapons and even a witch in a bottle.

◂ Blenheim Palace

Blenheim (see page 250) is best known as the birthplace of oil-painting, cigar-chomping hero of WWII, Sir Winston Churchill, but its history goes back to the early 18th century. The Palace itself is frankly huge, with an amazing interior and 2,000 acres of grounds, partly landscaped by 'Capability' Brown. Expect to spend the day, but still not see it all.

▸ Birdland

Not to be confused with the New York City jazz club of the same name, this is an actual land of actual birds (see page 74), home to the only group of king penguins in England. There are also flamingos, pelicans, penguins, cranes, storks, waterfowl, parrots, falcons, pheasants, hornbills, touracos, pigeons, ibis and many more.

◂ Ashmolean Museum

Opened in 1683, the Ashmolean (see page 167) is the oldest museum in the country. It contains important art pieces and artefacts, from Ancient Greece to the 20th century. It's a perfect balance between the academic, the engaging and the entertaining – you'll find yourself getting educated without even noticing.

Westonbirt Arboretum

If there's somewhere more spectacular to see autumn colours, not just in the Cotswolds but in Britain, we'd sure like to know about it. An astonishing collection of some of the oldest, biggest, rarest and most magnificent trees in the world (see page 220). A sure-fire crowd-pleaser at any time of year.

Cotswold Motoring Museum & Toy Collection

As well as its collection of vintage and classic cars and various motoring curiosities (see page 73), this is also the home of Brum, star of his own BBC TV show. The museum hosts a variety of exhibitions, so there should be something to keep everyone entertained.

Sudeley Castle

Visited by Elizabeth I, Henry VIII and Anne Boleyn, home to Catherine Parr and refuge to Charles I during the Civil War, there's no shortage of historical heavyweights attached to Sudeley (see page 217). Today you can enjoy a fascinating wander round the rooms and get a glimpse of how the Tudor half lived. The grounds are impressive too.

HISTORY OF THE COTSWOLDS

In the admittedly fairly unlikely scenario that you're being threatened with nasty consequences unless you can sum up the history of the Cotswolds in one word, the word to remember is 'wool'.

Those honey-coloured villages may make you think progress is something that happens somewhere else, but the Cotswolds have played host to great industries, great cities and great wars. Great people have come from here too: war-winning prime ministers, famous poets, playwrights and writers. In fact considering how much history has happened in these hills and valleys, they've no right whatsoever to still look this damned good.

The first Cotswolders were mesolithic nomads who hunted and gathered some 10,000 years ago in what was then a heavily wooded region. Around 4000 BC, neolithic (or New Stone Age) man began to farm. Neolithic Cotswolders cleared much of the primeval forest to make room for their animals and crops. They also left us their long barrows – huge, mysterious tombs, such as Belas Knap, near Winchcombe, and Nympsfield Long Barrow, near Nailsworth.

Bronze Age residents (2000–650 BC) redecorated the place, building round barrows and stone circles such as the supposedly

◀ Footpath at Uley Bury

magical circle at Rollright in the northeast Cotswolds. It's nigh-on impossible to count the same number of Rollright Stones twice in a row, which might lead you to think that the stones pop up and down behind your back through concealed trapdoors just to torment you. They also started building farming terraces called strip lynchets, and liked them so much they continued on until the early medieval period. You can see the remains of these around the region today.

The Iron Age (800 BC to Roman occupation) saw waves of Celts settle in what would become the United Kingdom. The newcomers built some 35 hill forts in the Cotswolds, most notably at Uley Bury (the most theatrically positioned), Painswick Beacon (the most dramatic), Crickley Hill (which has the most history) and Haresfield Beacon. During this period Cotswolders preferred to live on the hilltops, but in all other times the area's people built their settlements below the escarpment, in the valleys and combes (presumably because it's a bit less windy when you're nestled into a hillside).

Romans built Cirencester, Gloucester and Bath, the 182-mile Fosse Way (which travels right through the Cotswolds, running from Exeter to Lincoln – one section is now the A429), and lavish, mosaic-floored villas such as Chedworth and Great Witcombe. Cirencester, or rather *Corinium*, became the second largest city in Britain and a centre of a new trade: wool. The Romans discovered that while the well-drained Cotswolds hills, with their thin top-soil, were passable (if unspectacular) for crop-growing, they provided excellent pasture for woolly things. Thus began the region's legacy of large-scale sheep farming.

When the Romans all ran off home, the Saxons – for the nitpicky, the name covers several Germanic tribes – jumped in, and the Dark Ages ensued. The Saxons made little Winchcombe the capital of the not-inconsiderable kingdom of Mercia, and it's likely the phrase 'Cot's Wold' comes from this period. At the time, sheep were grazed in large 'cots' or enclosures on the wolds, around what's now Cutsdean in the north Cotswolds. A literal Anglo-Saxon translation of Cotswolds gives us 'sheep-hills', while a direct contemporary German translation yields 'high wooded land' (the hill tops were more wooded then). Competing theories suggest chieftains and gods named Cot or Cod.

The Normans arrived, a little aggressively it must be said, in 1066. William the Conqueror made Gloucester his base for a time, bringing further prosperity to the Cotswolds. The Normans built churches and carried out their epic Domesday Book survey. According to the Book, the area was heavily cultivated for the most part, but the west side was still very wooded – and, allegedly, in the entirety of the Cotswolds there was just one wall, which seems unlikely.

The Normans took the area's wool industry to a new level, clearing more land for grazing and putting the industry largely in church hands. Woolly things soon outnumbered (human) Cotswolders four to one. The Cotswold Lion sheep – big and hornless, with a white face and long, heavy fleece – emerged as the dominant breed. Their descendants can be seen at Adam Henson's Cotswold Farm Park (see page 133), near Guiting Power.

By the Middle Ages, the Cotswolds was one big grazing pasture. Wool wasn't just making the region rich, it was making the country rich. Wool exports accounted for more than half England's wealth, and half the nation's wool came from the Cotswolds. This increased income helped create a new middle class, and their money was often ploughed into building glamorous manor houses and so-called wool churches, such as the handsome examples in Winchcombe, Cirencester, Burford, Northleach and – the best of the bunch – Chipping Campden. Indeed, most of the Cotswolds' best-looking buildings owe their existence to this period of prosperity.

High taxes and competition from Spain forced a decline in the wool trade in the second half of the 15th century. It looked like the end of the Cotswolds' prosperity. But the region had another trick up its sleeve (pun intended).

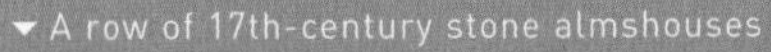

▼ A row of 17th-century stone almshouses

Starting in Temple Guiting way back in around 1185, the act of weaving, spinning and wool-cloth making had been spreading slowly throughout the region, initially as a cottage industry, before catching on and becoming a genuine industrial trade. By the end of the 16th century, cloth had replaced wool as the region's big earner. The Cotswolds sent finished cloth to India, Europe and the New World. By the 1700s, the five valleys around Stroud – Golden, Slad, Nailsworth, Painswick and Toadsmoor – teemed with water-powered mills. As many as 150 mills worked to dye fabric with the region's distinctive colours, Stroudwater Scarlet and Uley Blue. The long-lasting hues were derived from natural river salts, and gave British military uniforms their vividness.

The cute rows of terraced cottages you'll want to take photos of in Bibury, one of the most handsome Cotswolds villages, started out as cramped workers' cottages. It's rather ironic that they're now quite coveted. Seventeenth-century politician Sir Baptist Hicks started out as a clothier from Chipping Campden. He paid for the market hall you can still see if you visit the town, and went on to be lord mayor of London. Today you can best revisit this era in the Golden Valley (so named after the wealth the mills there created), near Stroud.

Greater social and aesthetic change came to the Cotswolds in the form of the Enclosure Acts. Between 1700 and 1840, rich land owners cordoned off large tracts of land that had traditionally

▼ Chipping Campden wool church

▲ The Cotswold Way, Painswick Beacon

been held in common. This privatising land grab deprived local people of their ancestral rights to graze animals and collect wood freely, and the resulting strife in part created Britain's modern working class. The Acts brought the region most of its signature drystone walls, often in the form of new boundary markers – though the technique dated back to the Stone Age, when the same style of construction was used for long barrows. Today the 4,000 miles of walls in the Cotswolds are roughly equivalent in length to the Great Wall of China.

The Cotswolds' lack of coal meant that the region's cloth mills were eventually out-manoeuvred by their Yorkshire rivals, who could use steam-powered trains to get their product to ships faster. Thankfully for the Cotswolds' scenic beauty – although not its 19th-century economy – the region never saw full-scale industrial overdevelopment. The long period of poverty that began in the 1850s ironically ensured an economic future for the Cotswolds as a tourist destination. Villages fell into a state of picturesque antiquarian decay. The region experienced genuine suffering, causing industrial action and mass migration to the New World (New South Wales, Australia has its own miniature Stroud and Gloucester).

There were still exciting times ahead for the region, albeit on a smaller scale. In the 1890s William Morris and his followers made Chipping Campden a thriving centre for the Arts and Crafts Movement. An antidote to industrialisation, this artistic and social vision included a strong strain of utopian neo-medievalism and an implicit call for a return to nature. Morris moved his family –

▲ Blenheim Palace

including his wife's lover, Dante Gabriel Rossetti – to Kelmscott Manor. Writers and artists followed, and Arts and Crafts buildings can still be seen in Campden, Painswick and Sapperton. Morris was also very active in preserving older buildings, especially those classic wool churches.

Beyond Morris' enduring legacy, the Cotswolds has had a disproportionately large impact on Britain's history and culture. Winston Churchill was born and brought up at Blenheim Palace (see page 250), in the Oxfordshire Cotswolds. William Shakespeare too is often claimed for the region. Many other writers and poets were from the Cotswolds, moved there or were inspired by the time they spent in the region. These include Laurie Lee (see page 35), Jane Austen, *Peter Pan* author J M Barrie, *Thomas The Tank Engine* author Rev Wilbert Vere Awdry, John Betjeman, J B Priestley, Edward Elgar, T S Eliot, Alexander Pope, W H Davies, Beatrix Potter, Charles Paget Wade and J K Rowling (who stole the name Dursley for her Harry Potter books).

Thanks to advanced farming methods, today some four-fifths of the Cotswolds are agricultural land. There are still sheep about, and some limestone quarries are subtly still going. Happily, traditional skills – potters, textile designers, glassmakers, blacksmiths, silversmiths and more – prosper in the area. Along with the Cotswolds' growing reputation as a foodie destination, local farmers' markets are enjoying a massive resurgence. Stroud's market is among the nation's largest. Tourism is now by far the region's biggest industry, bringing around £1 billion to the Cotswolds annually.

BACK TO NATURE

Up close the Cotswolds' bubble-wrap hills and curvy valleys may seem like the perfect aesthetic shapes, but the region's underlining geography and geology are as quirky as welly wanging.

Rather than the conventional up-and-down shape that we traditionally consider as 'hills', the region is a large, sloping plateau. The plateau builds slowly from Oxfordshire, so slowly – sneakily even – that you hardly notice the escalation. At the top of the hill-chain, the ground pretty literally plummets from beneath your feet. This is the Cotswold Edge, the western end of the escarpment. This stark juxtaposition of heaven and earth reveals vast views across the Vales of Evesham, Severn, Berkeley and Gloucester, falling away into the Malverns, and beyond them the moody mountains of Wales.

The Cotswolds may only reach a comparatively modest height of 1,082 feet (330m), but they're part of the country's largest continuous geological feature. The gigantic slab of limestone stretches all the way from Dorset to Yorkshire. The Cotswolds are the rock formation's most prominent part. Rivers have slowly sculpted the landscape over the centuries, creating dry and wet valleys.

▲ The Devil's Chimney, Leckhampton Hill ▲ Uley Bury

The area spanning northeast from Stroud to Chipping Campden is an elevated plateau, or 'high wold'. This windswept landscape feels invigoratingly open, with big skies and deep valleys that sometimes can't be seen until you're tumbling down into them. But around Stroud there are some long, deep, and wide valleys very different from the north wolds in character – the Five Valleys. From Tetbury heading east a gentle 'dip-slope' bridges the transition between the plateau and lowlands terrain. The dramatic Edge softens as you follow it south. The scarp is particularly characterful near Dursley, with its outlier hill Cam Long Down. The view is best enjoyed from Uley Bury hill fort.

The plateau is made of oolitic limestone. If wool defines the human history of the Cotswolds, this rock defines its physical creation, and therefore most things that have happened here. Almost everything about the Cotswolds – the shape of the terrain, the soil, plants and animals, man's industry, culture and history – is directly linked to the golden stone under these hills.

Oolitic limestone is a compressed mishmash of sediments, including clay, sand and the remains of gazillions of tiny sea creatures that lived 210 to 140 million years ago in the Jurassic period, in the warm tropical seas that once covered the area. The stone is rich with fossils. Ogle a Cotswold cottage up close, and you'll spy hundreds of crushed shells. Unquarried, the rock can resemble tightly packed fish egg. Hence the name – Oolite, or 'egg stone', from òoion, the Hellenic Greek word for egg.

Some 10,000 years ago, around the end of the last Ice Age, pressure from an ice cap to the north caused the giant limestone slab to buckle, forming the Cotswolds as we now know it. The melting snow and ice became rivers and streams, which gradually cut down through the limestone and gave the landscape its pleasingly smooth contours.

The limestone is comparatively soft and easy to shape when first taken from the ground, but it hardens over time. It thus makes an ideal building material. Locals have used this natural resource to build homes, long barrows and other structures since the Bronze Age (2000–650 BC). Indeed some of the walls in ancient long barrows are made according to the same method the Cotswolds' later inhabitants used to build the dry-stone walls the region's known for today.

In Cotswolds villages, the uniformity of the stone often masks the fact a given house might be hundreds of years older or newer than its neighbour. The Cotswolds have their own, timeless aesthetic. Oolitic limestone has a special, lingering glow in sunlight, which is especially pronounced at dusk. Often likened

▾ Blue flax at Broadway

to honey or syrup, the stone seems to preserve and magnify the sunlight's warm colour. As J B Priestley wrote in his seminal *English Journey* (1934), it is '[a]s if they know the trick of keeping the lost sunlight of centuries glimmering about them.' William Morris noted how Cotswold houses seem almost to grow out of the land underneath them.

The stone's colour varies across the region, tending to be more honey-golden and buttery in the north and a little greyer, more silvery and creamier in the south. Compare, for example, the colour of Broadway in the north – as golden yellow as it gets – with Painswick – as white as you'll see, albeit only halfway down the Cotswolds.

The limestone's thin topsoil has traditionally prevented the region from being extensively farmed, though modern farming methods have begun to change this. The Cotswolds' grasslands have survived relatively untouched since the Jurassic age. In fact the region has over 50 per cent of the country's unimproved (read: never substantially altered to make it more suitable for farming) Jurassic grassland.

The Cotswolds' designation as an Area of Outstanding Natural Beauty (AONB) – one tier below a National Park – recognises the

▾ The Cotswold Way crossing a golf course

▸ Berkeley Castle

region's 'rich, diverse and high quality landscape'. The Cotswolds are also home to five European Special Areas of Conservation, including Rodborough Common and Bredon Hill, three National Nature Reserves, including Wychwood Forest, and over 80 Sites of Special Scientific Interest.

Orchids can be found growing wild on the grasslands. Green-winged and early purple varieties arrive in late April and May, while common spotted, bee, frog, musk and pyramid crop up in summer, as do the rare and beautiful purple and gold pasque flower and Cotswold pennycress – arguably the region's signature flower. You may also see white oxeye daisies, bird's-foot trefoil, scabious, kidney vetch (which attracts common blue, rare chalkhill blue and Duke of Burgundy butterflies), hoary plantain, rock-rose, salad burnet, and knapweeds. Much of the woodland cover is ancient too, and in autumn the beech woods along the Edge are ablaze with colour.

The UK has half the world's bluebell population. Bluebells start flowering in the southwest, before fanning out across the country. These flowers often serve as indicators of ancient woodlands. In woods below the Cotswolds scarp in spring, you'll find carpets of bluebells wafting their natural perfume, as well as wild garlic.

In spring and summer, you can see the vivid clash of bright red poppies and the bright yellow rapeseed that makes the local farmland a tourist attraction in its own right. Snowshill's gently swishing fields of lavender may remind you of the vivid colour palette of *Crouching Tiger, Hidden Dragon*. You'll also likely see the thistle-esque teasel. The flower has a special historical place in the Cotswolds: the spiky heads were used in the manufacture of cloth, to raise the nap – the fuzzy surface – on velvet.

Many local places have taken their names from the landscape, such as Edge, Wotton-under-Edge and Sheepscombe, which wonderfully combines the natural surroundings with the region's traditional industry.

There's also plentiful birdlife, including buzzards, kestrels and sparrowhawks. The meadow pipit, with its puffed chest – often confused with the skylark – is perhaps the Cotswolds' signature bird. Bullfinches and yellowhammers dart between hawthorn and gorse. Migrating ring ouzels and wheaters stop off in spring (look on open hills and golf courses). Chaffinches, as well as skylarks and meadow pipits, stop by in autumn. If your tastes are more mammalian, the Cotswolds offer a chance to glimpse deer, foxes, rabbits, hares, grey squirrels and badgers (if they haven't all been shot). Many locals also believe in the presence of mysterious black cats.

LORE OF THE LAND

The wealth of the Cotswolds lies in much more than its immaculate villages built of warm stone. Ancient burial sites dot the land, and with them come tales of treasure. Near the Longstone is a long barrow, the Gatcombe Tump. Here an old woman from Minchinhampton who was able to charm away ailments, afterwards called Molly Dreamer, dreamed that she would find a long-lost pot of gold. She and her husband dug deep into the barrow until she had her hand on the pot, and was mouthing 'Come up! Labour in vain!' But as the words passed her lips a spirit appeared and frightened her off.

Near Bisley is a mound dubbed the Money Tump. Local legend holds that a wealthy chief dropped his riches there while fleeing Saxon invaders, and that the site is haunted by headless figures. A Roman general allegedly buried yet more treasure in nearby Golden Coffin Field. Despite many attempts over the centuries, these hidden fortunes have yet to be unearthed.

In this farming country, being in tune with nature was serious business. Taking note of the moon's phases was particularly important, as the guiding saw of the Chipping Campden farmer shows: 'Cut the lambs' tails in the rising moon and a south wind blowing, and never kill a pig when the moon be a-wasting [waning].' Farmers who disobeyed the rule would allegedly find it impossible to make good bacon, because the animal's flesh would not absorb salt properly. Broad Campden farmers also never sowed wheat except 'at the coming up of the moon'. Agricultural productivity also depended on locals' ability to predict the coming of rain. A Wotton-under-Edge rhyme runs: 'When Wotton Hill doth wear a cap [is covered in cloud], /Let Horton Town beware of that.' The sound of Woodchester's bells sent a meteorological message to nearby Rodborough. Damp air conducts sound much better than dry, thus:

Bring out your sou'westers
Say the bells of Woodchester.
All right old thing,
Answers Rodborough, ding ding.

The lore of the stones

Legend relates that 2,000 years ago, a king and his army marched through England as far as Little Rollright – an area now on the borders of Oxfordshire and Warwickshire, near Long Compton. Ascending a hill, the army encountered a witch. She called out to the king:

Seven long strides thou shalt take!
If Long Compton thou canst see
King of England thou shalt be.

Disastrously for the king the hill obscured his view, causing the witch to gloat:

As Long Compton thou canst not see
King of England thou shalt not be.
Rise up, stick, and stand still, stone,
For King of England thou shalt be none
Thou and they men hoar stones shall be,
And I myself an eldern [elder] tree.

So here the Rollright Stones stand: the ruler or King Stone, five Whispering Knights and 77 King's Men. In a circle 100 feet across, they wait for the magic spell that will make them human again. In a surprising gesture of solidarity, the witch likewise transformed herself into an elder tree. On Midsummer Eve, local people would cut an elder branch and congregate around the King Stone.

As the wound 'bled', some claimed to see the King's 'head' move. Witches and fairies would also gather at the stones at midnight to make merry, and at that time unmarried girls would press their ears to the Whispering Knights, hoping to hear the names of their future husbands.

A pair of holes pierces the Longstone, Gloucestershire's best-known megalith. Locals traditionally believe that at the chime of midnight the Longstone – also called Long John – and its neighbour the Tingle Stone run around the fields near Avening in which they stand. Long John is also said to bleed if pricked with a pin at midnight, and is further renowned for its healing properties. Mothers once passed children through the holes in the stone to prevent or cure rickets, smallpox, whooping cough and other then-fatal illnesses. Young couples would hold hands through the holes to ensure fertility.

Worst women

A tale from the 11th century recounts the exploits of the notorious witch of Berkeley Castle. She kept a tame jackdaw as her familiar, and one day, as the bird chattered to her more loudly than usual, she suddenly turned pale, later to hear that one of her sons and his family had been killed in an accident. Fearing her own impending doom she promptly called for two of her other children – one a monk, the other a nun – and confessed to them that she was a witch. The demonic bargain that had given her her powers ensured that her soul could not be saved, and so they were instructed, upon her death, to wrap her in a stag's skin and to then put the bundle into a stone coffin secured with three iron chains. By this means the witch hoped to cheat the devil out of his due.

▼ The Rollright Stones

The coffin was to remain in the church for three days, but while it lay there devils broke in and cut the chains. As one of the devils dragged the witch from the church, a black horse with iron hooks projecting from its back appeared. The witch was placed on the vicious saddle and pierced through. Her screams could be heard miles away.

Betty Barstoe, buried at the wayside in Betty's Grave, was called a witch for her supposed ability to make farm animals miscarry, prevent butter from solidifying or 'coming' and cream from setting, make gates fall from their hinges, and make people fall ill by dancing in the streets at midnight and spitting pins from her mouth. She was tried and burned, but after she was buried, other witches were said to gather at her grave and work their spells, stopping pedlars and other travellers on route to the market at Fairford. In another twist to the tale, it's said that Betty even left her grave and reappeared, only to be hanged and buried once again. The grave is still covered in flowers in the belief that only this can prevent her resurrection.

Most haunted

Ghosts stalk Cotswold villages in profusion, but though its spookiness seems to have no ill effects on its current residents, the prize for most haunted goes to Prestbury. Chief among the village's ghosts is a horseman who gallops at top speed down the Burgage, a street near Prestbury House, then suddenly screams to a halt. Locals believed the ghost was either a Royalist from Gloucester who was killed by Roundheads with a rope stretched across the road, or a messenger who was bound for Edward IV's camp at Tewkesbury in 1471. Revellers' ghosts come out to play on the grounds of Prestbury House (now a hotel), while a 'Black Abbot' haunts the churchyard, appearing only at Easter. In a cottage in the village, the ghost of a girl can be heard playing the spinet, while a spectral woman sings in a cottage nearby. An old woman in traditional country garb drifts across the fields, meeting the phantom sheep and shepherds that haunt the land.

Painswick also lays claim to extreme ghostliness. Its list of weirdness is long, and includes ghosts searching for buried treasure, black dogs, and creatures like goblins who dance around a milestone on the Gloucester road. Civil War soldiers and a grey lady also appear. People have heard strange cries and the sound of shuffling feet coming from Chirm Cottage in Kemps Lane. Scariest of all is the phantom coach that can be witnessed at midnight on New Year's Eve on the road from Painswick to Stroud. As the speeding coach crashes, you can hear the sounds of horses, coachmen and screaming passengers plunging to their doom, accompanied by the awesome crack of splintering wood. We can't recommend attempting to catch a glimpse (or hear a shuffle) of these otherworldly phenomena, as so doing may incur a terrible, sometimes even fatal curse...

WALKING IN THE COTSWOLDS

Visiting the Cotswolds and not putting your booted footprints on those lush green hills is like going to Paris and neglecting to see the Eiffel Tower or eat a croissant. This landscape was made for walking. The Cotswolds contain places of satisfying remoteness, authentic wildness and stirring drama. There are theatrically set hill forts, big views, stone circles, wildflower-splashed ancient grasslands, bluebell-carpeted woodlands, nature reserves and Sites of Special Scientific Interest (SSSIs).

Covering 790 square miles, this is the second largest protected landscape in England, after the Lake District, and the largest Area of Outstanding Natural Beauty in England and Wales. The region's crisscrossed with around 3,000 miles of often well-waymarked public footpaths. In terms of walking, the Cotswolds specialise in two things: the fabulous views from the limestone Edge, and appealingly clandestine valleys for you to get temporarily – and perfectly safely – lost in.

England and Wales have 15 National Trails: government-backed long-distance paths, usually considered to be the most scenic, as well as best waymarked and maintained, routes. One of them is

◀ Haresfield Beacon (previous page) ▲ Toadsmoor Valley

the Cotswold Way, which follows the hill chain as it ripples and bulges. The Way runs for 102 miles, from Chipping Campden at the north face of the hill-chain all the way down to Bath at the southern tip. The trail sticks closely to the Edge, giving the walker the best panoramas: right across the Vales of the Severn, Berkeley and Gloucester, the River Severn (the country's longest river), to J R R Tolkien's Forest of Dean, the jagged Malverns and the mountains of Wales.

There are many other long-distance paths too, such as the Gloucestershire Way, the Oxfordshire Way, the Macmillan Way, the Wysis Way and the Warden's and Windrush Ways, though they don't follow the escarpment like the Cotswold Way does. Not everyone has time to do the whole of the Cotswold Way, which takes most people 5–7 days, but if it's views you want there are plenty of short walks on the Way.

The Edge is higher and more spectacular in the north, and it's no coincidence that that's where you'll find Winchcombe, the unofficial capital of walking in the Cotswolds. The Cotswold, Warden's, Windrush and Gloucestershire ways all run through the town, as does the 42-mile Winchcombe Way. There are plenty of short walks to be enjoyed here, especially up to Belas Knap and/or Cleeve Common, the highest point in the Cotswolds. 'The town has "Walkers are Welcome" status,' says WinchcombeWelcomesWalkers.com, 'which means we will endeavour to make your stay and experience memorable.'

Other fantastic bits of the Edge can be easily accessed via short walks from the following places: going from north to south, Chipping Campden, Cheltenham, Broadway, Stanton, Birdlip, Painswick, Wotton-under-Edge, and Bath (not covered in this book). All are well worth visiting in their own right. Places you might not have considered visiting that have easy access to walking on the scarp include Selsley, Uley and Stroud. Leckhampton Hill, Crickley Hill and Cooper's Hill (of cheese rolling fame) are also well worth seeking out. Minchinhampton and Rodborough commons, and Bredon Hill, aren't on the Cotswold Way, but they also offer the sort of views that will cause you to get very annoyed with yourself if you didn't pack a picnic.

The Cotswolds also know a thing or two about how to produce the perfect valley, and discovering the results is an experience that amounts to almost a separate genre of walking. Nowhere does valleys quite like here: teasingly secretive, often intimate and overgrown, but also deep, wide and long. Some feel like their own little worlds. 'Those green little valleys at once make you feel so oddly remote, miles and miles from anywhere, clean out of the world,' wrote J B Priestley in *English Journey*.

The most famous valley in the Cotswolds is of course the Slad Valley, near Stroud, where Laurie Lee both grew up and set his multi-million-copy-selling autobiography *Cider With Rosie*. The five valleys around Stroud are the most logical places to go valley-hunting, while Toadsmoor, Miserden and Sapperton are path-less-trodden delights.

As well as views from the Edge and those famous valleys, there are hill forts (none better than Painswick Beacon and Uley Bury), long barrows (Belas Knap, Nympsfield Long Barrow, Leckhampton Hill) and stone circles (Rollright) to explore. Then there are those Jurassic grasslands, splashed with wildflowers and butterflies from late spring, most notably Cleeve (with several species of herb and grass), Selsley, Minchinhampton and Rodborough, and Haresfield commons.

There's plenty of woodland walking available too. In fact most Cotswolds walks involve trees. The region's glorious beech woodlands at times cover the steep escarpment. Beech trees aren't everyone's favourite as they can get dark in summer and don't let much else grow beneath them, but in autumn they light up in a gorgeous riot of bronze leaves.

If waterside walks are more to your taste, there are many rivers (the Thames is a Cotswolds river after all) and streams in the Cotswolds, as well as two canals. Other walks will take you past Roman ruins, castles, shams, follies and stately homes.

If you only have a short time in the Cotswolds and want to taste some of those classic villages as well as work up an appetite, the clever thing to do is to pick a route that includes several villages, such as a crowd-pleasing circuit of Stanton, Stanway and Snowshill (of *Bridget Jones's Diary* film fame). Or perhaps you might opt to take in Bourton-on-the-Water, Upper Slaughter, Lower Slaughter and Naunton. Getting some villages involved guarantees you that classic Cotswolds experience: a day out hiking the hills and valleys, topped off with a great feed and a couple of pints of something strange and local before you head to bed in the same handsome and satisfyingly historic establishment.

Walking destinations don't get much more beginner-friendly than the Cotswolds. It's not big and wild like the Brecon Beacons or Dartmoor, and you can't get genuinely lost for long – just find a road, and that'll take you back to civilisation soon enough. The more experienced walker might want to head to the Edge. You can get more of a workout there, and really feel like you've earned those big views.

Of course, going for a ramble is also a great way to escape the crowds.

Walking festivals and guiding

The following all have walking festivals:
Nailsworth (June, nailsworthhealthpartnership.org)
Dursley (October, dursleywelcomeswalkers.org.uk)
Winchcombe (May, winchcombewelcomeswalkers.com)

Some companies offer organised walking holidays and luggage-carrying options, including the Pudding Club (01386 438429; puddingclub.com); Contours Walking Holidays (01629 821900; contours.co.uk); Walking the Cotswolds (01386 841966; cotswoldwalking.co.uk) and Cotswold Walks (01386 833799; cotswoldwalks.com). Kington (kingtonwalks.org) includes the Wyche Way from Broadway to Kington, which opened in September 2015.

LAURIE LEE: LOTHARIO, BARFLY, AUTHOR

Laurie Lee, the Cotswolds' most famous son, had a complicated relationship with his home region. Born in 1914, Lee grew up in Slad, a village in a valley, not far from Stroud. His mother Annie raised eight children – four of which weren't hers – in a cottage with 'rooks in the chimney, frogs in the cellar and mushrooms in the ceiling'. She perpetually hoped for the return of the children's father, who had abandoned them to live in London with another woman.

Lee left school at 14 and took up an office job in Stroud, but left it to walk to London, with little but a fiddle and an aspiration to be a poet. Seeking adventure, Lee then took passage on a ship and walked through Spain at 19, playing his violin to earn his keep. 'I don't know what idiocies drove me in those days, but they were naïve, innocent idiocies in many ways', he told the BBC in later life. He left Spain in 1936, just as Civil War was breaking out.

Feeling guilty about having left the friends he'd made along the way to face the perils of war, he returned the following year to volunteer for the International Brigade. To re-enter the country, he had to cross the Pyrenees alone in a snowstorm. Lee claimed he was ultimately turned away because of his epilepsy, but not before being imprisoned and sentenced to death on suspicion of being a spy. By his mid-20s, Lee had had all the experiences that would become the material for his trilogy of autobiographies – books that would take him almost the rest of his life to write.

Rather than literature, Lee's passion was poetry, and he had some moderate success with it. He also worked as a journalist, scriptwriter and caption writer, and he made documentary films during World War II. Encouraged by editors and publishers who thought his poems about growing up in Gloucestershire were his best and most original work, Lee finally wrote about his upbringing in Slad in *Cider With Rosie*. Published in 1959 – some 20 years after the events look place – the book brilliantly captures a moment in history, conveying the unique texture of life in post-World War I rural Britain. The arrival of a motorcar in the village signals the end of an era. It's bucolic, nostalgic and funny, but also dark. The book depicts real poverty, an unsolved murder and 'self-slaughter'. It went on to sell six million copies, and became a canon text for English secondary schools.

◀ Slad (previous page) ▼ Laurie Lee

In an entertaining footnote, in *Cider With Rosie* Lee intimates that a fire at a piano factory was probably an insurance scam. Bentleys, a piano factory in Woodchester (in the Nailsworth Valley, on the other side of Stroud), successfully sued him for libel. His biographer Valerie Grove believes he genuinely didn't know of Bentleys, and might have just as easily called it a boiler factory – which it became in later reprints of the book. The whimsical choice of a piano factory ended up costing Lee a lot of money.

Despite the setback, Lee became financially comfortable and very famous. Yet the success suffocated him, and he struggled to find his creative edge. Constantly encouraged to come out with a follow-up book, 10 years later he wrote about his walk through Spain in *As I Walked Out One Midsummer Morning*. The third instalment of autobiography wouldn't be published until 1991. *A Moment Of War* chronicled Lee's involvement in the Spanish Civil War.

Some have doubted the veracity of some of the events described in the last book, which was published over 50 years after the period it recounts. The diaries Lee depended on to construct his narrative

▾ The River Coln

had also been stolen in the interim. Lee believed that 'the only truth is what you remember', although he also sometimes worried about what he called 'the censorship of self' and 'some failure between honesty and nerve'.

Along with poetry and alcohol, women were important in Lee's life, and his love life was complex. For example, his second daughter and his first grandchild were born on the same day, when he was 49. A pre-*Cider With Rosie* affair with the married Lorna Wishart led to the birth of his first child, who he rarely saw. At 36, Lee married Lorna's niece, Katherine, who was 18. According to biographer Valerie Grove, their relationship began when she was 14, after he'd dated both of her older sisters. Lee seemingly didn't put much stock in fidelity, either.

Like his father before him, Lee had tried to escape Slad. The success of *Cider With Rosie* brought him back, and in 1961 he bought a house right next to the legendary Woolpack Inn, his former local. The pub is easily found on the main road (B4070), and today it's filled with photos of the writer. Rose Cottage, where Lee lived (at least on weekends) from 1961 to 1997, is tucked directly behind it – he really couldn't have been any closer. The T-shaped Rosebank (formerly Bank Cottages), Lee's childhood home, is further up the road, along the bank about 20 yards northeast. In 1971 he bought the cricket pitch at nearby Sheepscombe to help ensure its future. Lee clearly loved this green corner of Gloucestershire, but paradoxically it wasn't stimulating enough for him. He spent many years commuting to London, spending the weekends in Slad, and frequently escaping abroad.

Slad was originally called Slade, meaning stream, and although you'd never know it from looking at the place, there were once prosperous cloth mills in the valley. In *Cider With Rosie*, Lee describes Slad Valley as '[n]arrow, steep, and almost entirely cut off... The sides of the valley were rich in pasture and the crests heavily covered with beechwoods.' If you get the chance to visit, you'll likely agree that the description still fits today – though how long it will continue to do so is uncertain, as the valley seems to be constantly under threat from developers. Lee later told the BBC that '[t]he sun sets down at the end of the valley over the Severn and there's this afterglow which catches those quarries and it just sits there glowing when the light is gone from everywhere else in the valley – it holds the light to the last drop.'

Despite having been a sickly child, Lee lived to 82, passing away in 1997. He's buried in the local churchyard, and his second daughter still lives in Slad, running his estate. His widow still lives in the 18th-century cottage they bought in Slad with the proceeds from sales of *Cider With Rosie*.

THE COTSWOLDS AT WAR

The Cotswolds may look the epitome of peacefulness, but this quilted landscape has seen some very significant battles and more than its fair share of bloodshed.

The Celts arrived in the Cotswolds in the Iron Age (from 500 BC), the beginning of a battle-filled era for the region. The Celts built hill forts along the Cotswold Edge to protect themselves against attacks from the Severn Valley. Arrowheads and the charred remains of bodies were discovered at Crickley Hill, excavated by Philip O. Dixon between the late 1960s and the early 1990s, and similarly on Bredon Hill the mutilated bodies of 50 men were found – left on the battlefield rather than buried.

The Romans arrived in AD 43. The Dobunni Celtic tribe that dominated the region from the southern Severn Valley to the Mendips was disappointingly quick to strike a deal with them, unlike their neighbours in Wales, the Silures, who violently resisted. When the Romans went home for good, tribal feuds broke out again, and Britain became an easy target for marauding tribes of Angles and Saxons from Denmark and Germany.

In the 5th century there's good reason to believe that the Battle of Badon, also known as the Siege of Mount Badon, where the Britons were led (according to legend) by none other than a certain

▲ Re-enactment of the battle of Tewkesbury
◀ Bredon Hill (previous page)

King Arthur and defeated an invading Saxon army, took place close to Bath. The victory led to around 50 years of peace for the region, but the peeved Saxons would be back.

In AD 577, the Cotswolds were invaded from two directions. A large Saxon army marched across the country, approaching from the Thames Valley, while the Angles took control of the region's northwest corner. The Dobunni leaders retreated to Bath, Gloucester and Cirencester, the region's three major cities.

The Saxons launched a surprise attack and seized the hill fort at Hinton Hill Camp, near Dyrham (north of Bath). The position commanded the Avon Valley and disrupted communications between the three cities. The Britons were still able to team up to attack Hinton Hill, but their three kings (Commagil of Gloucester, Condidan of Cirencester and Farinmagil of Bath) were killed, and the Britons were defeated. It was a pivotal moment in British history: the Saxons took charge of the three cities, and in so doing cut the Britons of southwest England off from their fellow Britons in the Midlands. The defeated Celts fled to Wales.

Oddly enough, the final battle in the Wars of the Roses – a bloody feud between the Houses of York and Lancaster, rival claimants to the throne of England – took place in the Cotswolds in 1471. The House of York dealt out a thrashing to their opponents at the Battle of Tewkesbury. Edward, Prince of Wales, was among the 2,000 casualties. He was the only son of Henry VI, and the only heir apparent to the English throne to ever die in battle. His death was instrumental in ending the lengthy conflict.

▲ Gargoyle, St Peter's Church, Winchcombe

The Cotswolds were at the centre of the English Civil Wars in the 1640s. Three major battles were fought there, including the War's first and last engagements. Broadly speaking, the populations of the north and west of England were Royalist, while those of the south and east of the country were Parliamentarian. This made the Cotswolds, which sit between these axes, a strong target for conflict. The struggle for power between King Charles I and the Parliamentarians, or Roundheads, finally turned to violence at Warwickshire's tiny Kineton in 1642. Both sides were marching towards London, aiming to take control of the capital, but Charles decided to confront his enemies. He lined his army up along Edgehill, while the Roundheads settled in the valley to the north. The Royalists advanced, but both sides lacked professional military experience. Artillery shells wildly missed their targets and the Roundheads fled the scene. By nightfall there was no clear winner, and the next day neither side really fancied continuing on. The result was a dissatisfying stalemate. The Roundheads sped to London to secure the capital, while Charles headed for Oxford, where he'd remain for the next four years.

In 1643 the Royalists attempted to seize Bath, meeting the Roundheads at Lansdown Hill. Heartbreakingly, the forces' two leaders, the Roundheads' Sir William Waller and the Cavaliers' Sir Ralph Hopton, had been childhood friends. Waller used the Edge's natural defence, hiding his artillery behind Celtic earthworks and forcing the Royalists' much larger army to attack uphill. Hopton's cavalry and infantry charges proved futile at first. He was persuaded to have another go and Cornish pikemen made inroads while musketeers sneaked through the woods to attack from the flanks. The Roundheads retreated a short distance, regrouping behind a dry-stone wall. Under the cover of darkness they retreated further, and in the morning it looked like a Royalist victory. However, the Roundheads had lost barely 30 men, while the Royalists' cavalry was decimated and was now too weak to attack Bath itself. Yet another draw.

In 1646 the last major battle of the war took place just north of Stow-on-the-Wold. With the Roundheads on the front foot, they attacked a Royalist army at dawn. The Royalists retreated into Stow itself, where the fighting (or rather the slaughter, according to some historians) continued in the market square until the Roundheads emerged victorious and imprisoned the remaining Cavalier soldiers in the church. There's a Royalist Hotel (now known as the Porch House) in Stow-on-the-Wold, among numerous other lasting reminders of the War in the Cotswolds.

Henry I built a hunting lodge in Woodstock in 1129, along with 7 miles of walls to create a park, which included lions and leopards. The lodge became a palace under Henry's grandson, Henry II, who spent time here with his mistress, Rosamund Clifford. Edward the Black Prince was born here in 1330 and the future Queen Elizabeth I of England was imprisoned here in 1554–55. Woodstock Palace was destroyed during the Civil War.

▾ St Edward's Church door detail, Stow-on-the-Wold

The town of Cirencester endured a lengthy siege, as did Gloucester. Dizzy Malmesbury changed hands seven times, and you can still see bullet marks on its abbey walls. You'll find similar scars on the church towers of Painswick and Winchcombe – the latter are bullet marks left by a Roundhead firing squad that lined Royalist prisoners up against the wall and there shot them dead. The Parliamentary army made the huge breach in Berkeley Castle's western wall. Similarly Sudeley Castle has battle scars – King Charles stayed here. Appropriately, he reputedly also stayed at Stow-on-the-Wold's Kings Arms in 1645. He's even said to have left Moreton-in-Marsh's White Hart coaching inn without paying his bill, the rapscallion!

Presumably eschewing royally named establishments, Oliver Cromwell supposedly stayed at Broadway's famous Lygon Arms in 1651 – as did Charles four years later. Charles is said to have disguised himself as a manservant while lying low at Cirencester's The Fleece. The same itinerant royal named the views from the Painswick Beacon as Paradise. The name remains to this day.

That was the last direct fighting in the region, though both World Wars would have a big impact. During World War I, open wolds were ploughed to grow extra food and woods were scavenged for timber. World War II saw numerous airfields built atop the plateaus, though dozens of them were abandoned after the end of the war.

▾ Sudeley Castle

LOCAL SPECIALITIES

There was a time when the Cotswolds' reputation for culinary sophistication might have been summed up by the image of a farmer slumped under a tree with a carrot in one hand and a half empty (or is it half full?) flagon of cider in the other. But that's long out of date.

The change has come about in part due to the amount of Londoners, Royals and celebrities who've purchased second homes in the Cotswolds. Their presence has raised house prices and made it very difficult for locals to buy properties in their own towns and villages, but the big grey cloud's silver lining is that standards in local pubs and restaurants have been raised to award-winning, Michelin star-earning levels. These eateries now equal or better any in the nation.

But that's not just down to Londoners. There's been a country-wide rise in ethical eating, Fairtrade products, organic food and locally sourced produce, but it's been firmly embraced in the Cotswolds. This is still a big farming region, after all – and it's close enough to Devon and Cornwall for fresh seafood to be delivered daily. Tetbury's Prince Charles has his own organic food range, Duchy Originals, sold in Waitrose, plus a Highgrove farm shop in Tetbury itself. Wherever you go in the Cotswolds, you'll chance upon restaurants serving fresh, locally sourced, ethically made, organic, independent food, along with farm shops and farmers' markets. The Cotswolds have become a gastronomic destination – foodies should look up the Food Tours of the Cotswolds (thecotswoldchef.com) and cookery courses.

MARKETS

Due to the region's history as a centre for the wool and cloth trades, the Cotswolds have a long tradition of markets, as well as many well-prepared market towns. So although the farmers' market phenomenon is fairly recent, it's also a continuation of the region's

◂ Banbury cakes ▴ Cheeses at Stroud farmers' market

traditional practices and values. The best of these markets is Stroud's (Saturdays). One of the largest in the country, it has featured on numerous television programmes. Other thriving farmers' markets to look for include Cirencester (second and fourth Saturdays of the month), Deddington (fourth Saturday), Stratford-upon-Avon (first and third Saturdays of the month), Stow-on-the-Wold (second Thursday of the month), Chipping Norton (third Saturday of every month), and Oxford's Covered Market (daily).

Farm shops are another great way to get high-quality produce straight from the source. The better ones include Tortworth Estate shop (near Wotton-under-Edge, tortworthestateshop.co.uk), Chedworth Farm Shop (cotswoldfarmfayre.com), Daylesford Organic Farm (daylesford.com), The Cotswold Food Store (cotswoldfoodstore.co.uk), Wayside Farm (near Evesham, waysidefarmshop.co.uk) and The Butts Farm Shop (near Cirencester, buttsfarmrarebreeds.co.uk), but look out for signs as you drive around, and check farmshopping.net. You'll also see roadside signs offering eggs, strawberries and other local produce at sub-supermarket prices.

FOOD

The region's reputation is centred on meats, especially Old Spot pork, Gloucester sausages, boar (from therealboar.co.uk), venison, meatballs (from lovemycow.com), award-winning organic burgers, local lamb, smoked venison, fish from Bibury trout farm, and salmon (from uptonsmokery.co.uk). The Cotswolds' fruit (particularly Blaisdon Red plums), vegetables (especially asparagus), honey, Tewkesbury mustard, ales and beer are also superb. But above all that, the Cotswolds' signature foodstuff is cheese. The region can boast more than 100 varieties, including mild and crumbly Single Gloucester (Godsells Cheese, godsellscheese.com), much rarer than its country-wide cousin Double Gloucester; yummy goats' cheeses (Windrush Valley Goat Dairy);

the Camembert-esque St Eadburgha (Gorsehill Abbey, gorsehillabbey.co.uk) and creamy organic Cotswold Brie (Simon Weaver, simonweaver.net).

Cotswolders also love their puddings. Look out for the Banbury cake (Eccles-esque, currant-filled pastry), a local speciality, and if you're ever near Nailsworth or Stroud, make sure you get up onto Rodborough Common to taste gorgeous, traditional Winstones Ice Cream. This small, family-run company is very popular with locals.

Food festivals to look out for include the Cotswold Show & Food Festival (July, cotswoldshow.co.uk), the Fairford & Lechlade Food & Drink Festival (May, fairfordlechladefoodanddrink.co.uk), the Cheltenham Food Festival (June, garden-events.com), and the Foodies Festival (Oxford, August, foodiesfestival.com).

DRINK

The region specialises in cosy, Cotswold-stone pubs, at their best when there's a fireplace (and that plump, purring cat). There's a good tradition of real ales here, too. Top tipples to look out for include Hook Norton's Hooky (golden bitter), Old Hooky (fruity) and Double Stout (dark, malty); The Patriot Brewery's Bulldog (golden ale) and Nelson (a classic bitter); Cotswold Spring's Codger (dry, crisp, with a hoppy finish), Stunner (a malty, fruity pale ale) and Rascal (fruity, citrussy wheat beer). Top real ale pubs include The Snowshill Arms, Cheltenham's Royal Oak, Tetbury's The Snooty Fox or Northleach's The Wheatsheaf Inn. A newcomer, but already a national CAMRA pub winner, is the Salutation Inn at Ham, near Berkeley.

Though the neighbouring counties of Herefordshire and Somerset have bigger reputations for cider making than the Cotswolds, you'll find some very tasty ciders here too. Start by visiting Coleshill House's Cotswolds Cider Company in Oxfordshire. Barnes & Adams are another local cider-maker, while Jo and Isaac Nixon at Prior's Tipple are artisan cider makers with a passion for creating excellent samples. For more information on Cotswolds beverages (soft and hard), visit cotswoldfinest.com.

The wildly popular Frocester Beer Festival (August, frocesterbeerfestival.com), the South Cotswold Beer Festival (July, yaterotary.pwp.blueyonder.com), the Winter Ales Festival (Tewkesbury, February, tewkesburycamra.org.uk), the Cotswold Beer Festival (Winchcombe, July, gloucestershirecamra.org.uk) and the Hook Norton Festival of Fine Ales (July, hookybeerfest.co.uk) all celebrate the region's contributions to drinking culture.

BEFORE YOU GO

THINGS TO READ

Cider With Rosie is the quintessential Cotswolds text. Laurie Lee beautifully describes a place in Gloucestershire, but also a place in time, capturing a key moment in history just on the cusp of its passing.

Hilarious travelogue writer and former *Times* subeditor Bill Bryson visited the Cotswolds in *Notes from a Small Island*. Radio 4 listeners voted to decide which book best represented Britain, and this won out. Starting from Oxford (after a few troubles with his rental car), Bryson calls in at Woodstock ('I must say I like [it] very much'), Blenheim Palace and Park ('a rural Arcadia', though he wasn't so complimentary about the Pleasure Gardens), Bladon ('nondescript'), Broadway ('absurdly pretty'), Broadway Tower ('sensational'), Snowshill (which seems to briefly please him), Snowshill Manor (which he was greatly intrigued by), Cirencester (where he praises the Corinium Museum's 'outstanding' collection) and finally Winchcombe, rounding off his time in the region with an 'enchanting walk' to see a Roman mosaic on nearby Cole's Hill.

Though William Shakespeare was from the region, the Cotswolds don't crop up often in his revered plays, with the exception of *Richard II*. This play gives us the lines:

> *'I am a stranger here in Gloucestershire,*
> *These high wild hills and rough uneven ways*
> *Draws out our miles, and makes them wearisome'*

Influential novelist J B Priestley visited the Cotswolds for his 1933 travelogue, *English Journey*, and marvelled at the oolitic limestone buildings. He wasn't smitten with Bourton-on-the-Water, but adored nearby Lower and Upper Slaughter. He likened the Cotswolds to a setting from a fairytale and pleaded for them to preserved as they were. 'The beauty of the Cotswolds belongs to England and England should see that she keeps it.' The region would eventually be granted the protected status of Area of Outstanding Natural Beauty. Bredon Hill, a big outlier hill just north of the Cotswolds escarpment, features in plenty of poetry, writing and art. Most famously it is depicted in poem 21 of A E Housman's *A Shropshire Lad*.

When he was stationed in France during World War I, Gloucester-born poet and musician Ivor Gurney wrote a poignant poem entitled *Crickley Hill*, which included the lines:

> *O sudden steep! O hill towering above!*
> *Chasm from the road falling suddenly away!*
> *Sure no men talked of you with more love.*

THINGS TO WATCH

Watch *Harry Potter* to see... Gloucester Cathedral, used in several of the films as part of Hogwarts. Many additional Hogwarts scenes were filmed at Oxford University's Christ Church College. You can see the fan-traceried vaulted ceiling in the tower housing the staircase and landing used in *Harry Potter and the Philosopher's Stone* (2001) and *Harry Potter and the Chamber of Secrets* (2002). The Tudor architecture of the grand Dining Hall in Christ Church College was the inspiration for the set design of Hogwarts Great Hall.

Watch 2002 James Bond film *Die Another Day* to see... parts of Bourton-on-the-Water – albeit mostly a local car park, which was covered in artificial snow for the filming so that Bond and his Aston Martin could be dramatically chased across it. The film also made use of an ex-RAF aircraft runway at nearby Upper Rissington in the same ice chase scene.

Watch *Bridget Jones's Diary* (2001) to see... pretty Snowshill, near Broadway. Filming included the village green and a local house featuring as the home of Bridget's parents. For the scene when she visited them at Christmas time, the village was covered in artificial snow.

Watch *Emma*, the 1996 TV dramatisation of Jane Austen's famous novel (starring Kate Beckinsale and Prunella Scales), to see... Sudeley Castle and Stanway House, near Broadway, both of which formed parts of Mr Knightley's home, Donwell Abbey.

Watch 2004's *The Libertine* to see... Stanway House. Johnny Depp plays a debauched 17th-century poet, the womanising Earl of Rochester. Stanway House also featured in 2004's *Vanity Fair*, which starred Reese Witherspoon as the main character, Becky Sharp.

Watch 2010 TV hit *Downton Abbey* to see... Bampton. Most of the exterior shots of the drama series were filmed in this Oxfordshire village.

Watch *The Bourne Ultimatum* (2007), *Brideshead Revisited* (2008), *The Oxford Murders* (2008), *Inspector Morse* (1987–2000) and *The Madness of King George* (1994) to see... Oxford.

Watch BBC's period drama *Tess Of The d'Urbervilles* (2008), an adaptation of the Thomas Hardy novel, to see... Owlpen Manor and Chavenage House, near Tetbury.

Watch *Amazing Grace* to see... Gloucester's docks.

Watch *Lark Rise to Candleford* (2008), *House of Elliot* (1991–94), *Noel Edmund's House Party* (1991–99), *Poirot: The Mysterious Affair at Styles* (1990), the remake of *Poldark* (2015) and many more TV programmes to see... Chavenage House.

Watch BBC TV's adaptations of *Cider With Rosie* (2015) to see... Miserden, where the outdoor scenes were filmed, and *Wolf Hall* (2015) to see... Chastleton House and Berkeley Castle.

THINGS TO KNOW

- Prince Charles, Princess Anne, Jeremy Clarkson, Damien Hirst, Alex James, Lily Allen, Stella McCartney and Kate Moss are just a few of the celebrities with Cotswolds abodes. The quickest way to make yourself unpopular with locals, however, is to start asking questions about them. Local people aren't particularly interested in tabloid fodder, especially as the newcomers have helped drive house prices through the roof (excuse the pun). The only exceptions to this general apathy might be the two royals, who've lived in the area a long time.
- There's no general agreement on what the word Cotswolds means, though it's probably of Saxon origin and probably originally conveyed something like 'sheep enclosures on the hills'.
- Covering nearly 790 square miles and spanning six counties (Warwickshire, Worcestershire, Gloucestershire, Oxfordshire, Somerset and Wiltshire), the Cotswolds is the largest of the 38 Areas of Outstanding Natural Beauty (AONB) in England and Wales.
- About 80 per cent of the Cotswolds is farmland. This farmland is divided by around 4,000 miles of dry-stone walls – that's roughly equivalent in length to the Great Wall of China.
- The Cotswolds is crisscrossed with around 3,000 miles of public footpaths, which are often well-waymarked.
- The Cotswolds is part of the largest geological feature in the country: a slab of limestone that stretches from Yorkshire to Dorset.
- Some Cotswolds plants are so rare that they have specific legal protection under the Wildlife and Countryside Act 1981.

- The Cotswolds region contains five European Special Areas of Conservation, three National Nature Reserves and over 86 Sites of Special Scientific Interest.
- 120,000 people live in the Cotswolds Area of Outstanding Natural Beauty, and the majority of them commute to jobs outside it.
- The highest point in the Cotswolds is Cleeve Hill (1,083 feet/330m), near Winchcombe.
- Some of the most important research in the early days of geology was undertaken in the Cotswolds, so the area is strongly connected to the development of the subject. The theory of strata was developed near Bath.
- The first officially recognised dinosaur was found in the Cotswolds in 1824, at Stonesfield.

THINGS TO PACK

Map and walking boots
To get up into those beckoning hills

Camera
To capture the views from the top

Wild flower book
Even the locals don't know what half of them are

Autograph book
In case you catch sight of any of the Cotswolds celebrities

Sunglasses
So you can pretend you might be a celebrity

Credit card
It's not the cheapest holiday destination

Trousers a size too big
You'll need them after a couple of big Cotswolds dinners

▾ A finger signpost for Stow-on-the-Wold and Toddington

Hand cream
For repairing the damage after you end up taking that dry-stone wall-building course (see cotswoldsruralskills.org.uk)

Reading glasses
For *Cider With Rosie*

HOW TO GET AROUND

Though trains call at the region's cities (Gloucester, Oxford) and some of the larger towns (Cheltenham, Banbury, Kemble, Moreton-in-Marsh, Stratford-upon-Avon, Stroud), and local buses will get you to most of the villages eventually, the Cotswolds aren't blessed with a great public transport network. Your own wheels – two or four – are definitely the way to go. Plus, then you'll have better access to quiet little Cotswolds secrets like Bisley and Minchinhampton.

That said, the traffic can be a headache at peak times, particularly in midsummer on the A429 between Stow-on-the Wold and Cirencester. Likewise, you should try to avoid the A40 between Burford and Cheltenham on Bank Holidays and Sunday evenings, especially when travelling eastwards. Coming and going, the M4 and M5 are good bets – just check the traffic reports first.

Cars aside, there are two very enjoyable train journeys to be had in the Cotswolds, more for leisure's sake than for reasons of practicality. The historic Gloucestershire Warwickshire Railway (gwsr.com) offers a chuffing steam train ride. The much-loved Cotswold Line goes between Oxford and Hereford, through some of the north Cotswolds' most beautiful scenery, especially the stretch from Evenlode to Moreton. The Line also features in two notable poems: *Adlestrop*, by Edward Thomas, and Sir John Betjeman's *Pershore Station, or A Liverish Journey First Class.*

WHERE TO STAY

Even before the Cotswolds were a tourist destination, places such as Broadway were popular stop-offs for long-distance coaching journeys. The region's thus very well prepared for visitors. There are all types of accommodation, though the scale is weighted more towards the boutique and luxury B&B end than the budget end – there aren't many hostels or campsites compared to, say, Devon or Wales. Though of course the cities and larger towns, particularly Cheltenham and Oxford, are appealing, and have more amenities, if what you're after is a classic Cotswolds experience, the more obvious honeypot villages are in the north. These include Chipping Campden, the most elegant of the lot, Burford, Bibury, Bourton-on-the-Water and Broadway. All are very photogenic, but all get crowded in the summer and most weekends. To dodge the coach-loads a little, perhaps look to stay in Winchcombe,

Blockley or Snowshill in the north, or further south in Painswick, Nailsworth or Tetbury. All are picturesque places with great character.

Also think about what it is you want from the Cotswolds. If it's to tag as many syrupy villages, manor houses and gardens as possible, the north has more A-listers. The central area (Painswick, Nailsworth, Stroud, etc.) has fewer crowds and more varied walking. It's also closest to the best farmers' markets and restaurants, which are, loosely speaking, located at the Tetbury-Stroud-Cirencester axis.

For a list of hotels and B&Bs in picturesque stone cottages, visitcotswolds.co.uk is a good starting point. You could also check the tourist board website for a free Welcome to the Cotswolds brochure (cotswolds.com).

If you're keener on camping, see Campsites, page 56. Other good Cotswold campsites include Thistledown Farm near Stroud (01453 860420; thistledown.org.uk), Cotswold Camping near Charlbury (01608 810810; cotswoldscamping.co.uk) and Far Peak Camping near Northleach (01285 720858; farpeakcamping.co.uk).

WHEN TO VISIT

Every season has good reason to visit. Crowd-free winters are ideal for crisp, enlivening walks, long pub lunches by the fire – and lower hotel prices. Spring brings bluebells, daffodils and bleating lambs. Summer's great of course, but the honeypot villages in the north get swamped with bus tours and day-trippers. But then again, the more sunlight, the more those buildings glow. Autumn's just peachy: the villages and hills are quieter, plus those beech woodlands are gloriously ablaze, especially at the magnificent Westonbirt and Batsford arboretums.

VISITING WITH KIDS

Kids might get bored being dragged around to village after village, which may all look the same to them after a while. However, most village visits can easily be combined with short but rewarding walks. Animals are usually crowd pleasers, and Cotswold Wildlife Park (Burford), Adam Henson's Cotswold Farm Park (Guiting Power), Slimbridge Wetland Centre or Bourton-on-the-Water's Birdland should keep them entertained. If the weather's uncooperative, think about visiting manor houses and mansions (see 10 Mansions and Manor Houses, page 245), castles (Sudeley or Berkeley) or, if there's a break in the clouds, get out to those spectacular gardens. The historic Gloucestershire Warwickshire Railway (gwsr.com) is another option. If the weather's good, the Cotswold Water Park (near Cirencester, waterpark.org) is well worth splashing out at.

▲ Gloucestershire Warwickshire Railway

THINK LOCAL

In places such as Chipping Norton, it may look like everyone's a lord or a millionaire, although that's not the case across most of the Cotswolds. In fact an influx of wealthy Johnny-and-Jenny-come-latelies has pushed house prices beyond the reach of some locals. Good new businesses fail here as they do elsewhere, bullied by global-brand competitors. Wherever you can, please shop locally in the independent cafes and shops rather than grabbing something from one of the ubiquitous chains. Being independently minded is very much what the Cotswolds are about.

FURTHER INFORMATION

The best starting point, especially for the great outdoors and things like dry-stone walling courses, is escapetothecotswolds.org.uk. Another good resource for information is the-cotswolds.org, and the area's official tourist information site is cotswolds.com.

Local tourist information centres include Bourton-on-the-Water (01451 820211); Chipping Campden (01386 841206); Cirencester (01285 654180); Moreton-in-Marsh (01608 650881); Stow-on-the-Wold (01451 870998); and Tetbury (01666 503552). Most are open usual office hours, as well as on weekends.

FESTIVALS & EVENTS

As well as various arts, literary and music festivals in the Cotswolds, there are many original, traditional and quirky celebrations.

MAY

Cotswold Olimpick Games
Chipping Campden
olimpickgames.co.uk
If you can only make one Cotswolds event, make it this one. The Cotswold Olimpicks started in 1612, and they continue today with torch-lit processions, Morris dancing, tug of war, shin kicking and welly wanging. It is unique and brilliant.

Cheese-Rolling at Cooper's Hill
Brockworth
Spring Bank Holiday
cheese-rolling.co.uk
A mock Double Gloucester cheese is rolled down a precipitous slope and people run/fall after it, breaking a few bones, while someone from the nearby village of Brockworth inevitably nabs the prize. Idiosyncratically Cotswoldian.

Randwick Wap & Spring Time Cheese-rolling Ceremony
Randwick (near Stroud)
Randwick also has a cheese-rolling ceremony, preceded by a colourful procession of costumed villagers led by the Mop Man, who wields a wet mop to clear crowds. Plus there's a dunking in the pond. The festival is thought to date back 700 years.

Tetbury Woolsack Races
Tetbury
tetburywoolsack.co.uk
Men and women race up a steep hill carrying 60lb (35lb for the ladies) sacks of wool on their backs. The event, celebrating Tetbury's past as a prosperous wool town, dates to the 17th century. There's also a street fair.

Levellers' Day
Burford
This day of music, fancy dress, debate and entertainment celebrates three Levellers who quit Oliver Cromwell's New Model Army, and were executed here.

Morris Dancing
Dancing with bells and sticks is still a strong tradition here, thought to date to at least the 13th century. The dances are a celebration of rural life, and often include elements that mimic country skills, such as harvesting and sewing. May Day and St George's Day are good times to catch the spectacle.

JUNE

Ramsden Fete
Ramsden
ramsdenvillage.co.uk
Not just your average collection of cupcake and second-hand Lego

stalls. The Ramsden Fete offers a strong man contest, jousting, egg throwing, tug of war, morris dancing (of course) and much more glorious silliness.

Summer Solstice
Rollright Stones
rollrightstones.co.uk
Join the Cotswold Order of Druids at the mysterious Rollright Stones, near Chipping Norton, to see in the longest day of the year. There's also a Samhain ceremony in early November.

Longborough Festival Opera
near Moreton-in-Marsh
lfo.org.uk
A boutique opera event, set in a converted barn on a country estate in North Gloucestershire. 2013's edition played Wagner's entire *Ring Cycle* to celebrate the composer's bicentenary.

▶ JULY

Banbury Hobby Horse Festival & Town Mayor's Sunday
Banbury
When they all turn out for this parade, the number and variety of horse-related costumes that exist in the world will stagger you. There's Maypole dancing and lots of horsing around.

Artburst
Painswick
painswickartsfestival.com
A lively arts festival with nine days of workshops, open studios, demos and exhibitions covering the whole gamut of arts with fun activities for kids.

▶ AUGUST

Treefest
Westonbirt Arboretum
forestry.gov.uk/westonbirt
A celebration of traditional woodcrafts and woodland skills. See falconry and axe carving.

Football In The River
Bourton-on-the-Water
Six-a-side, 15 minutes each way, kicks off at 4pm – only the pitch is the Windrush River, which runs through the centre of Bourton-on-the-Water. This tradition of moist matches has been around for over 70 years and takes place on August Bank Holiday Monday. Spectators should expect to get wet too.

▶ SEPTEMBER

Painswick Ancient Clypping Ceremony
Painswick
In Painswick's 'Clypping' ceremony (see page 177), children join hands around the church while singing the Clypping Hymn. The annual observance is thought to date back to 1321.

Tetbury Food and Drink Festival
Tetbury
tetburyfooddrinkfestival.com
From Gloucester Old Spot sausages to wines from Bow in the Cloud Vineyard, this popular festival is all about local Cotswold produce.

▶ DECEMBER

Boxing Day Duck Race
Bibury
biburycricketclub.co.uk
Hundreds of festive fans gather in pretty Bibury for the increasingly popular duck races. Two races orchestrated by the local cricket club, one of 150 'decoy' ducks and a second of over 2,000 plastic yellow fellows. It's a good quack.

Marshfield Paperboys
Marshfield, Boxing Day
The town crier leads a procession of 'Mummers' dressed in paper costumes through the streets, as the 'paper boys' perform the town's unique mumming play. There are carols and encores too.

CAMPSITES

For more information on these and other campsites, visit theaa.com/self-catering-and-campsites

Tudor Caravan & Camping ►►►►
tudorcaravanpark.com
Shepherds Patch, Slimbridge, GL2 7BP | 01453 890483 | Open all year
This park benefits from one of the best locations in the county, situated right alongside the Sharpness to Gloucester canal and just a short walk from the famous Wetland Centre at Slimbridge. The site has two areas, one for adults only and a more open area with a facility block. There are both grass and gravel pitches, with electric hook-ups. As it's next to the canal, there are excellent walks, plus the National Cycle Network route 41 can be accessed from the site. There is a pub and restaurant adjacent to the site.

Apple Tree Park Caravan and Camping Site ►►►►
appletreepark.co.uk
A38, Claypits, Stonehouse, GL10 3AL
01452 742362 | Open all year
This family-owned park is on the A38, not far from the M5. A peaceful site with glorious views of the Cotswolds, the park is well located for visiting Slimbridge Wetland Centre and makes an excellent stopover for M5 travellers.

Bo Peep Farm Caravan Park ►►►►
bo-peep.co.uk
Bo Peep Farm, Aynho Road, Adderbury, Banbury, OX17 3NP
01295 810605 | Open Mar–Oct
Charmingly named Bo Peep Farm is a park with good views and a spacious feel. Four well laid out camping areas, including two with hard standings and a separate tent field, are planted with maturing shrubs and trees. In keeping with the area the two facility blocks are built in attractive Cotswold stone. The 'Dovecote Barn' offers on-site food at selected times. There are four miles of walks on site through woods and along the river bank. There is also a bay where you can clean your caravan or your motorhome.

Lincoln Farm Park Oxfordshire ►►►►►

lincolnfarmpark.co.uk
High Street, Standlake, OX29 7RH
01865 300239 | Open Feb–Nov

This attractively landscaped family-run park is in a quiet village near the Thames. There are top class facilities throughout the park, and excellent leisure facilities in the Standlake Leisure Centre, complete with two indoor heated swimming pools, gym, solarium and sauna. A warm welcome is assured from the friendly staff.

Cotswold View Touring Park ►►►►

cotswoldview.co.uk
Enstone Road, Charlbury, OX7 3JH
01608 810314 | Open Easter or Apr–Oct

This is a good Cotswold site, well screened, but with attractive views across the countryside. Breakfasts and takeaway food are available from the shop, and the site has camping pods for hire. It's a perfect location for exploring the Cotswolds and for anyone heading for the Charlbury Music Festival.

Briarfields Motel & Touring Park ►►►►

briarfields.net
Gloucester Road, Cheltenham, GL51 0SX | 01242 235324 | Open all year

Briarfields is a well-designed, level park, with a motel, where the facilities are modern and very clean. It became an adults-only location in the 2015 season. The park is well-positioned between Cheltenham and Gloucester, with easy access to the Cotswolds. And, being close to the M5, it makes a perfect overnight stopping point.

Greenhill Leisure Park ►►►►

greenhill-leisure-park.co.uk
Greenhill Farm, Station Road, Bletchingdon, OX5 3BQ | 01869 351600 | Open all year (restricted opening Oct–Mar, no dogs, games room closed)

Greenhill is an all-year round park set in open countryside near the village of Bletchingdon, and is well-placed for visiting Oxford and the Cotswolds. Fishing is available in the nearby river or in the park's two well-stocked lakes. Pitches are very spacious and the park is very family-orientated. The owner's motto is 'Where fun meets the countryside'. The facilities are also very good and include an excellent new reception, shops and a bar/cafe.

Wysdom Touring Park ►►

Cheltenham Road, Burford, OX18 4PL | 01993 823207 | Open all year

Owned by Burford School, this small 'adults' only' park is very much a hidden gem, just a five-minute walk from Burford, one of the prettiest towns in the Cotswolds. The pitches have good privacy; all have electric and there are many hardstandings for caravans and motorhomes. The unisex toilet facilities are very clean.

A–Z of The Cotswolds

VISIT THE MUSEUMS | GET OUTDOORS | EXPLORE BY BIKE | GO BACK IN TIME | TAKE A TRAIN RIDE | MEET THE WILDLIFE
TAKE IN SOME HISTORY | HIT THE BEACH | EAT AND DRINK | GET INDUSTRIAL | VISIT THE GALLERIES | GO CANOEING
TRY HORSE-RIDING | PLACES NEARBY | CATCH A PERFORMANCE | GO ROUND THE GARDENS | TAKE A BOAT TRIP

Badminton MAP REF 256 C5

Badminton joins Mexico's Tabasco as a place a lot less famous than its name has become. Unlike the sauce, however, the sport of thwacking a feathery flying thing across a high net doesn't strictly come from this place of the same name. The game was imported here from India in 1873 and takes its name from Badminton House, the demesne of the Dukes of Beaufort. But this little village is also pretty famous for its annual, high-profile three-day horse trials. They've taken place on the estate since 1949, and the roads get pretty gridlocked around here when they're on in early May. The village is worth a quick look, even if Badminton House itself is closed to the public. The village's yellow, lime-washed houses seem out of step with their Cotswolds neighbours.

Badminton House is a Palladian structure, built for the first Duke of Beaufort in 1682 and remodelled by William Kent in 1740. It's considered a fine example of period style and the interior – which, unfortunately, you won't be seeing – is wonderfully decorated. The park was partly the work of famous landscape architect 'Capability' Brown. Some of the formal layout is on a quite extraordinary scale: the tree-lined Great Avenue is several miles long.

Great Badminton, the 18th-century church on the grounds of the estate, is notable for its monuments to the Beaufort family. One of these, by Grinling Gibbons, is so big that the church had to be altered to accommodate it. The boxpews are exceptionally large, like old-fashioned snug bars.

The area around Badminton was known locally as 'Beaufortshire', famous as home to the Beaufort Hunt.

PLACES NEARBY

The brilliantly named Sodburys – the villages of Chipping, Old and Little – (see page 189) and an impressive Iron Age hill fort are only about five minutes away, across the other side of the A46. And it only takes another five minutes to tootle down the A46 to visit Dyrham Park (see page 119), an excellent National Trust site with a manor house, gardens and herds of deer. Westonbirt Arboretum (see page 220) is not far away either.

Barnsley & Barnsley House MAP REF 257 F2

barnsleyhouse.com

GL7 5EE | 01285 740000 | Usually open daily; contact first

Little Barnsley is right up there with the very prettiest Cotswolds villages. And there, coyly keeping its charms hidden until the last moment, stands Barnsley House. After the abrupt

▲ Badminton Horse Trials

entrance drive has been negotiated, the first and lasting impression is one of harmony. The House is both a restaurant (often using freshly picked vegetables from their own kitchen garden) and a hotel, but chances are that even if you only popped in for a nose about, you'll end up at least buying lunch. And if you only popped in for lunch, chances are you'll be staying the night. The honey-coloured Queen Anne house stands serenely amid 4 acres of intimate gardens, which are well worth a visit. Restaurant guests have free access to these, but call ahead. Rosemary Verey and her late husband, David, began to design the gardens in the 1950s. On an axis from the drawing-room door, a stone path – its texture softened by clumps of geraniums and rock roses – runs straight to the centre of the south lawn, which is flanked by the soft, muted colours of aquilegias, stachys, phlomis and other flowers. Beyond this, a purple sycamore, an atlas cedar and a silver-grey white poplar provide a marvellous contrast of foliage colours, textures and shapes.

A delightful knot garden sits near to the house's western side, its little box hedges set amid gravel in the manner of 16th- and 17th-century formal parterres. In the 1960s David Verey moved a temple from Fairford Park to the southeast corner of the garden, creating a peaceful vista that leads the eye over the richly covered lily pond, through two iron gates flanked by statuesque cypresses, and finally to a charming wall fountain beyond.

Alongside Mrs Verey's potager, or decorative kitchen garden, runs a wonderful laburnum tunnel. In spring this tunnel is thickly covered with yellow panicles that reach down to meet the tall, mauve alliums that rise from beneath its shade.

The potager, inspired by the one at the Chateau de Villandry in the Loire valley, and by *The Country Housewife's Garden*, written in 1617 by William Lawson, is a remarkable creation. The layout of the potager is typical of Barnsley House garden – a charming mixture of nonchalance and formality. Brick paths in many different patterns criss-cross the area. The beds themselves are planted with red and green varieties of lettuce and other vegetables, while sweet peas grow close to gooseberries, onions, cabbages, lavender and strawberries.

In perfect harmony with the stone wall behind them, two stone statues of country girls holding baskets generously filled with flowers flank the gateway to the potager beyond.

The annual Barnsley Festival takes place in May, founded by Rosemary Verey in 1988. On the day of the festival the gardens of Barnsley House are open to all comers, as well as those of nearby Barnsley Park Estate, not normally open to visitors.

10 classic towns & villages

- **Barnsley** page 60
- **Bibury** page 66
- **Bourton-on-the-Water** page 70
- **Broadway** page 77
- **Castle Combe** page 83
- **Chipping Campden** page 96
- **Painswick** page 176
- **The Slaughters** page 184
- **Tetbury** page 219
- **Winchcombe** page 233

PLACES NEARBY

On the B4425, near Cirencester, is Abbey Home Farm Shop.

Abbey Home Farm Shop
theorganicfarmshop.co.uk
GL7 5HF (though they warn that satnavs will misdirect you)
01285 640441
Offers lots of great food, but there's also an award-winning cafe with vegan options, as well as accommodation (including yurts and a lakeside cabin).

The Falcon Inn
falconinnpoulton.co.uk
London Road, Poulton, GL7 5HN, 01285 850878
This centuries-old pub offers a reliable pint of real ale from independent breweries, and marries contemporary comforts with age-old tradition. There's a fresh, zingy menu too.

Berkeley Castle MAP REF 256 B3

berkeley-castle.com

Berkeley, GL13 9BQ | 01453 810303 | Open Apr–Oct Sun–Wed 11–5 (last admission 4)

We probably shouldn't grumble really – at least not within earshot of locals – but if the Cotswolds do lack something, it's castles. Well, and beaches. But let's deal with the castles for now. Not including Castle Combe, which is a misleadingly-named village, there are only two castles in the Cotswolds: Sudeley (see page 217) and Berkeley. And really, Sudeley is a Renaissance manor house rather than a genuine military fort. Berkeley, on the other hand, is a real castle, belonging to the more aggressive Middle Ages.

For over 850 years the gaunt profile of Berkeley Castle has kept watch over the Severn and the Welsh Borders, seeming to grow powerfully out of the outcrop of rock on which it stands. With its forbidding towers and dense walls of purple stone, it was for centuries the home of one of the region's most powerful families. Few can trace their ancestry back to the Anglo-Saxons, but the Berkeleys of Berkeley Castle descend directly from the Master of the Horse to Edward the Confessor. Their descendants have lived here for more than 800 years.

Events of great importance have taken place inside its thick walls. The West Country barons met in the castle's great hall before placing their demands before King John at Runnymede in 1215. In 1327, the unfortunate Edward II was first imprisoned and then murdered in a room in the keep. During the Civil War Berkeley Castle was besieged for three days by Parliamentary forces, and though the castle was not seriously damaged, the large breach the Parliamentarians made in the wall of the keep remains to this day.

Berkeley Castle was founded after Henry II granted a Charter to Robert Fitzharding in 1154. Visitors still enter the shell keep via a Norman doorway in the inner courtyard. Most of the building that we see today dates from the 14th century. The Drake Room and Tower Room contain a later – but nonetheless remarkable – collection of ebony furniture from the Portuguese East Indies, which, by tradition, once belonged to Sir Francis Drake. In the picture gallery there are seascapes by van de Velde, portraits by Lely, a groom and horses by Stubbs and a hunting painting, *The Old Berkeley Hounds*, by Benjamin Marshall. Hunting is an ever-present subject at Berkeley. The dining room is hung with portraits of three Masters of the Berkeley Hounds, by Raoul Millais, William Orpen and John Teesdale. Beyond the medieval kitchen is the housekeeper's room, where the Godwin Cup – believed to have belonged to King Harold's father – is displayed.

The great hall still retains a medieval atmosphere, with its 13-foot (4m) thick walls hung with Oudenarde tapestries illustrating the story of Queen Esther, an unusual painted screen dating from the 16th century and a magnificent timber roof. Over the fireplace hangs a fine portrait of Admiral Sir Cranfield Berkeley by Gainsborough. A well-preserved Berkeley Arch gives access to the grand staircase. This lovely wooden stair (1637) leads to the morning room, which was once the chapel. The ribs of its ceiling are painted with verses from the Bible, translated into Norman French in 1387 by John Trevisa, a friend of scholar and philosopher John Wycliffe. The verses are an early example of the practice of rendering the Bible in the vernacular. The walls of the staircase are hung with

▼ Berkeley Castle and gardens

magnificent early Brussels tapestries depicting the stories of Isaac and Rebecca and Sodom and Gomorrah, woven by the de Pannemaekers from cartoons by Raphael. Among the wall decorations is a Doom painting above the chancel arch, intended to urge people away from the path of sin.

From the castle, the views over the gardens to the river are superb. The terraces have grass walks with borders of low plants, backed by shrubs and climbers, while the bowling alley is flanked by a high wall and ancient clipped yews. Beyond, cattle graze in the water meadows, creating as beautiful and peaceful a scene as can be found anywhere in the country.

The Butterfly House has close to 42 species of fluttery things, including specimens from as far afield as Japan and Indonesia, and the Atlas, the world's largest moth. All are of course kept in one of those super-humid rooms that makes you feel instantly sleepy.

TAKE IN SOME HISTORY

Dr Jenner's House
jennermuseum.com
Church Lane, High Street, GL13 9BN | 01453 810631
Open May–Sep Sun–Wed 12–5 (also daily Easter and Oct half term)

At the risk of being morbid, you might never have been born if it wasn't for Edward Jenner (1749–1823), son of the local vicar. This fine fellow pioneered a vaccine against smallpox in 1796, and this beautiful Queen Anne house was his home. The house and the garden, with its thatched Temple of Vaccinia, are much as they were in his day. The displays record Jenner's life as an 18th-century country doctor, his work on vaccination and his interest in natural history. You can discover the story of a man who changed the world in the house where history was made. Jenner is buried in the chancel of the church.

EAT AND DRINK

The Malt House
themalthouse.uk.com
Marybrook Street, GL13 9BA
01453 511177

In the middle of Berkeley and near the castle, this pub is popular with walkers tackling the spectacular Severn Way, which runs along the nearby estuary shoreline. Comfy accommodation and good food tempt passers-by into making overnight stops.

PLACES NEARBY

The Slimbridge Wetland Centre (see page 187), which has the world's largest collection of swans, geese, ducks and flamingos, isn't far away. If you're in the mood for a walk, head east towards Dursley (see page 117) or Wotton-under-Edge (see page 252) to meet the Cotswolds Edge and to see some spectacular views from the top.

Bibury MAP REF 258 A3

Poet, artist, socialist and Arts and Crafts Movement luminary William Morris described Bibury as the 'most beautiful village in England', which is quite a claim in an area as blessed with handsome villages as this. Bibury is certainly in the upper echelon, and if you're looking for that one 'Cotswold' shot, you'll find it here, where the trout-filled River Coln glides alongside the almost-never-not-being-photographed row of picturesque cottages on the main street.

Bibury has Saxon origins, though most of what makes the village, as well as neighbouring settlement Arlington, so attractive dates from around the 17th century, when it prospered as a weaving centre. The interest-filled church of St Mary's sits in a well-tended churchyard at the far end of the main street, at the heart of the original village. It retains some of its original Saxon work – the chancel arch jambs, and fragments of a cross shaft.

TAKE IN SOME HISTORY

Arlington Row

Arlington Row, a terrace of low-gabled weavers' cottages just across the river, towards the church end of the village, is the most photographed street in Bibury, and perhaps in the entirety of the Cotswolds – and for good reason. Seeing them may provoke one of those 'have I just stepped back in time?' moments. Originally they were used by workers weaving wool for Arlington Mill at the other end of the village – they used the Rack Isle in front of the cottages, now a bird sanctuary, for drying wool. The cottages are owned by the National Trust, and still occupied. The path in front of Arlington Row continues up the amusingly named Awkward Hill, which is lined with attractive cottages, or skirts Rack Isle, parallel to the river, and continues on to 17th-century Arlington Mill.

▼ The River Coln and Arlington Row

SEE A LOCAL CHURCH

St Mary's Church

The church has a Saxon core, which can be seen in the lower parts of the chancel arch and in the Saxon cross shaft set into the chancel wall. The original church was extended and embellished throughout the Middle Ages: there's a 13th-century south aisle with lancet windows, a large Perpendicular window to the right of the porch, and a Norman north doorway. The churchyard has a fine assortment of tombs and gravestones, a number of which commemorate the local clothiers and weavers who financed the development of the church over several centuries. Part of the churchyard is known as the Bisley Piece as a result of a curious story. It seems that the village of Bisley once possessed what was called a 'bone hole', around which there are several legends. Some 600 years ago, a priest is supposed to have fallen in and died. The incident apparently angered the Pope himself, and consequently the pontiff forbade burials in Bisley (see page 215) for two years. Instead, at considerable inconvenience, the residents had to bury their dead at Bibury, 15 miles away.

10 hidden gems

- **Bisley** page 215
- **Blockley** page 68
- **Chedworth** page 88
- **Guiting Power** page 133
- **Ilmington** page 140
- **Minchinhampton** page 147
- **Minster Lovell** page 149
- **Miserden** page 95
- **Snowshill** page 189
- **Stanton** page 192

EXPLORE BY BIKE

The Carter Company
the-carter-company.co.uk
HP22 5EZ | 01296 631671
Cycling holidays in the Cotswolds, including a Cotswolds Valleys Tour that takes in Bibury and Burford.

GO FISHING

Bibury Trout Farm and Fishery
biburytroutfarm.co.uk
GL7 5NL | 01285 740215
Open Apr–Sep 8–6; closes at 5pm Mar and Oct, 4pm Nov–Feb

Next door to Arlington Mill you'll find Bibury Trout Farm and Fishery, where budding fishermen can catch their own fish or buy them from the shop. Children will love it too, as they can have fun in the play area or watch the trout leaping.

EAT AND DRINK

Catherine Wheel
catherinewheel-bibury.co.uk
Arlington Row, GL7 5ND
01285 740250
Catherine Wheel is a former blacksmith's that opened as an inn in 1856. A warm welcome, good ales and quality food remain its hallmarks. The beautiful Cotswold-stone

building, stable courtyard and orchard date back to the 15th century, and plenty of historical features remain.

The William Morris Tea Rooms
thewilliammorris.com
11 The Street, GL7 5NP | 01285 740555
You are bound to want to loiter in this delightful village, so treat yourself to an afternoon cream tea here, which is also a tiny two-roomed B&B.

PLACES NEARBY

Nearby are two villages with good pubs, while Barnsley (see page 60) lies to the west.

Ablington
The pretty neighbouring hamlet of Ablington comprises a collection of cottages, barns and manor houses. It was home to Reverend Arthur Gibbs, the 19th-century author of *A Cotswold Village*.

Coln Community Café
colnstores.co.uk
Main Street, Coln St Aldwyns, GL7 5AN | 01285 750294
Join the locals in this community-run cafe and store and find out what makes a small Cotswolds village tick. The cafe is a good start or finish point for a walk along the river to Bibury.

Blenheim Palace

see **Woodstock & Blenheim Palace**, page 246

Blockley MAP REF 262 B4

This pretty village with a misleadingly graceless name sits beside the fast-flowing Blockley Brook. It's less well known than many of its more crowded neighbours – partly because the big tour buses struggle on the narrow lanes around here. So with a satisfying degree of privacy you can visit Blockley and discover its subtle appeal. The village, with its pretty mill stream, is dotted with houses of varying ages. It was formerly a silk town, employing 600 people in the six mills here in the 1880s, just before the failure of the industry in the area. Many of the weavers' cottages remain, with the older ones clustered towards the village centre and the 19th-century silk workers' cottages terraced along the northern edge. One of the old mills can be seen beyond a pool near the church. A beautiful garden, Mill Dene, has been created around another of the old mills.

The church of St Peter and St Paul, with its Norman chancel, is unusually large, a testament to the village's early status. Within are a Jacobean pulpit and some interesting brasses. There are plenty of good walks to be taken around Blockley and the surrounding area.

▲ Blockley

GO ROUND THE GARDENS

Mill Dene Garden

milldenegarden.co.uk
School Lane, GL56 9HU
01386 700457 | Open Apr–Oct
Wed–Fri 10–5, Sat 9–1

A charming English garden that triumphs against its steep gradient and is full of humour. Remarkably, the creators admit that they knew nothing about gardening when they started out decorating this 2.5-acre site. There are plenty of inviting seats dotted about so you can take it easy, and they serve cream teas too.

PLACES NEARBY

To the north of Blockley you'll find the busier and prettier Chipping Campden (see page 96) or yellow Broadway (see page 77), a village of great popularity with tourists, but one that's nevertheless well worth a look. To the south is Moreton-in-Marsh (see page 151), which is better than it sounds. Nearby Batsford (see page 153) is an estate village with a Victorian church which contains some excellent monuments, while Batsford Park has an arboretum and a falconry centre.

Bourton-on-the-Water MAP REF 262 B5

Bourton-on-the-Water – especially in photographs – looks the very epitome of loveliness. 'The Venice of the Cotswolds', as it likes to call itself in a rather bold and un-English manner, has unique features not found in other Cotswolds villages, namely the five graceful footbridges that the River Windrush flows under in the village centre. They're backed by an appealing combination of Jacobean and Georgian facades in classic Cotswold stone. Bourton's church, St Lawrence's, likewise comprises a mixture of elements: it has a medieval chancel, a Victorian nave and a distinctive domed Georgian tower – complete with skull on the exterior, which serves as a salutary reminder of our mortality.

The cherry on the top of Bourton's (pricey, yet delicious) sundae, and the chief reason for its popularity, though, is that it offers a lot more attractions than most Cotswolds villages, where there's sometimes little to do other than look about a bit and click your camera a few times. These range from the excellent Birdland (featuring everything from penguins to birds of prey) to a model village (representing Bourton in miniature), a perfume factory, a motor museum, the Dragonfly Maze, and a model railway exhibition – all near the High Street and within walking distance of each other. Bourton has loads to do and is particularly child friendly in a region that isn't always obviously so.

Naturally however, with great popularity comes great crowds, and so many people visit Bourton that this must be the busiest place in the Cotswolds. It's become something of a victim of its own success; *all* the bus tours seem to stop here, bringing with them an abundance of gift shops and the likes.

▼ The River Windrush, Bourton-on-the-Water

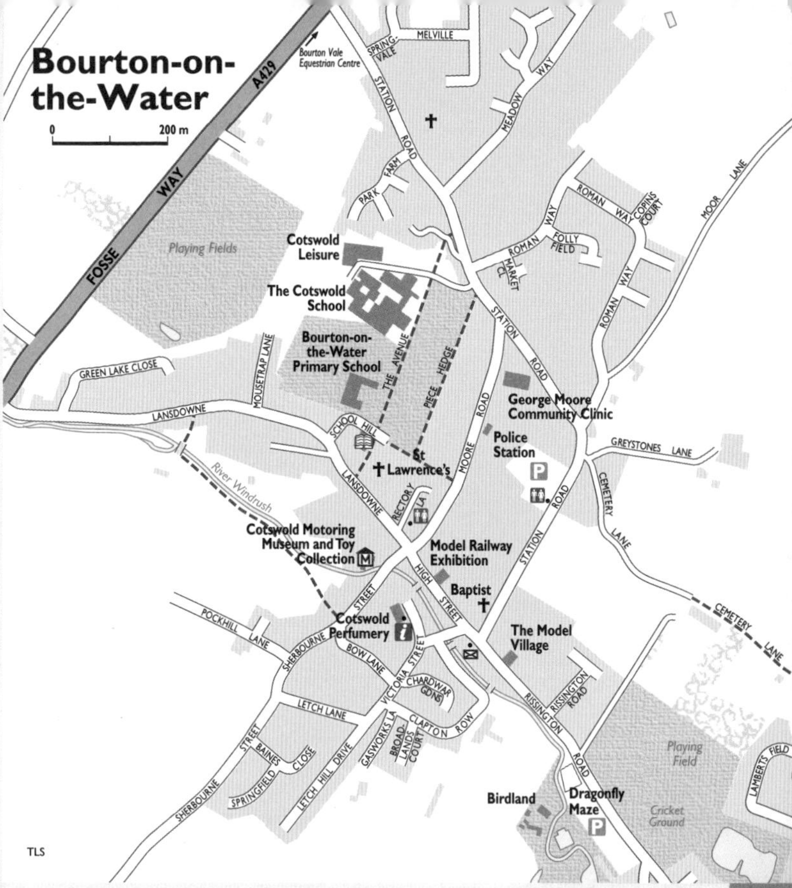

In peak season Bourton may have more the atmosphere of a theme park than a sleepy village.

The region isn't particularly hilly, but there's good valley-walking to be enjoyed nearby – especially the circuit linking Upper Slaughter, Lower Slaughter and Naunton. Alternatively, the climb up to the Rissingtons is a shorter and quieter option. Nearer at hand, to the east of Bourton there are a series of disused gravel pits which, now filled with water, have become sanctuaries for waterfowl. Following the path across Station Road from the car park makes for a very pleasant walk.

If you can, visit Bourton on a winter, spring or autumn weekday, and you may well love it. During standard visiting hours at any other time, you'll have to fight with the hordes for your prized photo – don't say you weren't warned. The absolute best day to visit Bourton, though – and to embrace the crowds, figuratively rather than literally – is the August Bank Holiday, when the typically quirky Cotswoldian Football in the River festival occurs (see page 55). A 30-minute game of football takes place in the normally calm Windrush River, with bridges for goalposts. Spectators shouldn't expect to remain dry.

VISIT THE MUSEUMS

Cotswold Motoring Museum & Toy Collection

see highlight panel opposite

Bourton Model Railway Exhibition

bourtonmodelrailway.co.uk
High Street, GL54 2AN | 01451 820686 | Open Jun–Aug 11–5, weekends only Sep–May (closed Jan)

Covering over 500 feet, these guys have some of the finest operating indoor model railway layouts in the country – so they say, anyway, and who are we to argue? Over 40 British and continental model trains run automatically on three main displays. There's also memorabilia, working fun fair models, and much more for those who love to keep it rail.

MEET THE BIRDLIFE

Birdland

see highlight panel overleaf

ENTERTAIN THE FAMILY

The Model Village

themodelvillage.com
Old New Inn, Rissington Road, GL54 2AF | 01451 820467
Open daily 10–6 (4 in winter)

The Model Village is a fascinatingly intricate one-ninth-scale replica of the centre of Bourton-on-the-Water, containing all the buildings from the Old Water Mill to the Old New Inn and the ford. There's a model village within the model village. Mini Bourton took local craftsmen five years to build and was officially opened in 1937, on the Coronation Day of King George VI and Queen Elizabeth.

Dragonfly Maze

thedragonflymaze.com
Rissington Road, GL54 2EE
01451 822251 | Open daily 10–5

Slowly negotiate your way to the centre (if you're lucky) of the high-hedge maze using clues on the flagstones en route. And if it isn't challenging enough, simply ask about 'the extra puzzle'. Perfectly suited to equally frustrate and amuse both children and adults.

TOUR THE FACTORY

Cotswold Perfumery

cotswold-perfumery.co.uk
GL54 2BU | 01451 820698
Open Mon–Sat 9.30–5, Sun 10.30–5 (in summer daily until 5.30)

This is one of Europe's few combined manufacturers and retailers of perfume, offering excellent factory tours and perfumery courses. 'We started with just one perfume – it was dreadful,' remembers John Stephen, the owner who turned his hobby into a business around 50 years ago.

TAKE OFF

Ballooning In The Cotswolds

ballooninginthecotswolds.co.uk
GL5 3EX | 01453 753221

Get in a basket to appreciate the Cotswolds from above. You can get an early morning start, or wait for the late afternoon/evening time slot. Flights are subject to weather. Allow up to four hours, with about an hour in the air.

Cotswold Motoring Museum & Toy Collection MAP REF 262 B5

cotswoldmotoringmuseum.co.uk
The Old Mill, GL54 2BY | 01451 821255 | Open mid-Feb to mid-Nov daily 10–6

Vintage car collections, classic cars and motorcycles, quaint caravans, original enamel signs and a collection of motoring curiosities might sound like an enthusiast's special delight, but this museum is very much aimed at children, too. A regularly changing exhibition takes a sideways look at some of the 20th century's motoring icons. Past exhibitions have included *Wallace & Gromit: The Curse of the Were-Rabbit*, and The Who film *Quadrophenia*.

Birdland MAP REF 262 B5

birdland.co.uk

Rissington Road, GL54 2BN, 01451 820480 | Open Easter–Oct daily 10–6, Nov–Mar 10–4 (last admission 1 hour before closing)

Birdland has the only group of king penguins in England. There are also flamingos, pelicans, owls, cranes, storks, waterfowl, parrots, falcons and many more feathered friends. The Desert House is home to the more delicate species, and the new Jurassic Journey is a trail of discovery for all things 'dinosaur'. It is also a reminder that today's bird species are directly descended from dinosaurs. Plenty to keep the kids – and adults – entertained.

EXPLORE BY BIKE

Hartwells Cotswolds Cycle Hire
hartwells.supanet.com
High Street, GL54 2AJ
01451 820405
Hartwells has a large choice of mountain bikes, hybrid and touring cycles, and tandems. Rentals include free parking.

SADDLE UP

Bourton Vale Equestrian Centre
bourtonvaleequestrian.co.uk
College Farm, Fosseway, GL54 2HN
01451 821101
Escorted riding in small groups around the Slaughter villages for 1 to 2 hours. All ages and abilities. Pre-booking essential.

EAT AND DRINK

Dial House ❀❀
dialhousehotel.com
High Street, GL54 2AN
01451 822244
This hotel occupies one of this popular village's oldest houses, built in the 18th century from honeyed Cotswold stone. The kitchen delivers finely tuned Anglo-French cooking.

10 places to take the kids

- **Birdland and Dragonfly Maze, Bourton-on-the-Water,** page 72 and opposite
- **Chedworth Roman Villa,** page 87
- **Cogges Manor Farm,** page 243
- **Cotswold Farm Park,** page 133
- **Cotswold Water Park,** page 191
- **Cotswold Wildlife Park,** page 81
- **Minchinhampton Common,** page 148, **Rodborough Common,** page 213, **Selsley Common,** page 212, or **Cleeve Common,** page 236, **a great place** for kite-flying, Frisbee-throwing or just a run around
- **Prinknash Bird and Deer Park,** page 179
- **Slimbridge Wetland Centre,** page 185
- **Westonbirt Arboretum,** page 220

PLACES NEARBY

The Cotswold Farm Park (see page 133) is only 10 minutes' drive away. The Slaughters (see page 184) – Upper and Lower – are almost as good-looking as Bourton, and slightly less crowded. West of Bourton is a group of interesting villages – **Notgrove, Turkdean, Hazleton** and **Cold Aston** – that are all worth a visit.

Naunton

Normally a place like Naunton, tucked into the bottom of a classic shallow but steep Cotswold valley, would be a pleasing attraction by itself. But because it's close to three other attractive villages it gets overlooked. The best way to visit it is on a walking loop from Bourton-on-the-Water, taking in both Slaughters as you stroll.

Bredon Hill MAP REF 261 D3

Bredon Hill is quite the oddity around these parts. A traditional hill – one you can walk all around the bottom of in one go and everything – in the Cotswolds. Imagine! The landscape north of Tewkesbury, just within the borders of Worcestershire, is dominated by the 981-foot-high bulk of Bredon. This huge outlier was part of the escarpment many centuries ago. The countryside here is quite different from that of the Cotswolds proper. The landscape is more in tune with the surrounding Vale of Evesham, and building in stone is much less common. The hill itself is an excellent place for both rambling and brambling: in the autumn, the lanes and tracks that criss-cross Bredon's slopes are thick with blackberries.

The earthworks at the summit are the remains of Iron Age hill fort Kemerton Camp, probably abandoned in the 1st century AD after a big battle against the invading Belgae. The slashed remains of 50 bodies were discovered here, grouped around the main entrance where they presumably fell in battle.

There are also Roman earthworks and ancient standing stones here. The Banbury Stone is nicknamed 'Elephant Stone', for reasons that become obvious once you see it, while two stones near the summit are called the King and Queen Stones. Locals once believed that passing between the King and Queen Stones would cure illness. The summit's chunky tower is called Parsons Folly, and was built in the mid-18th century as a summer house.

Bredon Hill features in plenty of poetry, writing and art, and is most famously immortalised in A E Housman's poem 21 from *A Shropshire Lad:*

In summertime on Bredon
The bells they sound so clear
Round both the shires they ring them
In steeples far and near
A happy noise to hear.

PLACES NEARBY

Below the hill are several villages of interest. At **Beckford**, silk continues to be printed by hand, while at **Kemerton** a footpath takes you through the exotic gardens of the old priory. **Overbury**, with its variety of half-timbered and stone houses, is one of the loveliest villages in Worcestershire. **Bredon** itself was immortalised in John Moore's affectionate story of mid-20th century rural life, *Brensham Village*. The village is noted for its magnificent 14th-century threshing barn with its aisled interior, now owned by the National Trust.

Broadway MAP REF 262 A4

Without wishing to cause an argument, Broadway is one of the five, or possibly three, most handsome villages in the Cotswolds. Yet, with its broad main street – there's a clue in the name – ploughing busily up the lower slopes of the escarpment, it's hardly a typical one. Most of the houses on the high street date from the 16th, 17th and 18th centuries. Some were inns, for Broadway was an important staging post on the London to Worcester route, following the construction of the road up Fish Hill in the early 18th century. The Lygon Arms, now one of the most famous hotels in the country, is a reminder of that period. Later the village was the object of the attentions of William Morris and other creative luminaries, including American novelist Henry James and pioneering designer Gordon Russell.

Most of the village can be discovered on foot. In Russell Square, you'll find a museum devoted to 20th-century furniture designer Gordon Russell. Broadway's original church, St Eadburgha's, is out on the Snowshill Road, and is worth a visit. Broadway Tower, an impressive Gothic folly built on the second highest point in the Cotswolds, overlooks the town. From here you can look out over a 62-mile radius and peer (allegedly) into 16 counties. The view is definitely worth the steep climb up the hill when following the Cotswold Way.

VISIT THE MUSEUM

Gordon Russell Museum
gordonrussellmuseum.org
15 Russell Square, WR12 7AP
01386 854695 | Open Mar–Oct Tue–Sun 11–5, Nov–Feb closes at 4; closed Jan and Mon

Schooled in the Arts and Crafts tradition of the Cotswolds, Gordon Russell was a furniture designer and maker, calligrapher, entrepreneur, educator, and a champion of accessible, well crafted design. He believed that good design has a lasting impact on people's lives. The museum celebrates his life and work during his 60 years in Broadway with a collection of furniture that embraces styles from the Arts and Crafts to 1930s streamlined Modernism, and from Utility Furniture to 1980s luxury postmodernism.

GET OUTDOORS

Broadway Tower & Country Park
broadwaytower.co.uk
Broadway, WR12 7LB
01386 852390

Members of the Arts and Crafts Movement used the Tower, completed in 1798, as a holiday retreat – artists William Morris, Dante Gabriel Rossetti and Edward Burne-Jones were frequent visitors. The vantage point was also used to track enemy planes during the World Wars. Nowadays there's a former nuclear bunker (weekends only), a dog-friendly cafe, a shop, a museum and lots of stairs to climb to the top. There are deer in the park, too.

EAT AND DRINK

Tisanes Tea Rooms
tisanes-tearooms.co.uk
21 The Green, WR12 7AA
01386 853296
They serve wonderful cream teas, as well as an unusual and extensive variety of sandwiches and lunches, in this pretty 17th-century stone building on the High Street.

PLACES NEARBY

Buckland, within walking distance of Broadway, is a pretty village with a fine 15th-century parsonage that is said to be England's oldest. The church contains a Jacobean pulpit, 15th-century glass and a panel thought to have come from Hailes Abbey (see page 235), near Winchcombe.

Buckland Manor
bucklandmanor.com
WR12 7LY | 01386 852626
Privately owned 13th-century Buckland Manor is one of those places that's so fancy you won't ever feel you belong – which can make a visit all the more pleasurable. Everything's dripping in luxury, expense and elegance. In summer, take tea on the garden patio. And you could always add a glass of champagne to your order...

Burford MAP REF 258 C3

Yet another memorably handsome, classic Cotswolds town. Albeit not quite as oooh-inducing as the Biburys of this world, it's more characterful than instantly cute. Just off the main Oxford road, Burford is all but invisible to passing motorists. Drive north from the roundabout, however, and almost immediately, from the brow of the ridge, Burford slips away before you in a cascade of attractive inns and charming cottages. The wide main street, lined with shops and pubs, passes the church on the right before crossing the Windrush on a medieval bridge (1322) by the old mill. Burford's prosperity has historically depended on wool, quarrying, and coaching. There were burgesses here in the 13th century, and the town grew rapidly in the first Elizabethan era to become an important wool centre. The nearby quarries at the Barringtons, Upton and Taynton produced some of the Cotswold stone used in the construction of some of England's finest buildings – Blenheim Palace, St Paul's Cathedral and the colleges of Oxford. In the 18th century, at the dawn of the coaching era, Burford became an important stop on the route east to Oxford and London. In the days immediately following the opening of the turnpikes, when Burford was an established coaching

▲ Burford

town, its inns competed with each other for travellers' custom. 'Burford Bait' was the name given to the famously large meals they provided, which probably relied on venison poached from Wychwood Forest. The coaching era, however, came to an end with the ascendancy of the railway, which had the audacity to bypass Burford.

Burford provides some enjoyable strolling. While the High Street is the main thoroughfare, Sheep Street to the west and Witney Street and Church Lane to the east have much to offer too. Sheep Street has some very fine inns – the Bay Tree Hotel and the Lamb Inn (the old brewery next door houses the Tourist Information Centre) – while Witney Street boasts perhaps the finest building in town, the 17th-century Great House. From Witney Street, Guildenford leads to Church Lane, where a row of lovely almshouses (founded in 1457) are close to St John the Baptist church. Opposite the almshouses sit the old buildings of Burford Grammar School, which was founded in 1577 by wealthy cloth merchant Simon Wysdom. He also constructed the Weavers' Cottages, which are grouped near the medieval bridge.

The 15th-century parish church is impressive. Among the chapels and monuments, perhaps the finest is the effigy of Sir Lawrence Tanfield, James I's Lord Chief Baron of the Exchequer, erected in 1628. Another fine memorial honours Edmund Harman, barber-surgeon to Henry VIII, and includes Britain's first representation of Amazonian Indians from the New World. The autograph of a Leveller, one of 340 Roundhead mutineers kept in the church for three days during the Civil War, is inscribed on the rim of the font: 'Anthony Sedley prisner 1649' (sic). Taking Priory Lane, which meets the High Street near the bridge, leads you past the handsome Elizabethan Priory and around to Falkland Hall (1558).

At the corner of High Street and Sheep Street you'll find the pillared Tolsey, a Tudor house where wool merchants used to meet and which now houses a museum of considerable interest. Further down you'll see the wide arch of the old George Hotel, where Charles II used to stay with his mistress Nell Gwynn, which later became an important coaching inn. Their son was created Earl of Burford.

Due to the proximity of the Bibury races, which used to take place near Aldsworth, Burford was also once famous for its saddlery business. As a result of Charles II and Nell Gwynn's visits to the town when the races were on, Burford saddles received an unspoken royal appointment.

ENTERTAIN THE FAMILY

Cotswold Wildlife Park and Gardens

see highlight panel opposite

SEE A LOCAL CHURCH

The 'wool' Church of St John the Baptist

burfordchurch.org

Lawrence Lane, at the lower end of Burford High Street, beside the River Windrush, OX18 4RY

St John's began life as a Norman church, as the central tower and west wall, with its typical Norman door, can attest. It was rebuilt in the 13th century, but in the 15th century the nave was remodelled to add enormous Perpendicular windows. A fine clerestory and a splendid three-storey porch were also constructed.

One curiosity to be found at St Johns is the memorial tablet to Edmund Harman, barber-surgeon to Henry VIII. It is carved with one of the earliest known representations of South American Indians.

The brightly coloured pulpit was assembled in 1878 from fragments of 15th-century wooden tracery. The wooden chantry chapel opposite the door survived the Reformation thanks to the local squire, who used it as a private pew.

In a small chapel north of the chancel, there is an early 17th-century canopied tomb occupied by Sir Lawrence

Cotswold Wildlife Park and Gardens MAP REF 258 B3

cotswoldwildlifepark.co.uk
OX18 4JP | 01993 823006 | Open daily 10–6, until 5pm Nov–Mar (last admission 4.30 Apr–Oct, 3.30 Nov–Mar)

Two miles south of Burford, this 160-acre landscaped zoological park (surrounding a Victorian Gothic-style manor house) contains more than 260 different animal species. Many of the animals, such as Asiatic lions, lemurs, rhinos and wild camels, are endangered. Visit the reptiles, hide away in the bat house, spot the sloths or walk through the lemur enclosure. There's an adventure playground and skymaze, a children's farmyard, and train rides during summer. There are opportunities to feed the penguins and the bats. The park has also become one of the Cotswolds' leading attractions for garden enthusiasts. Its exotic summer displays and varied plantings offer something of interest all year round.

Tanfield, Lord Chief Baron of the Exchequer, and his wife. At their feet kneels their grandson, Lucius Cary, Viscount Falkland, the Cavalier courtier and poet who was killed at the Battle of Newbury in 1643.

G E Street restored the church in 1877, removing most of the original plaster in the process – much to the ire of William Morris, who founded the Society for the Protection of Ancient Buildings (SPAB) as a direct consequence. Thankfully this new society ensured that many of the region's fine churches and other buildings were preserved as they were.

A plaque on the outside of the church commemorates three Roundhead soldiers who were executed here in 1649. They were the ringleaders of a band of mutinous troops known as Levellers, 340 of whom were imprisoned by Cromwell in the church during the Civil War. One inscribed his name on the lead font, which can still be seen.

EXPLORE BY BIKE

The Carter Company
the-carter-company.com
01296 631671
Cycling holidays in the Cotswolds, including a Ramble and Ride in the Cotswolds Tour that takes in Burford and Bourton-on-the-Water.

EAT AND DRINK

The Angel at Burford ®
theangelatburford.co.uk
14 Witney Street, OX18 4SN
01993 822714
The Angel is a gem of a pub, albeit an upmarket one, with a row of Hook Norton real ales on the pumps and a roaring log fire during cooler months. It's the kind of place where your dog is made welcome, as well as you. There's a serious approach to food, too, with due respect paid to local suppliers and the seasons. Look out for the summer beer festival.

The Bay Tree Hotel ®
cotswold-inns-hotels.co.uk/baytree
Sheep Street, OX18 4LW
01993 822791
A Cotswold country inn smothered in wisteria with flagstone floors and leaded windows overlooking a garden is an appealing prospect, and The Bay Tree fits the bill. Candlelit in the evenings, the dining room is a cream-coloured space offering cooking that takes a modern approach.

The Bull at Burford ®®
bullatburford.co.uk
105 High Street, OX18 4RG
01993 822220
The Bull started life as a coaching inn in 1610, so it's seen some high-profile visitors over the centuries – Lord Nelson and Charles II, to name just two. The Bull's classy restaurant features bare Cotswold-stone walls, age-blackened beams and original artwork. The modern French-influenced dishes show welcome ambition.

PLACES NEARBY
South of Burford is the excellent Cotswold Wildlife Park (see page 81), the only place to see descendants of the Cotswold Lion sheep. To the east are pretty Minster Lovell (see page 149) and Witney (see page 242).

Castle Combe MAP REF 257 D5

Wiltshire's Castle Combe is Stanton's (see page 192) biggest rival to the coveted Prettiest Village in the Cotswolds title – that is, if it's not the prettiest in the whole country. The historical village, which always seems to be sun-kissed, is tucked away in a stream-threaded, wooded combe.

So beautifully preserved in aspic is it that, as well as garnering regular clusters of tourists, it has also captured the attention of filmmakers and thus earned itself a tidy living in recent years as a film-set. Steven Spielberg's *War Horse* (2011) is among its more recent credits. When the sound technicians, makeup artists and Jeremy Irvine have left town, though, Castle Combe settles back into unruffled pastoral tranquillity, a picture of serenity.

Entering Castle Combe, you'll see 15th-century Cotswold-stone cottages with steep gabled roofs, all surrounding a turreted church and a stone-canopied market cross. There is also a medieval manor house, a fast-flowing stream in the main street leading to an ancient packhorse bridge, and a perfectly picturesque river. The timeless valleys and tumbling wooded hillsides that surround the village make for some lovely strolls.

The nearby castle, which gave the village its name and of which little more than earthworks remain, began life as a Roman fort. The Saxons used it before it became a Norman castle in 1135, and the home of the de Dunstanville family. In the 13th and 14th centuries, the village established itself as an important weaving centre. Sir John Fastolf, the lord of the manor, erected fulling mills along the By Brook and 50 cottages for his workers. Castle Combe prospered greatly with the growth of the cloth trade in Wiltshire, becoming more like a town. It hosted a weekly market and an annual fair. For centuries the villages produced a red and white cloth, known as 'Castle Combe'. Cloth manufacture began to decline in the early 18th century when the diminutive By Brook was unable to power the larger machinery being introduced. People moved to larger towns seeking work, and Castle Combe became depopulated and returned to an agricultural existence. An annual fair, centred around the market cross, continued until

1904, and Castle Combe remained an 'estate' village until 1949, when the whole village was sold at auction.

A favourite view of the village can be had from the old weavers' cottages, across the bridge. The greatest tribute to the wealth of the weaving industry is reflected in St Andrew's Church, which probably dates from the 13th century; at the base of the tower stands the faceless clock, among the most ancient working clocks in the country. The church's impressive Perpendicular tower was built in 1436, when the church was enlarged.

Outside the village is the motor racing circuit which hosted national championship races until the early 2000s. Motor sports and other popular events are still held here.

There's almost no parking in the village itself, so when you're encouraged to park up at the top of the hill – a request that may leave you eyeing the maker with suspicion – you're better off obeying.

PLAY A ROUND

Manor House Hotel and Golf Club

manorhousegolf.co.uk

SN14 7JW | 01249 782206

Open Mon, Tue, Thu and Fri. Other days pm only

Set in a wonderful location within the wooded estate of the 14th-century Manor House, this course includes five par 5s and some spectacular par 3s. Manicured fairways and hand-cut greens, together with the River Bybrook meandering through the middle, make for a very picturesque and dramatic course.

EAT AND DRINK

The Bybrook at The Manor House Hotel ®®®

manorhouse.co.uk

Castle Combe, SN14 7HR

01249 782206

The dining room is a sober setting, exuding class with its mullioned windows, muted colours and pristine white linen, while the cooking aims to cut a contemporary dash with tip-top ingredients and a tendency towards complexity. Much of the produce is grown in the kitchen garden, and much of the rest is sourced from organic growers in the village.

Charlbury MAP REF 259 D2

The Evenlode valley area of the Cotswolds hides its villages well. Charlbury is a small, busy town looking across the valley towards Wychwood Forest. It has a large number of shops and inns, and a railway station designed by Isambard Kingdom Brunel. Although primarily a prosperous sheep town, it was also a centre of glove manufacture in the 18th century. Behind the main street is a small green, the Playing Close, which has a

Jacobean-style drinking fountain at one end and which is surrounded by handsome villas and cottages tucked behind solid iron railings. Charlbury's church, St Mary's, on the other side of the main street, is largely Perpendicular in style, with Norman pillars and arches on the north side. Unexpectedly, it has a rather Victorian interior. The town museum in Market Street is dedicated to the traditional crafts and industries of the area.

SEE A LOCAL CHURCH

Church of St Mary the Virgin

charlburychurch.co.uk
Church Lane, OX7 3PS

The interior of this church is something of a surprise. It was much altered in the 19th century, and in the early 1990s the main altar was moved to the nave's west end, creating more space and enhancing the church's architectural features – particularly the fine Norman arcade on the north aisle. The five-light windows at the east end of both chancel and aisle are good examples of 14th-century Decorated tracery. A sundial from 1776 is preserved on a south-facing buttress.

EAT AND DRINK

The Bull Inn

bullinn-charlbury.com
Sheep Street, OX7 3RR
01608 810689

This handsome stone-fronted 16th-century free house presides over Charlbury's main street. Log fires and the beamed interior add to the charming period character. Outside, the vine-covered terrace is a lovely backdrop for a drink or meal in summer. The Bull Inn serves Bull Bitter, brewed for the pub.

PLACES NEARBY

At **Finstock**, a few miles south of Charlbury, the poet T S Eliot was baptised in 1927. Novelist Barbara Pym, who died in 1980, lived here for the last eight years of her life. You will also find a couple of parks nearby at Cornbury and Ditchley.

Cornbury Park

cornburypark.co.uk
OX7 3EH

Beyond the River Evenlode is Cornbury Park, a gift from Charles I to Henry Danvers. A pleasant walk can be had through the grounds, though the largely 17th-century house itself is not open to the public.

Ditchley Park

ditchley.co.uk
OX7 4EP | 01608 677346

Ditchley Park, west of Charlbury, is open to the public by appointment only. James Gibbs built this 18th-century mansion for the 2nd Earl of Lichfield, while 'Capability' Brown did the landscaping. The grounds consist of a 3,000-acre park, a lake, temples and woodlands. The house was the meeting place of Winston Churchill and Harry Hopkins during World War II.

Chavenage House MAP REF 257 D3

chavenage.com

Near Tetbury, GL8 8XP, 01666 502329 | Open May–Sep Thu & Sun 2–5 (last tour 4). Also Easter Sun & Mon

Numerous TV programmes and films have been shot at this beautiful, Elizabethan house. It served as Trenwith in the BBC's *Poldark* (2015), and appeared in the 2008 adaptation of *Tess of the d'Urbervilles*, as well as several tales related to ghosts, ghouls or spectral goings-on; this creaky old manor house has a long history of hauntings that dates back to the owner, Nathaniel Stephens. A relative of Oliver Cromwell by marriage, Nathaniel was Parliament's member for Gloucestershire. Cromwell sent his son-in-law, Henry Ireton, to Chavenage to persuade him to vote for the arrest and trial of Charles I – and convinced him to state in Parliament that the best cure for a sick plant is 'cutting off its head'.

Nathaniel's daughter was horrified and laid a curse on the family, and sure enough, a few months later Nathaniel was struck down by a fatal illness. When he died, a black coach and horses arrived, driven by a headless coachman, and the ghost of Nathaniel was literally spirited away – or so the story goes.

The room where Cromwell slept has reputedly witnessed several ghostly happenings. One visitor was apparently so terrified that she packed her bags and fled, walking the seven miles to Kemble Station in the middle of the night. Other weird occurrences include appearances from a 'grey lady', an apparently restless heavy wooden bed that lifts off its legs, and sightings of a ghostly monk in the chapel.

▼ Chedworth Roman Villa

Built in 1576, the Elizabethan house contains stained glass from the 16th century and even earlier, as well as fine furniture and tapestries. Chavenage is a typical Elizabethan E-shaped house, with a central porch and two projecting bays. The main door also has a sanctuary ring and a spy hole, which probably came from the priory. With its tall windows containing late-medieval glass, its fine 16th-century screen and the minstrels' gallery above it, the main hall retains the atmosphere of Elizabeth's reign.

Queen Anne is thought to have lodged at Chavenage. The splendid bed that stands in her room is supposed to have been converted for the use of her personal physician.

At the bottom of the stairs there is a memorial chest which dates from the beginning of the 17th century, while the ballroom has fine court cupboards and Cromwellian chairs upholstered in leather. The present chapel was built in the early years of the last century, but it contains a lovely Elizabethan monument and an important Saxon font.

PLACES NEARBY

The nearest place to this surprisingly remote manor is handsome Tetbury (see page 219), a former wool town. To the north is Nailsworth (see page 155), a mill town tucked into a steep wooded valley.

Chedworth Roman Villa MAP REF 257 F2

nationaltrust.org.uk

Yanworth, GL54 3LJ | 01242 890256 | Open Apr–Oct daily 10–5, mid-Feb to Mar and Nov 10–4

With the obvious exception of Bath's baths, you'll struggle to find a better insight into Roman Britain than the one offered by this National Trust property. Chedworth Roman Villa was rediscovered in 1864 by a gamekeeper. Set in a wooded combe, with 50 rooms, it was one of the largest mansions in the country and was home to some of the richest people in the country during its heyday in the 4th century. What remains are the lower parts of the walls – which give us enough information to identify the purposes of each of the rooms – and compelling fourth-century mosaics featuring, among other things, representations of the four seasons. The mosaics can be viewed via state-of-the-art walkways. Two bath houses and a temple with spring provide us with insight into non-mod cons such as latrines and underfloor heating. In terms of mod cons, there's also a cafe. You can park on site, but consider parking in Chedworth and enjoying a half-hour or mile-long walk from the village. There is, in general, good walking to be had nearby.

PLACES NEARBY

Most people will come to the area to visit the Villa, but relaxed little Chedworth, a mile away, is worth a look as well. At Colesbourne you will find a handsome, stone-built inn.

Chedworth

Because it's spread around a valley head, the village is said to be the longest in England. The church has a 12th-century tower, and the 17th-century Seven Tuns pub has a waterwheel and good beer.

Four miles north of Cirencester on the A429, you'll find the Chedworth Farm Shop.

The Colesbourne Inn

thecolesbourneinn.co.uk
Colesbourne, GL53 9NP
01242 870376

The Colesbourne Inn is just a short meadow walk from the source of the Thames. Dating back to 1827, the inn oozes historic charm and character. The seasonal menus combine traditional pub classics with modern ideas.

Cheltenham MAP REF 261 D5

If you're looking for a spa town in this part of the country, this probably isn't the one that you're thinking of, overshadowed as Cheltenham is by nearby Bath.

It's not an architectural match for its similarly-spa-boasting rival at the bottom end of the Cotswolds, but Cheltenham is a fine place nonetheless – and, crucially, unlike its southern cousin, Cheltenham is not usually swamped with tourists. Built against the base of the Cotswolds escarpment, overlooked by Cleeve and Leckhampton Hills, it's a useful base for visiting the escarpment hills, as well as the Severn Vale, the Forest of Dean and the Wye Valley. It also doesn't have quite the reputation it should for its festivals: there's a Folk Festival in February, the National Hunt Festival horse racing festival in March; Jazz in April; the Science Festival in June; the Summer Cricket Festival and the Music Festival in July; and the Literature Festival in October. That's a lot of festivals.

The discovery of a spring in 1716 rocketed what was then a market town of comparative insignificance to prominence as a fashionable spa town. The wealthy rushed to Cheltenham to bathe and to try to cure their myriad ills, which ranged from worms to constipation. The Regency era (1811–1820) building boom has left behind a town of considerable elegance, with handsome, wide streets lined with tasteful villas and terraces.

The centre is fairly compact and easy to explore on foot. The original town ran along the current High Street, which is now home to major chain stores and shopping arcades. The Regency town spread southwards along the Promenade, one

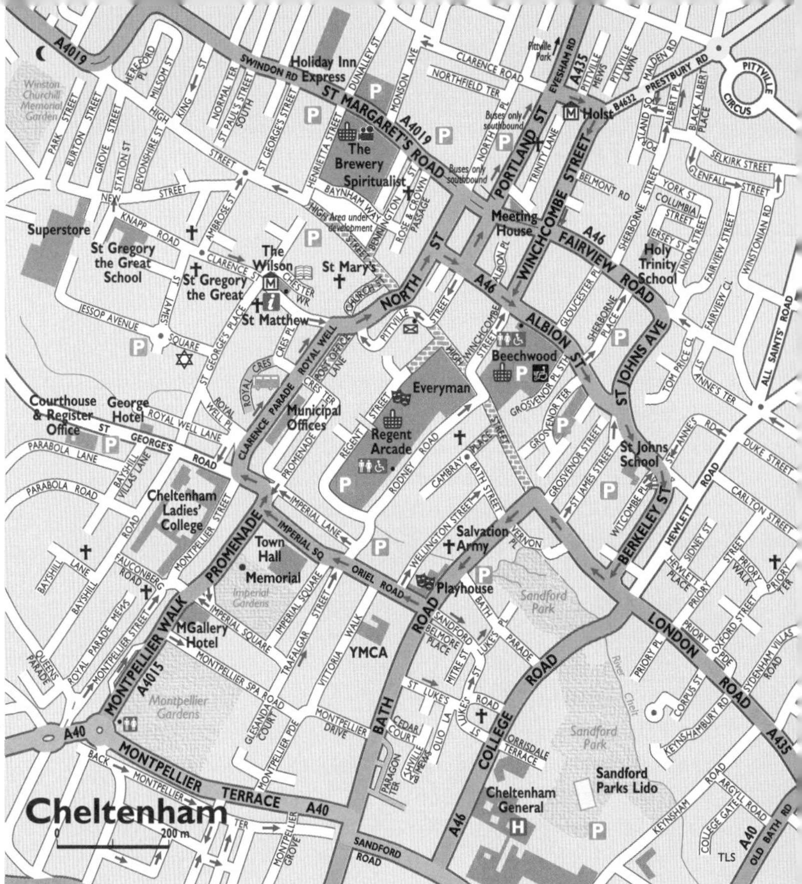

of the finest thoroughfares in the country, and which is today lined with elegant shops. The magnificent terrace at the northern end, built to house those coming to take the waters, now houses the Tourist Information Centre. In front of this terrace stand the Neptune Fountain and a statue of Edward Wilson, the Cheltenham botanist and explorer who accompanied Captain Scott on his ill-fated expedition to the South Pole. The Promenade continues gently uphill, passing the Imperial Garden and the Town Hall on the left, and reaching the imposing, porticoed facade of the MGallery (formerly Queens Hotel), which was built on the site of the Imperial Spa.

The road narrows between the shops here. It is worth walking along Queens Circus and a short way down Fauconberg Road – on the right is Cheltenham Ladies' College, part of which conceals the original Royal Well. On the left is one of Cheltenham's loveliest lanes, Montpellier Street, which is lined with interesting shops. A small alleyway on the left leads back towards the main road, passing old Montpellier Arcade on the left. At the top of the road is the Rotunda. Although it's now a bank, this was originally the Montpellier Spa. Its design was apparently based on the Pantheon in Rome. The well-preserved interior is worth a look.

There's plenty more Regency architecture to enjoy in the area close to Montpellier, notably to the west in Lansdowne. Heading southeast will take you to Suffolk Square, just beyond which, along Suffolk Parade and Suffolk Road, are some independent antique and curio shops.

North of the High Street is Pittville. Its showpiece, the Pittville Pump Rooms, were designed between 1825 and 1830 by John Forbes, a local man. The Pump Rooms constitute a magnificent architectural ensemble, and they were to have been the focal point of Joseph Pitt's Pittville Estate. The project ran out of money before reaching completion, but Forbes still left his mark on his hometown. His legacy survives in the Pump Rooms, Pittville Park (with its lake surrounded by villas in an array of fantastic styles), Pittville Lawn, Clarence Square and Wellington Square. In the Pump Rooms, which are often used for concerts and recitals, you can taste the waters originally recommended for gout, rheumatism and constipation.

Cheltenham is noted for the ironwork that decorates many of the early buildings of the town. Distinctive balconies of finely wrought iron adorn many of the elegant buildings, adding a continental atmosphere to the streets and squares. Particularly fine examples are to be found along Oxford Parade, Royal Parade and Suffolk Square.

Cheltenham also has a growing reputation as a great place for eating.

VISIT THE MUSEUMS

The Wilson

cheltenhammuseum.org.uk
Clarence Street, GL50 3JT
01242 237431 | Open daily 9.30–5.15

This gallery and museum has four floors, with archive collections and space for local heroes, including explorer Edward Wilson, Captain Robert Scott's right-hand man on his 1912 Antarctic expedition. There are also large galleries for temporary exhibitions: international and national touring shows, highlights from other collections and family-focused stuff. The Arts & Crafts collection is housed in a new gallery, and there's a Tourist Information Centre on the ground floor.

Holst Birthplace Museum

holstmuseum.org.uk
4 Clarence Road, GL52 2AY
01242 524846 | Open Tue–Sat 10–4 (10–5 Jun–Sep and Sun 1.30–5); closed mid-Dec to Jan

Cheltenham's other famous son is the composer Gustav Holst, the composer of *The Planets Suite*. Holst was born in Cheltenham in 1874. The house in Clarence Road where he grew up is now a museum dedicated, in part, to the life of the composer, and in part to an evocation of life in the Regency and Victorian city. There's a Gustav Holst Way medium-distance trail in the north Cotswolds too, which calls in at places relevant to his life.

Pittville Pump Room
cheltenhamtownhall.org.uk
Pittville Park, GL52 3JE
01242 523852 | Open Wed–Sun 10–4 (events permitting)
Cheltenham's elegant signature building is the Pump Room (free admission), designed between 1825 and 1830 by local man John Forbes as a grand spa. Though the project ran out of cash before it could be fully realised, at least this centrepiece was finished. Inside, you can sample the (honking) spa waters from a marble fountain. The rooms are often used for concerts and recitals, so it's best to check if it's open when you want to visit.

GO TO THE RACES

Cheltenham Racecourse
cheltenham-thejockeyclub.co.uk
GL50 4SH | 01242 513014
16 race days per year
The track is best known for the Cheltenham Festival, which is held there in March. This is the top three-day meeting of the National Hunt season. It features the Gold Cup and Champion Hurdle, and attracts more than 50,000 spectators. The Hall of Fame tells the story of the history of the racecourse.

GO SHOPPING

The Courtyard
Montpellier Street, GL50 1SR
Times vary, but generally open Mon–Sat 9–5.30
Escape the chain stores by visiting this two-level complex of chic boutiques, specialist shops, antiques dealers and stylish eateries, clustered around a piazza and an elevated walkway.

GO TO THE THEATRE

Playhouse Theatre
cheltplayhouse.org.uk
47–53 Bath Road, GL53 7HG
01242 522852

Everyman Theatre
everymantheatre.org.uk
Regent Street, GL50 1HQ
01242 572573

▼ Holst Statue, Imperial Gardens

▲ View over Cheltenham

TAKE OFF

Ballooning In The Cotswolds

balloonninginthecotswolds.co.uk

Cheltenham, GL5 3EX

01453 753221

see page 72

EXPLORE BY BIKE

Compass Holidays

compass-holidays.com

The Studios, Beechurst House, The Reddings, GL51 6RT | 01242 250642

This local Cotswold company runs walking and cycling short breaks and holidays around the region.

SADDLE UP

Ullenwood Court Riding Centre

ullenwoodriding.co.uk

Ullenwood, Cheltenham, GL53 9QS

01242 575020

Ullenwood Court offers escorted rides through lovely countryside or tuition by BHS qualified staff, as well as pub rides. They also cater for people with disabilities.

GO SWIMMING

Sandford Parks Lido

sandfordparkslido.org.uk

Keynsham Road, GL53 7PU | 01242 524430 | Open May–Sep; check website for times

One of the largest outdoor pools in the country set in the gardens of Sandford Parks, with a heated main pool, children's pool and paddling pool.

GO WALKING

Cotswolds Walking Holidays

cotswoldwalks.com

01386 833799

As their name suggests, this husband and wife team run walking holidays in the Cotswolds area.

PLAY A ROUND

Cotswold Hills Golf Club

cotswoldhills-golfclub.com
Ullenwood, Cheltenham, GL53 9QT
01242 515264 | Open daily all year

A beautiful, free-draining, gently undulating parkland course high on the Cotswolds, with stunning panoramic views of the surrounding countryside.

Lilley Brook Golf Club

lilleybrook.co.uk
Cirencester Road, Charlton Kings, GL53 8EG | 01242 526785
Open daily all year

This challenging parkland/downland course on the lower slopes of Leckhampton Hill also has outstanding views of Cheltenham, the Malverns and the Black Mountains.

EAT AND DRINK

Le Champignon Sauvage ®®®®

lechampignonsauvage.co.uk
24–28 Suffolk Road, GL50 2AQ
01242 573449

The cookbooks that have issued forth from this supremely civilised place over the years provide fascinating snapshots of British restaurant dining of the past quarter-century. The modern French food is served in a sunny yellow and cornflower blue room hung with striking modern paintings. The scene is refined, comfortable and relaxing.

The Curry Corner ®®

thecurrycorner.com
133 Fairview Road, GL52 2EX
01242 528449

On the edge of Cheltenham's main shopping area, The Curry Corner occupies a Georgian townhouse-style property, but has a chic, contemporary look. Genuine Bangladeshi home cooking is the theme, so spices are flown in from far-flung countries like India, Morocco and Turkey, with fresh produce sourced locally. This policy, combined with high technical skills and good judgement, results in dishes that zing with layers of flavour.

The Daffodil ®

thedaffodil.com
18–20 Suffolk Parade, Montpellier, GL50 2AE | 01242 700055

Where converted banks were once the dominant restaurant trend, old Art Deco cinemas now follow. The Daffodil occupies what was once Cheltenham's first picture palace, which opened in the early 1920s with a screening of now-forgotten horse-racing thriller, *Thunderclap*. Nothing of the drama is lost in the building's refashioning as a modern eatery. Its open kitchen sits where the screen once did, and the sizzling Josper charcoal oven is matched by sizzling live jazz.

Ellenborough Park ®®®

ellenboroughpark.com
Southam Road, GL52 3NH
01242 545454

With its impressive facade and its elevated position in rolling parkland overlooking Cheltenham racecourse, historic Ellenborough Park's palatial grandeur cannot be overstated. Ellenborough has a swanky spa, business facilities, smart bedrooms and two restaurants. The Brasserie is a useful second string to its bow, but the establishment's event is the fine-dining Beaufort Dining Room, with its Tudor fireplaces, stained-glass oriel windows and acres of burnished oak panels. It's an impeccable setting for the finely crafted, inspired cooking. There are first-rate cheeses, too, with a fabulous selection from across the British Isles to choose from.

The Gloucester Old Spot
thegloucesteroldspot.co.uk
Tewkesbury Road, Piff's Elm, GL51 9SY | 01242 680321
With its quarry tile floors, roaring log fires, farmhouse furnishings and real ales, local ciders and perries, this pub ticks all the boxes. There's a May Day bank holiday cider festival, too. Game and rare-breed pork make appearances on the menu. The newly renovated gardens are just the place to enjoy lunch or a drink.

Lumière ❀❀
lumiere.cc
Clarence Parade, GL50 3PA
01242 222200
Refurbishment has given Lumière an elegant and serene ambience, with its crisply starched linen, pinstriped carpet, banquettes and gilt mirrors.

Monty's Brasserie ❀❀
montysbraz.co.uk
George Hotel, 41 St George's Road, GL50 3DZ | 01242 227678
The George delivers all the Regency style one hopes for in Cheltenham, with plenty of period details inside and out. Monty's matches its good looks with a lively menu backed with daily specials, all of which are based on good-quality ingredients. There's also a cocktail bar in the basement.

PLACES NEARBY

A number of villages in the vicinity of Cheltenham are worth visiting, including **Prestbury**, which is both home to a racecourse and said to be the most haunted village in Britain. It has a good pub. **Syde** and **Brimpsfield**, 5 miles to the south of Cheltenham, are noted for their interesting churches. Two other churches of note can be found at **Bishop's Cleeve** and **Stoke Orchard**.

Church of St James the Great
Stoke Orchard, GL52 7SH
If churches are your thing, north of Cheltenham in Stoke Orchard, near the M5, is the Church of St James the Great, which dates from 1170. It's the inside that makes the church so special. Its walls are covered in a wonderful jumble of paintings, the fragments and layers of which were painted over the course of several centuries, including the early 13th. This arrangement of paintings is unique in Britain.

St Michael and All Angels Church

Bishop's Cleeve, GL52 8LJ

Bishop's Cleeve's St Michael and All Angels Church has excellent Norman architecture and decorative work. Built on a Saxon foundation that may date back to the 700s, the current church takes its shape and character from the 1170s, when the Normans rebuilt it. There is a small museum about the church's history over the south porch, which includes charming murals painted by a Georgian schoolmaster as visual lessons.

Miserden and Misarden Park Gardens

misardenpark.co.uk

GL6 7JA | 01285 821303

Garden open Apr–Sep Tue–Thu 10–4.30

Perched above the wooded valley of the River Frome, stately Miserden is another off-the-beaten-track little village worth visiting if you've time. The main attraction, other than walks in the valley, is Misarden Park Garden, home to flowers, shrubs, fine topiary, roses, and much more. The 17th-century Manor House (not open) overlooks the Golden Valley. No one knows why the two are spelled differently.

Camp Riding Centre

ridingschoolgloucestershire.co.uk

The Camp, Miserden, GL6 7HJ

01285 821219 | Open daily all week & some evenings

Camp Riding Centre offers tuition for adults and children, as well as half-day and full-day treks, in beautiful hill country.

The Royal Oak Inn

royal-oak-prestbury.co.uk

The Burgage, Prestbury, GL52 3DL

01242 522344

Close to the racecourse, this 16th-century pub serves local cask ales, real ciders and delicious food in a snug dining room or on the patio overlooking the pretty beer garden. There's a beer festival at Whitsun bank holiday and an August bank holiday cider festival.

10 arts festivals

- **Feb, Folk Three,** cheltenhamfestivals.com
- **April/May, Cheltenham Jazz Festival,** cheltenhamfestivals.com
- **April, Site Festival,** sitefestival.org.uk
- **May, Nailsworth Festival,** nailsworthfestival.org.uk
- **May/June, Wychwood Music Festival,** wychwoodfestival.com
- **June, Longborough Festival Opera,** lfo.org.uk
- **July/August, Guiting Festival,** guitingfestival.org
- **August, Stroud Fringe,** stroudfringe.co.uk
- **August, Didmarton Blue Grass,** didmarton-bluegrass.co.uk
- **October, Tetbury Music Festival,** tetburymusicfestival.org.uk

Chipping Campden MAP REF 262 B3

The loveliest village in the Cotswolds? It depends on your definition. It's certainly the most elegant, though it arguably gets a bit too busy to be the loveliest overall (that's Stanton, surely). But it has character, history and handsomeness, and you should definitely visit, ideally for May's unfathomably brilliant Cotswold Olimpicks (see page 54). The curving main street is lined with houses. Each is grafted to the next, but each also has its own distinctive embellishments. As the name suggests (chipping means market, via the word 'cheap'), Chipping Campden was once a market town. In fact it was one of the most important of the medieval wool towns in the Cotswolds. Campden then dozed for centuries until C R Ashbee moved his Guild of Handicraft here from London in 1902. The Court Barn Museum displays work from that era.

Campden's church, at the north end of the town, is the finest wool church in the Cotswolds, with a magnificent tower and a spacious, almost austere interior. It contains the largest brass in the county, memorialising wool merchant and church patron William Grevel. The Gainsborough Chapel houses the fine 17th-century marble tomb of Sir Baptist Hicks and his wife. The Hickses built the nearby stone almshouses in 1612, as well as Campden House, which was razed during the Civil War.

Grevel House is on the High Street, opposite Church Street. It once belonged to the aforementioned William Grevel who, in addition to being largely responsible for the church's current form, is supposed by some to have been the original model for the merchant in Chaucer's *Canterbury Tales*.

Just off Leysbourne, which is the northern extension of the High Street, is the Ernest Wilson Memorial Garden, a charming little botanical enclave snug in the shadow of the church. The garden is named for and commemorates an eccentric plant collector who was born here in 1876. In the middle of the village, supported by stone pillars, is the 1627 Market Hall.

Dover's Hill, the scene of the annual Olimpick Games, overlooks the village. The Cotswold Way, a glorious, 102-mile National Trail, starts here, and goes all the way down the limestone escarpment to Bath.

VISIT THE MUSEUM

Court Barn Museum
courtbarn.org.uk
Church Street, GL55 6JE
01386 841951 | Open Apr–Sep Tue–Sun 10–5, Oct–Mar Tue–Sun 10–4; closed Mon except BH

Artists, designers and craftspeople have worked in and around Chipping Campden since the time of the Arts and Crafts movement. This museum celebrates these practitioners, including

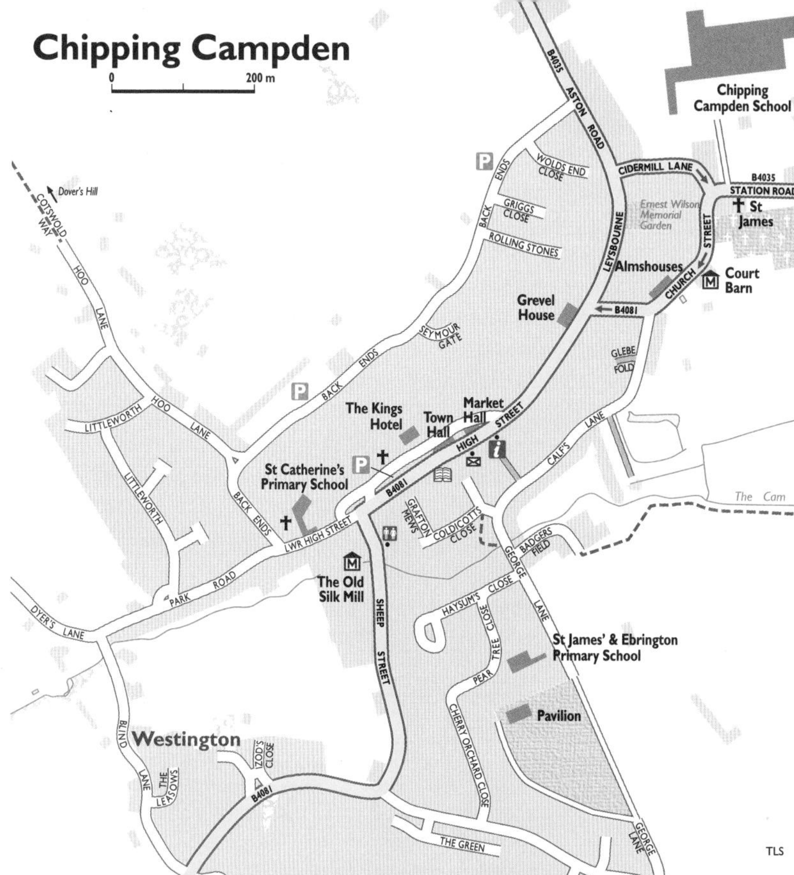

the talented C R Ashbee, and their skill. There are informative displays and video, a shop, and even workshops. It's great stuff.

SEE A LOCAL CHURCH

St James wool church

stjameschurchcampden.co.uk
Church Street, GL55 6JG
01386 841927

This is the quintessential Cotswolds wool church. The tower is the first feature you see: solid and square, it was built in about 1500 and houses eight bells that date from 1618 to 1737. Inside, the first impression is of grace and light. This is in part due to the window over the nave arch, a Cotswolds speciality. The church's treasures include a unique pair of altar hangings from about 1500. There are also excellent monuments, many to the rich wool merchants who poured their wealth into the creation of the building.

GO WALKING

For some cracking views along the escarpment and across the Vale of Evesham, simply follow Cotswold Way markers (which start at the Market Hall) for about 30 minutes. These will guide you along the high street, out of town and uphill to Dover's Hill.

EAT AND DRINK

The Bakers Arms

bakersarmscampden.co.uk
Broad Campden, Chipping Campden GL55 6UR | 01386 840515

Ease into the compact little bar, squeeze into a space near the inglenook and live the Cotswold dream, with local Stanney Bitter mirroring the colour of the mellow thatched stone cottages in this picture-postcard hamlet. The menu offers traditional tasty home-style cooking.

The Bantam Tea Rooms

bantamtea-rooms.co.uk
High Street, GL55 6HB
01386 840386

This traditional, welcoming, family-run tea room, built in 1693, is situated among the wonderfully preserved buildings of golden Cotswold stone, many of which date back to the 14th and 17th centuries. Try one of their freshly baked cakes, or even a Bantam Afternoon Tea. You can choose from a variety of traditional, fruit or herbal brews. If you fancy a picnic or a snack for the road, all of their tasty treats are also available to take away.

Eight Bells

eightbellsinn.co.uk
Church Street, GL55 6JG
01386 840371

Originally built in the 14th century to house the stonemasons who constructed

▼ Chipping Campden

nearby St James' church, this lovely inn was rebuilt in the 17th century and used to store the peal (or the set) of eight church-tower bells while they awaited installation. The cobbled entranceway leads into two atmospheric beamed bars with open fireplaces and, in the floor of one fireplace, a surviving priest's hole. Rough-hewn stone walls add further period character. Outside, an enclosed courtyard and terraced garden overlook the almshouses and church. Enjoy the Hook Norton and Purity real ales and freshly prepared, seasonal dishes. Specials, a prix-fixe menu and a children's menu are also available.

The Kings ❁❁
kingscampden.co.uk
The Square, High Street, GL55 6AW
01386 840256
Sympathetically restored and packed with character, The Kings' oldest parts include the 16th-century stone mullioned windows on the first floor. It may be a classic Georgian town house built out of honey-hued Cotswold stone, but it wears the style of a smartly casual modern operation, with comfy banquettes, mismatched furniture and polished wooden floors in the brasserie, and, in the beamed restaurant, unclothed antique tables and a log fire. It serves uncomplicated modern British cooking. The large grassed garden and dining terrace is good to find in a town centre pub.

The bar offers at least two real ales, including local Hook Norton, as well as daily papers and traditional pub games (but no noisy gaming machines). Bar snacks include a good range of sandwiches and baguettes, while main meals are served in the informal bar brasserie or the relatively formal two AA-Rosette restaurant overlooking Chipping Campden's square. The packed, imaginative formal restaurant menu features modern food built on splendid seasonal ingredients.

Noel Arms Hotel
noelarmshotel.com
High Street, GL55 6AT
01386 840317
This golden Cotswold-stone 16th-century coaching inn is one of the oldest hotels in the Cotswolds. Charles II reputedly stayed here. Packhorse trains used to carry bales of wool, the source of Chipping Campden's prosperity, through the carriage arch and on to Bristol and Southampton. The Noel Arms' traditional appeal has been successfully preserved and seamlessly interwoven with contemporary comforts. You can absorb the history while sipping a pint of Wye Valley Butty Bach in front of the log fire in Dover's Bar, reading the papers over a coffee and pastry in the coffee shop or enjoying brasserie-style food in the restaurant. Indunil Upatissa provides an alternative to the modern English dishes by

creating his trademark curries daily. Enthusiasts come for his Curry Club on the last Thursday evening of every month.

The Seagrave Arms ❁❁
seagravearms.co.uk
Friday Street, Weston Subedge, GL55 6QH | 01386 840192
This Grade II listed former farmhouse dates from around 1740, and looks out over some of the lushest scenery in England. The Seagrave has been sympathetically restored and retains many of its original features. It offers open log fires in winter and a sheltered courtyard in summer. The kitchen sources from local farms and suppliers, bakes its own bread, and makes its own chutneys and ice creams – local cheeses come with apple chutney. The Seagrave also has luxurious accommodation and the bar serves great beers from Purity, Hook Norton, Wye Valley and Cotswold breweries, a range of British bottled craft beers, and Hogan's traditional cider from the Malvern Hills. You can eat in the dining room, the former games room or the sheltered courtyard.

Three Ways House ❁
threewayshousehotel.com
Chapel Lane, Mickleton, GL55 6SB
01386 438429
Three Ways House is the Cotswolds seat of the Pudding Club, so skipping dessert just won't do. The Victorian building has heaps of period charm, although the restaurant itself has a more contemporary, eclectic look, and makes good use of mirrors to increase the sense of space. The cooking is punchy, big-hearted British stuff. A flag-waving dedication to local raw ingredients is balanced with a multicultural approach to flavour combinations.

The Volunteer Inn
thevolunteerinn.net
Lower High Street, GL55 6DY
01386 840688
This convivial, log-fire warmed, honey-coloured, stone-floored bar is a welcoming retreat for guests hunting through the town's antiques shops or pausing on a stroll along the Cotswold Way. Once a recruiting centre for volunteer militia, today's clients sign on for some very interesting dishes from the Inn's Maharaja Restaurant. These can be washed down with a pint of Doom Bar bitter or Stowford Press cider. The grassy beer garden is a quiet town-centre retreat.

PLACES NEARBY

To the north of Chipping Campden are the spectacular gardens of Hidcote Manor Garden (see page 135). To the west is another north Cotswolds honeypot, Broadway (see page 77). The town itself, and Broadway Tower in particular, are definitely worth a visit. A little further to the east is Shipston-on-Stour (see page 181), formerly an important wool town.

Chipping Norton MAP REF 262 C5

Chipping Norton is mostly famous these days for its celebrity incumbents – or should that be non-incumbents? Referred to by the media as the 'Chipping Norton set', they include Rebekah Brooks, former editor of *The Sun*, David Cameron (though he's got another house in London, apparently) and Jeremy Clarkson (ex-Top Gear), all of whom live near – but not technically in – Chipping Norton, ironically enough. Former Blur bass guitarist Alex James lives nearby too, making artisan cheeses. Depending on your political and cultural leanings (or interest in celebrity-spotting in the wild) you might consider this to be either a positive or a negative, though less high-profile residents are keen to emphasise that that's not all there is to the town.

Moving swiftly on then, Chipping Norton is a busy market town. The Bliss Tweed Mill, built in 1872 by Lancashire architect George Woodhouse, sits in a fold to the west of the town. For the Cotswolds, the large Victorian structure serves as an unusual reminder of the Industrial Revolution – although it's now been converted into flats. The Market Square, dominated by the 19th-century Town Hall, with its Tuscan-style portico, is the heart of Chipping Norton. Opposite the Town Hall, you'll find a museum with displays on the town's history.

Elsewhere you'll find a varied collection of shops, hotels and houses, some dating back to the 17th century, though most are 18th-century – a testimony to the wool trade. From the square, the town slopes down Church Street, past a row of almshouses dating back to 1640, towards St Mary's, a magnificent church in the Perpendicular style, containing some fine brasses and impressive tombs. Its most unusual feature is a hexagonal porch with a vaulted ceiling. Behind the church are motte-and-bailey earthworks that show the town was of some importance in the Norman period. In Middle Row, look out for the 16th-century Guildhall.

VISIT THE MUSEUM

Chipping Norton Museum
chippingnortonmuseum.org.uk
High Street, OX7 5AD
01608 641712 | Open Easter–Oct Mon–Sat 2–4
The pleasingly unglamorous volunteer-run museum and history society has a large collection of artefacts, which range in provenance from Roman Britain to World War II. It has extensive archives.

GO FISHING

Chad Lakes
chadlakes.co.uk
Chad Lakes Fishery, Bledington, near Chipping Norton, OX7 6XL
01451 831470
Coarse fishing in the heart of the Cotswolds countryside.

PLAY A ROUND

Wychwood Golf Club

thewychwood.com
Lyneham, OX7 6QQ | 01993 831841
Wychwood was designed to use the natural features of its location. It's set in 170 acres on the fringe of the Cotswolds, and blends superbly with its surroundings. Lakes and streams enhance the challenge of the course, with water coming into play on eight of the 18 holes. All greens are sand-based, built to USGA specification.

EAT AND DRINK

The Chequers ®

thechequerschurchill.com
Church Road, Churchill, OX7 6NJ
01608 659393
This unassuming stone building has modern gastro-pub style in spades, but that's not to say you can't just have a pint in the cosy bar. The ambience is relaxed. The small oyster bar is also home to a delicious array of charcuterie and cheeses. The kitchen has an eye for top-notch local produce; this place is all about simple dishes done well.

The Crown Inn

crowninnenstone.co.uk
Mill Lane, Church Enstone, OX7 4NN | 01608 677262
This 17th-century stone inn is cosy and welcoming, with log fires in the inglenook and old historic photos of the village on the walls. The Crown specialises in fresh fish. All the ingredients come from local suppliers. There's also a picturesque cottage garden.

Daylesford Farm Cafe ®

daylesford.com
Daylesford, near Kingham, GL56 0YG | 01608 731700
Enjoy organic handmade bread, pastries, seasonal-fruit yoghurts and even handmade brown sauce at this beautifully designed cafe, or a traditional afternoon tea. There's also a cookery and farm school, and a farm shop. There's even a yoga studio with a lovely rural view. You could spend a full day here.

The Kingham Plough ®®®

thekinghamplough.co.uk
The Green, Kingham, OX7 6YD
01608 658327
The Plough is quintessentially English, with stylish rustic-chic decor, venerable beams and exposed stone walls. In the bar are great beers from small breweries such as Purity or Cotswold and scrumpy, and large comfy armchairs and sofas to enjoy them in. There's also proper bar food. Chef proprietor Emily Watkins, who used to work at Heston Blumenthal's The Fat Duck, happily deploys traditional and trendy cooking techniques to deliver intelligent interpretations of modern British cuisine.

The Kings Head Inn ®

kingsheadinn.net
The Green, Bledington, OX7 6XQ
01608 658365

The Kings Head is a textbook example of a switched-on village pub. Outside, honey-hued Cotswold houses huddle around the village green, where ducks and bantams play in a trickling brook. Inside, you'll find wobbly flagstone floors, log fires and head-skimming beams. The place is still the village boozer, serving a fine pint of Hook Norton, while the cooking is a definite notch or two above your average pub.

Wild Thyme Restaurant with Rooms ❁❁
wildthymerestaurant.co.uk
10 New Street, OX7 5LJ
01608 645060

The mood is relaxed at this chic restaurant. Black beams are all that attest to the age of the building. Otherwise the scene is one of rustic modernity – chunky country-style tables, bare wooden floors and exposed stone or whitewashed walls. There's modern art, too, matching the modernity of the kitchen's output – smart, contemporary British food that deals in intelligent flavour combinations.

Wyatt's Tea Room
wyattsgardencentre.co.uk
Hill Barn Farm, Great Rollright, OX7 5SH | 01608 684835

Part of a farm shop, this spacious and very clean tea room is justifiably popular. Light lunches – homemade soups, freshly-baked bread, quiches, ploughman's, home-baked cakes and 'luxurious lattes' – and mouth-watering teas can be enjoyed throughout the year.

10 places to eat

- **The Bell**, Sapperton, bellsapperton.co.uk
- **Le Champignon Sauvage**, Cheltenham, lechampignonsauvage.co.uk
- **Cotswolds88Hotel**, Painswick, cotswolds88hotel.com
- **The Kings Head Inn**, Bledington, kingsheadinn.net
- **The Kingham Plough**, Chipping Norton, thekinghamplough.co.uk
- **Lords of the Manor**, Upper Slaughter, lordsofthemanor.com
- **Lumière**, Cheltenham, lumiere.cc
- **The Priory Inn**, Tetbury, theprioryinn.co.uk
- **Three Ways House**, Mickleton, puddingclub.com
- **Wild Garlic Restaurant and Rooms**, Nailsworth, wild-garlic.co.uk

PLACES NEARBY

The Rollright Stones

The Cotswolds only has one stone circle of note, but it's a pretty good one, not to mention a sneaky beast. It's one of three distinct ancient monuments on the side of the A3400 road between Shipston-on-Stour and Chipping Norton, near Long Compton. The monuments are believed to have been built at different times for different

▲ The Rollright Stones

purposes. The names of the megaliths, the King's Men, the Whispering Knights and the King Stone, derive from a legend explaining their origins. Long ago a band of soldiers met a witch. She told them that their leader might take seven long strides, and then 'if Long Compton thou canst see, King of England thou shall be'. The aspiring monarch risked all, saw nothing and was, along with his followers, turned to stone. The Whispering Knights, clustered together off in their own tight circle, were traitors who planned to overthrow the king once he became ruler of all England.

There's a more banal origin story for the Stones too. The three monuments are said to date from 3000–2000 BC, during the Bronze Age. Scholars believe that there were originally 105 King's Men, but there are now only 77, 100 feet in diameter. The remaining 77 are mysteriously difficult to count. If you can count them three times in a row and get the same total, it's said you will receive a wish. The Whispering Knights are believed to be all that remains of a neolithic long barrow. The Stones are open to the public, but note that parking is limited.

Little and Great Rollright

The nearby village of Little Rollright has a fine 17th-century manor house and a handsome little church built in the Perpendicular style, which contains some magnificent 17th-century stone monuments. Great Rollright has fine views looking southwards over the rolling countryside. Its historic buildings include the Norman church, with its gargoyles and carved doorway. Wyatt's Tea Room is close by, and you can purchase organic food and plants there.

Churchill

Just 3 miles southwest of Chipping Norton and close to Stow-on-the-Wold is the village of Churchill, the birthplace of Warren Hastings, the first

Governor-General of Bengal. It was also the birthplace of William 'Strata' Smith, 'the Father of English Geology', who produced the first geological map of England. Their stories are well told in the Churchill and Sarsden Heritage Centre in the Old Church, which also contains village records and maps dating back to the 17th century.

Hook Norton

Hook Norton, northeast of Great Rollright, is known these days, above all, for its beer, which is brewed in a Victorian red-brick brewery next door to the village museum. A huge railway viaduct running across the valley shows the village's past importance as an ironstone centre.

Hook Norton Brewery

hooky.co.uk
Brewery Lane, Hook Norton, OX15 5NY | 01608 730384
Tours Mon–Fri 11 and 2, Sat 10.30 and 1.30

Knock back a beer after taking a tour around the over-150-year-old Hook Norton Brewery. In business since 1849, Hook Norton is one of only 32 family-owned breweries left in the country. It's also the finest extant example of a Victorian tower brewery. The owners still transport the beer to pubs around the village using a traditional shire-horse-drawn dray.

Long Compton

Long Compton, strung out along the A3400 and not far from the Rollright Stones, is an attractive village with pretty thatched cottages and a handsome Perpendicular church. You approach the church through a lychgate, which is thought to be a cottage with its lower floor removed.

Jurassic Way

Not far from the Rollright Stones is the Jurassic Way, a long-distance footpath connecting Banbury and Stamford. It runs for 88 miles and largely follows the line of a Jurassic limestone ridge, passing through a wide variety of different landscapes. It links with the 290-mile Macmillan Way, which passes through Stow-on-the-Wold.

Cirencester MAP REF 257 E3

It's hard to imagine that, after London, Cirencester was once the most important city in England. Very hard indeed – as handsome as it is in places, Cirencester's just, well, comparatively *small* and Cotswoldsy. Part of the Cotswolds' charm is that its best places don't feel important in a political or business sense. But once, this place really was.

The town was founded as a military headquarters around AD 49 during Roman occupation. It was then called Corinium

Dobunnorum. A number of important roads radiated from the city – the Fosse Way, Ermine Street and Akeman Street. The Saxons renamed Corinium 'Cirencester'. Ciren, from *coryn*, means the 'top part'. This refers to the River Churn, the highest source of the Thames. *Ceastre* means 'fort'. One wonders why the Saxons bothered with the rebranding effort when they also practically destroyed the town, preferring instead to build smaller settlements outside the walls. Only in the Middle Ages did Cirencester regain something of its former glory, when it became the most important of the Cotswold wool towns. Satisfyingly, markets still take place each Monday and Friday.

The town is most easily explored on foot. There are a number of well-signposted car parks within easy reach of the city centre, while the market square is the most convenient place to begin discovering the town. The 15th-century parish church of St John the Baptist, one of the largest parish churches in England, is the main attraction. Its magnificent Perpendicular tower was built by a group of local earls with the reward Henry IV gave them for foiling a rebellion. The church's east and west windows are filled with medieval stained glass, and clerestory windows illuminate its fine roof. The exterior's best-known feature is its three-storeyed south porch, which overlooks the market square. The abbots built the porch in the late 15th century as an office for the abbey, and after the Dissolution destroyed the abbey itself the porch became the town hall. One of the finest examples of its type in the country, the building was returned to the church only in the 18th century. Inside you'll find several memorial brasses bearing the matrimonial histories of well-known wool merchants, some interesting church plate and a decorative, painted, wine goblet-style pulpit.

The Victorian Corn Hall, on the Market Place opposite the church, has been beautifully restored and hosts several markets throughout the week. The Brewery Arts Centre, just off Cricklade Street (which runs south from the square), is a hub of visual and performing arts. The old brewery also houses craft studios.

On Park Street, close to Cirencester Park, is Corinium Museum. The museum brings many aspects of local history and various finds to life, including the mosaics that were made in the area in the Roman era. Many are displayed in tableaux form. The museum is also the home of the Tourist Information Centre.

Close by is Thomas Street, on which you'll find a 15th-century Weavers Hall almshouse, also known as St Thomas's Hospital. Nearby Coxwell Street is lined with merchants'

▲ Corinium Museum

houses. Farther north, on Spitalgate Lane, you'll find another group of almshouses and the arcade of the nave of the Hospital of St John. East from here is the mysterious-looking Spital Gate, all that remains of the old abbey. From here, a walk through the Abbey Grounds – where the remnants of the Roman walls can be seen at the eastern boundary – will take you back to the town centre.

No visit to Cirencester would be complete without a glimpse, at the very least, of Cirencester Park, probably the finest example of geometric landscaping in the country. It is approached by walking up Cecily Hill, one of the prettiest streets in Cirencester, which leads to the wrought iron entrance gates. The first Lord Bathurst conceived the park in the early 18th century. The house (not open to the public), hidden behind one of the largest yew hedges in the world, was built to his own design. The park was landscaped with the help of, among others, the poet Alexander Pope, who celebrated the construction of the park in verse. In fact there is a corner known as Pope's Seat near the polo ground. The grounds are privately owned, but open to walkers and riders. Cirencester Park is an excellent place for walking, especially along the Broad Ride, which stretches from the entrance almost to Sapperton.

Apart from the wall in the Abbey Garden, the only other surviving local souvenir from the Roman occupation is the superb 2nd-century Roman Amphitheatre, which is one of the largest and best preserved in the country. Only the earthworks can be seen.

The King's Head, complete with royal keystone over the door, sits on the Market Square. Despite outward appearances, the hotel dates back to 1340. In 1642 the Royalist Lord Chandos took refuge in the hotel, thus saving his life, while in 1688 Lord Lovelace, of William of Orange's army, was captured here.

The plate of Cirencester's parish church is among the most interesting in the country. The Boleyn Cup, made in 1535 for Anne Boleyn, second wife of Henry VIII, is particularly interesting. The church is also notable because it has the oldest 12-bell peal in the country, which rings out the 'pancake bell' every Shrove Tuesday.

VISIT THE MUSEUM

Corinium Museum

coriniummuseum.org

Park Street, GL7 2BX

01285 655611 | Open Mon–Sat 10–5, Sun 2–5

Corinium was one of Britain's largest Roman towns, and as such the museum is known for its Roman mosaic sculpture and other Roman material. The museum also features archaeological and historical material from prehistoric times to the 19th century from Cirencester and the Cotswolds generally, housing medieval, Tudor, Civil War and 18th- to 19th-century displays. Anglo-Saxon treasures from Lechlade bring this little-known period to life.

SEE SOME LOCAL CHURCHES

Church of St John the Baptist

Gosditch Street, GL7 2PE

Dubbed the Cathedral of the Cotswolds, Cirencester's brilliant 'wool' church is the largest and, many would say, the finest of them all. The richly ornamented three-storey south porch and imposing tower certainly preside over the Market Place with all the grandeur of a cathedral. The interior is just as astonishing.

Roman Cirencester (Corinium) had become the second most important town in Britain, and by late Saxon times there was already a very large church here. By the early 12th century Cirencester had an Augustinian abbey, and it was about then that the first church was built on this site.

Parts of it survive in the present church, most of which dates from successive renovations and additions throughout medieval times. The Lady chapel dates from 1235–50, the tower from around 1400, various chantry chapels from the mid-15th century, and the porch from about 1490. The nave was rebuilt between 1515 and 1530, acquiring the soaring, slender pillars and huge Perpendicular clerestory windows that are key factors in creating the church's light-filled, elegant interior. Little more than a hundred years after these improvements were made, this glorious building was a temporary prison. In 1642 the Royalists locked up more than 1,000 citizens of Cirencester here overnight after a Civil War battle.

Many interior features are worth seeking out. Don't miss the exquisite fan vaulting or the wineglass pulpit – a stone masterpiece from about 1440, with delicate openwork tracery and decorative paintwork in burgundy and gold.

North Cerney All Saints
Dark Lane, a lane running west from the A435, GL7 7BX
This unusual and lovely church gets its character from an eclectic mix of work from the 12th, 15th and 20th centuries. Transepts and a new roof were added to the original Norman church in the 1470s, creating a cruciform shape that makes for an oddly charming juxtaposition with the saddleback tower at the west end. Look out for animal carvings on the exterior walls.

The interior, full of colour and beautiful craftsmanship, owes much to a 20th-century benefactor. William Iveson Croome, a knowledgeable local historian, worked with architect F C Eden to restore and refurnish the church. They thoughtfully executed work on the rood loft and the gilded reredos, also purchasing contemporary glass and period furnishings.

GET CRAFTY

New Brewery Arts
newbreweryarts.org.uk
01285 657181
Arts and crafts workshops and courses and a tempting shop.

TAKE OFF

Ballooning In The Cotswolds
balloninginthecotswolds.co.uk
Cirencester | 01453 753221
see page 72

SADDLE UP

Talland School of Equitation
talland.net
Dairy Farm, Ampney Knowle, near Cirencester, GL7 5ED
01285 740155
Talland offers flexible courses, including residential, and tuition for all ages and abilities. Large indoor and outdoor schools. People with disabilities catered for.

PLAY A ROUND

Cirencester Golf Club
cirencestergolfclub.co.uk
Cheltenham Road, Bagendon, GL7 7BH | 01285 652465
Open daily all year
An undulating open Cotswold course with excellent views.

EAT AND DRINK

The Crown Inn
thecrowninn-cotswolds.co.uk
Frampton Mansell, GL6 8JG
01285 760601
This old inn, a 17th-century cider house in the Golden Valley, is full of low beams and has cosy open fireplaces and real ales. Fresh, local food is served in the restaurant and at

the three inviting bars. In warm weather, there is plenty of seating in the garden.

The Crown of Crucis

thecrownofcrucis.co.uk
Ampney Crucis, GL7 5RS
01285 851806

This 16th-century former coaching inn retains its historical charm while feeling comfortably up-to-date. 'Crucis' refers to the Latin cross in the nearby churchyard. The pub overlooks the village cricket green and stands beside Ampney Brook in the heart of the Cotswolds. The quiet stream meandering past the lawns creates a perfect picture of quintessential rural England. With its traditional beams, log fires and warm, friendly atmosphere, the busy bar offers a large selection of draught and real ales, including their own Crown Bitter, and a choice of wines by the glass. Bar food is served all day, and the restaurant offers a fine dining menu.

The Fleece at Cirencester

thefleececirencester.co.uk
41 Market Place, GL7 2NZ
01285 658507

Charles II reputedly hid in this 16th-century pub disguised as a manservant. Settle by one of the log fires with a pint of Wainwright, and select your fare from a menu that mixes traditional and modern influences, using produce from ethical suppliers. The Fleece also serves afternoon tea, offers rooms, and is conveniently located in the heart of Cirencester.

PLACES NEARBY

South Cerney and the Cotswold Water Park (see page 190) lie to the south of Cirencester. The Cotswold Water Park is the best place in the region for sporting activities (if you don't mind getting a bit soggy), from windsurfing to sailing, bike riding and more. Travelling west towards Stroud (see page 211) makes for a lovely drive. You'll pass **Sapperton**, with its Arts and Crafts Movement connections, and then travel on through the Golden Valley and Chalford (see page 212), where there are fine walks to be had in the steep wooded valleys and abandoned canals to explore. The area can also yield great insights into Stroud's industrial past as the centre of the cloth trade. Then pop up onto Minchinhampton Common (see page 148) to enjoy vast views from the Jurassic grasslands, or down to Nailsworth (see page 155). Chedworth's Roman Villa (see page 87) and its mesmerising mosaic are to the north, and unfairly pretty Bibury (see page 66) is to the northeast.

The Duntisbournes

A string of villages along the small River Dunt just to the north of Cirencester, the Duntisbournes have a special character. Their saddleback church towers have something almost French about them. Duntisbourne Abbots was the home of Dr Matthew Baillie, the Scottish-born physician who attended George III during his many years of illness. Duntisbourne Leer is prettily forded by the Dunt, as is Middle Duntisbourne, which is barely more than a farm at the bottom of a steep valley. The church at Duntisbourne Rouse is particularly dramatically situated.

Rodmarton Manor

rodmarton-manor.co.uk
GL7 6PF | 01285 841442
Open May–Sep Wed, Sat and BHs 2–5

Rodmarton Manor is one of the finest legacies of the Arts and Crafts Movement, and one of the last country houses to be built and furnished in the old traditional style when everything was done by hand with local stone, local timber and local craftsmen. There are gardens to wander about too.

St Michael's Church

Duntisbourne Rouse, GL7 7AP

This enchanting little church, on the slope of a Cotswold hillside, is just as ancient as it looks and feels. The nave reveals its origins: here are two Saxon doorways, in addition to other distinctive Saxon herringbone masonry and quoins with long-and-short stonework. There are traces of early wall paintings. The tiny crypt chapel below the Norman chancel has a small, unglazed, round-headed east window to let in the morning sun. A medieval cross in the churchyard completes the idyllic scene. The saddleback tower that helps lend the building its timeless air was actually a later addition to the church, and dates from 1587.

Coln Valley MAP REF 257 F2

The River Coln, a tributary of the Thames, carves through the Cotswolds. It rises on the escarpment not far from Cheltenham (see page 88) then gently descends the slopes, passing through a number of pretty villages en route.

One of these, **Withington**, has an unusually large church with a fine Norman doorway and a handsome wall monument to Sir John Howe and Lady Howe of Cassey Compton. The village was the subject of a Time Team investigation when they spent three days excavating a Roman villa. The 17th-century mansion of **Cassey Compton** is now a magnificent farmhouse (not open to the public). It lies in splendid isolation in the middle of the valley, and forces the Yanworth road to curve around it.

Near here the river passes close to Chedworth Roman Villa (see page 87) and **Fossebridge**, a steep point on the Roman

Fosse Way where an ancient inn continues to attract passing customers. On the other side of the Way, the Coln furrows across the meadows of **Coln St Dennis** – a small, quiet village built around a modest green, with a small Norman church. Look for the mysterious inscription to Joan Burton on the interior wall of the tower, as well as the Norman corbel stones that now line the nave.

Further on you'll find the pretty hamlet of **Calcot**, and then almost immediately **Coln Rogers**, a village with a church remarkable for its Saxon plan and the Saxon window north of the chancel. At the old mill in **Winson**, where the road zigzags, there are charming gardens, and towards the centre of the village you'll find some converted barns. The compact green is overlooked by a classical-looking manor house. After Winson come Ablington (see page 68) and gorgeous Bibury (see page 66).

Finally, before going on to Fairford (see page 121) and Lechlade (see page 144), the Coln arrives at **Coln St Aldwyns**, where a magnificent horse chestnut tree shades the green.

▼ The River Coln, Cassey Compton

The New Inn is a fine local pub. A pretty churchyard surrounds the church, which has memorial windows commemorating John Keble, the 19th-century reformer, and his father. It is possible to walk along the Coln from here to Bibury.

Corsham Court MAP REF 257 D6

corsham-court.co.uk

SN13 0BZ | 01249 701610 | Open 20 Mar–Sep Tue–Thu, Sat–Sun 2–5.30, Oct–19 Mar open Sat–Sun 2–4.30 (last admission 30 mins before closing); closed Dec

If you fancy visiting a classic Cotswolds manor house but don't fancy the attendant crowds, come here – it's an interesting place in a quiet corner of the region.

Corsham Court is an Elizabethan manor house. It was built in 1582 on the site of a medieval royal manor that had, for centuries, been part of the dower of the Queens of England. Paul Methuen, a wealthy clothier and ancestor of the present owner, bought Corsham in 1745. 'Capability' Brown's designs were employed in the house as well as the grounds, and John Nash made further changes to Corsham.

In the 19th century Frederick Methuen, Lord-in-Waiting to Queen Victoria, married Anna Sanford. The young heiress brought with her a collection of Old Masters, many of which were outstanding and important. Since then the Methuens, though primarily a military family, have shared a love of art and a commitment to preserving their inheritance. The fourth Lord Methuen studied painting under Walter Sickert (of the Camden Town Group) and, as a soldier in liberated France, served as Field Marshal Montgomery's advisor on the preservation of monuments and art. In later years Methuen let a large part of the house to the Bath Academy of Art, although the present Lord Methuen continues to make Corsham Court his home.

The character of the house as we see it today dates principally from the middle of the 19th century. The staterooms are splendid, as much for their architecture and furnishings as for the paintings they contain. The picture gallery, designed by Brown, is a triple cube, 72 feet in length, with an intricately plastered ceiling and walls of crimson silk that match the Chippendale furniture. Van Dyck's superb *Betrayal of Christ* hangs here, together with Rubens's *Wolf Hunt* and works of the Italian School. In the elegant dining room are two Reynolds portraits of the children of Paul Methuen. Corsham also possesses an exquisite *Annunciation* from the studio of Filippo Lippi, a haunting portrait of the ageing Queen Elizabeth I and a sculpture of a sleeping cherub by Michelangelo. It further contains furniture by Chippendale, Adam, Cobb and Johnson. The garden has flowering shrubs, herbaceous borders, a Georgian bath house and peacocks.

Corsham itself, right on the edge of the Cotswolds, is worth a wander around. You won't find many tourists here, but you will find a handsome, historical market town, which was once prosperous due to the thriving wool trade and a quarry. The high street's 17th-century buildings are the best-looking things in town: a row of gabled Flemish cottages and the Hungerford Almshouses and Schoolroom. The Georgian town hall is also impressive. There are some good independent shops about, including good-value cafes and bookshops.

EAT AND DRINK

Guyers House Hotel @@
guyershouse.com
Pickwick, SN13 0PS | 01249 713399
Set in six acres of lovely English gardens, which include a tennis court and croquet lawn, Guyers House is a classic country-house hotel. When it comes to dining, the kitchen keeps fruitful connections with the local food network, as well as furnishing the larder with fresh, seasonal ingredients from its own vegetable and herb garden. Although the setting is traditional, the menu comes up with some surprising compositions that work well.

The Methuen Arms @@
themethuenarms.com
2 High Street, SN13 0HB
01249 717060
The Methuen Arms is a contemporary boutique inn situated at the hub of Corsham village life. Bare elm floorboards, log fires, ancient beams and exposed stone walls give the Methuen a rustic-chic look. There are hand-pulled real ales at the bar, and the extensive menu offers simple, modern tasty dishes. The kitchen promises top-grade local ingredients.

PLACES NEARBY

Travelling west on the A4 towards Bath takes you downhill to pretty little Box and the gorgeous valley of By Brook. There's a spectacular viewpoint by a bus stop where people often stop to take photos. You'll know when you see it. Limestone has been quarried here since the 9th century, but Box is more famous for its tunnel.

Isambard Kingdom Brunel constructed the Great Western Railway link between Bristol and London from 1835 to 1841, and it included what was then the world's longest tunnel (2 miles). The tunnel, which passes through Box Hill, has a dramatic neoclassical facade and pillars. That's bold enough, but apparently Brunel also planned for the sun to shine directly down the tunnel on his birthday, 9 April. Unfortunately atmospheric refraction meant that he was two days out. Nevertheless, the tunnel entrance is still an impressive sight today.

Box also provided a home for and inspiration to *Thomas the Tank Engine*-author Wilbert Awdry. It's also home to musician Peter Gabriel and his recording studio, as well as record-breaking adventurer David Hempleman-Adams. There's some fine walking to be done in the By Brook valley, which has woods and combes worth exploring.

Little Box Cafe
littleboxcafe.com
On the A4, next to the Post Office, Box, SN13 8NA
Why aren't there more cafes like this one? Winningly bohemian, down to earth and friendly, it's a small space – as the name suggests – but the food's fantastic and excellent value. Their vegetable dhal curries have a loyal following, and their hearty vegetable soups are similarly homemade and very tasty. They also do all-day breakfasts, and the cakes are as good as they look.

The Northey Arms ❁
ohhpubs.co.uk
Bath Road, Box, SN13 8AE
01225 742333
The Northey has stylish, relaxing decor, ingredients are sourced through local suppliers and the bar features regular guest ales and beers.

The Quarryman's Arms
quarrymans-arms.co.uk
Box Hill, Box, SN13 8HN
01225 743569
Superb views of the Box Valley can be enjoyed from this 300-year-old pub, from where you can also see Solsbury Hill. A display of Bath stone-mining memorabilia bears witness to the years Brunel's navvies spent driving the Great Western Railway through Box Tunnel deep beneath the pub. The honeycomb of Bath stone workings attracts potholers and cavers, who slake their thirsts on local ales and ciders.

Deerhurst MAP REF 260 C4

Deerhurst is an attractive farming village. Its cottages, which come in a variety of architectural styles, include some fine examples of cruck timber-framing. Deerhurst is splendidly located on the wide, grassy east bank of the Severn. Its claims to fame are a largely Saxon parish church and an almost-complete Saxon chapel.

Dating from the 8th century, St Mary's Priory was once part of an important 10th-century monastery. The priory is the only remaining Saxon monastic church in the country, and has several Saxon doors and windows. The extremely rare 9th-century font is said to be the finest in England. Particularly striking is the double-headed window high up on the west wall, which is possibly made up of Roman stones. The animal-headed label stops (the carved ends of dripstones) in the middle doorway below this window date from the early 9th century. On the surviving arch of the Saxon apse, now on the east exterior, you'll find the Deerhurst Angel, a carving from the 9th century.

SEE SOME LOCAL CHURCHES

Odda's Chapel

english-heritage.org.uk
Deerhurst, GL19 4BX | Open daily Apr–Oct 10–6, Nov–Mar 10–4

Odda's Chapel used to be concealed behind walls added over the course of later centuries. The chancel had been divided by floors, while the nave had become a kitchen. Only in 1865 was this complete Saxon chapel revealed. The Odda Stone, an inscribed tablet discovered inside, dates the construction of the chapel to 1056.

St Mary's Priory Church

Deerhurst, GL19 4BX

St Mary's is one of the most complete buildings to survive from before the Norman conquest. The building has many elaborate Saxon features, including a carved baluster, tiny triangular windows, and, high up on the west wall, a beautiful pair of windows with pointed tops. There are several excellent pieces of Saxon sculpture here, thought to date from the 9th century, including an angel in the ruined apse. The font, one of the oldest in England, is interesting, covered in intricate interleaving carved patterns. At some point the font was appropriated for use as a washtub on a farm. It was reclaimed in the course of restoration work.

An early painted figure was recently discovered on a panel high up in the east wall of the nave. It may date from the 10th century, which would make it the oldest wall painting in any church in Britain.

▾ St Mary's Priory Church

PLACES NEARBY

To the north of Deerhurst is the medieval market town of Tewkesbury (see page 223). Make sure you follow the Battle Trail. There's also a stunning collection of ancient wall paintings at the Church of St James the Great (GL52 7SH) at **Stoke Orchard** to the east.

Dursley MAP REF 256 C3

J K Rowling used the name of this town for the unpleasant Dursley family in her popular books about a bespectacled schoolboy who can do a few magic tricks. Although the busy market town beneath the Cotswold Edge has been severely modernised, its old centre remains intact. Dursley was once an important cloth manufacturing town. The delightfully arcaded Georgian market hall, and the Market House (which is now the town hall) sit bang in the centre, along with a statue of Queen Anne.

The church is not blessed with a harmonious interior, but it does have a fine vaulted porch in the Perpendicular style. The Gothic tower's spire collapsed in 1698, and it was rebuilt at the beginning of the 18th century with a grant from Queen Anne. The north door of the church was blocked to prevent the church from being used as a thoroughfare for the collection of water from the Broad Well.

Although in the immediate area Woodmancote offers a better selection of 18th-century houses, Dursley is a pleasant, old-fashioned sort of place, and exploration of its centre is very rewarding.

GO WALKING

Twinberrow Wood, on the slopes of Stinchcombe Hill, is home to the Dursley Sculpture and Play Trail. Various community groups created the trail to encourage children to appreciate the woods, and the result is worth checking out. To find the trail, take the A4135 from Dursley towards Tetbury. At the top of the hill take a sharp right. Continue along this road until you see the sign for the Sculpture and Play Trail. There's parking on both sides of the road. Map available from valevision.org.uk.

EAT AND DRINK

The Old Spot Inn
oldspotinn.co.uk
Hill Road, GL11 4JQ
01453 542870

This classic 18th-century free house is a former Campaign For Real Ale Pub of the Year, so it's worth visiting to sample the regularly changing, tip-top real ales on pump and to savour the cheerful buzzing atmosphere of this cracking community local. It sits smack on the Cotswold Way, and was once three terraced farm cottages known as 'pig row.' It's apt, then, that it should take its name from the Gloucestershire Old Spot pig. Devoid of modern-day intrusions, the traditional low-beamed bars are havens of peace. Only the sound of crackling log fires and the hubbub of chatting locals fills the rambling little rooms. Food is wholesome and homemade. There's also a pretty garden for summer alfresco sipping.

PLACES NEARBY

Sleepier, more old-fashioned Wotton-under-Edge (see page 252) is just down the road from Dursley, while historic and moody Berkeley Castle (see page 63) is to the west. North Nibley (see page 254) lies to the southwest. The mill town of Nailsworth (see page 155) and handsome Tetbury (see page 219) are about 15 minutes' drive to the east. Closer to hand, the dramatic hill fort at Uley Bury and Owlpen Manor (see page 230) are both to the northeast.

Cam

The village of Cam lies just to the north of Dursley. The parish church of St George, apparently rebuilt in 1340 by Thomas, Lord Berkeley to save his soul after the murder of Edward II took place at Berkeley Castle in 1327, contains a Jacobean pulpit. Nearby Cam Peak and Cam Long Down are Cotswold outliers – outliers of the Cotswold escarpment, the surrounding softer rock has been eroded around them, leaving them stranded.

Stinchcombe Hill

Just to the northwest of Dursley is Stinchcombe Hill, considered by many to be the marker for the most westerly point of the geographic Cotswolds. From its summit, Drakestone Point, you can take in far-reaching views along the escarpment to the Forest of Dean and the River Severn.

Stinchcombe Hill Golf Club

stinchcombehillgolfclub.com
Stinchcombe Hill, GL11 6AQ
01453 542015

Stinchcombe sits high on the hill, with splendid views of the Cotswolds, the River Severn and the Welsh hills. It's a downland course with good turf, some trees and a variety of greens. Protected greens make this a challenging course in windy conditions.

Nibley Knoll

Southwest of Dursley is Nibley Knoll, with its distinctive needle-shaped monolith rising out of the hillside. This is the Tyndale Monument. It was built in 1866 to honour William Tyndale, born in nearby North Nibley in 1494. Tyndale was the first man to translate the Bible from Latin into English. Climb the 111-foot-tall monument to get an excellent view.

Frocester

Nestled just below the Cotswold escarpment, Frocester was originally a Roman settlement, although there is evidence of human settlement right back to the Bronze Age. The remains of a large Roman villa were found in the grounds of Frocester Court, much of it excavated by the owner, amateur archaeologist Eddie Price, with the support of professionals. Frocester Court (not open to the public) is the site of 13 listed buildings, including a 13th-century tithe barn.

▲ Dyrham House

Dyrham Park MAP REF 256 C5

nationaltrust.org.uk

SN14 8ER | 0117 937 2501 | House open Mar–20 Dec daily 11–5; garden, shop & tearoom mid-Feb to 20 Dec 10–5; park open daily 10–5. Check for occassional closures and later opening times

Dyrham, a picturesque and flowery village eight miles to the north of Bath, bears a name associated with a battle of enormous consequence for Britain. It took place on nearby Hinton Hill in AD 577. The invading Saxons defeated the Britons, permitting the capture of the Romano-British cities of Bath, Cirencester and Gloucester.

There was once a Tudor house here. The National Trust-owned Dyrham Park we see today, however, was built for William Blathwayt, Secretary at War during the reign of William III. The present house is entirely a creation of the William and Mary period at the end of the 17th century. From fairly modest beginnings, Blathwayt rose through the Civil Service to hold a number of top government jobs. He found favour with William III, both for his administrative abilities and because he spoke Dutch. Blathwayt also made an advantageous marriage to the heiress of the Dyrham estate. After the death of both his in-laws and his wife, he began to replace their family home.

The baroque mansion, set in a valley and surrounded by 272 acres of gardens and rolling parkland, was constructed in two stages. Huguenot architect Samuel Hauduroy presided over the first wave in 1692. William Talman, designer of Chatsworth, and one of the foremost architects of his day, undertook the second phase of the work around the turn of the century. Between them they created a splendid house that displays unusual restraint for the time. The Blathwayt family lived here until 1956, when the government acquired the house. In 1961, the National Trust acquired it in turn. In 1993, the house was used as a backdrop for the film *Remains of the Day*.

Dyrham Park has changed little over the years. All the furniture, paintings and china you can see in the house today were collected by Blathwayt himself. The magnificent collections of blue-and-white Delftware and Dutch paintings of the period reflect Blathwayt's regular journeys to Holland in the company of William III.

There are Dutch-style water gardens, too. These include a statue of Neptune and one of the earliest-known greenhouses. Thanks to the great landscape architect Humphry Repton, swathes of the park are now designed in accordance with the more naturalistic English style. A herd of fallow deer grazes in the parkland, as they have done since Saxon times.

Children are well catered for with two play areas with sections for the under-5s and under-10s, including tractors to drive, towers to climb, balancing beams and den-building.

EAT AND DRINK

Tollgate Teashop
tollgateteashop.co.uk
Oldfield Gatehouse, on the A46, SN14 8LF | 01225 891585
On the side of the busy A46, in a stone building with arched windows and wooden floors, is the Tollgate Teashop, a listed building that was once an old turnpike dating back to the early 19th century. You can indulge in a delicious cream tea while listening to peaceful classical music and smelling their fragrant wood-burning stove. Tollgate offers a selection of good teas.

PLACES NEARBY

To the west of Dyrham Park is the small village of Hinton.

The Bull at Hinton
thebullathinton.co.uk
Hinton, SN14 8HG
0117 937 2332
This 17th-century former farmhouse and dairy is packed with character, with original beams in the bar and dining room. Meals are freshly prepared using ingredients mostly sourced locally and seasonal fruit, herbs and vegetables grown in the pub's allotment.

Evesham MAP REF 261 E2

Built in a protective loop of the River Avon in the middle of a fertile vale that has become Britain's foremost fruit-growing area, Evesham is an agricultural centre and a market town, well known for its asparagus.

The medieval town grew up beside the 8th-century Benedictine abbey, one of the grandest ever built. Abbeys like Evesham once dominated this region, and were instrumental in developing orchards and gardens for the production of fruit and vegetables. Unfortunately little of this once-mighty abbey survives today. Detached Evesham bell tower is probably England's finest example of the kind. The tower, 14th- and 16th-century gateways and two medieval churches, constitute the principal remains of the once mighty abbey. The churches were originally the abbey chapels, and the bell tower was a combined gatehouse and campanile. The bell tower's peal of 12 bells certainly lives up to the grandeur of their setting, and is nationally acclaimed as a benchmark against which other English-hung rings are compared.

One of the abbey buildings houses the Almonry Museum and Heritage Centre, which contains a mock-up Victorian kitchen and exhibits that commemorate the Battle of Evesham (1265). Here the troops of Prince Edward, later King Edward I, killed Simon de Montfort, the leader of the opposition to Henry III. After the rebellion of 1263–64, de Montfort had become de facto ruler of England. He had also called the first directly elected parliament, securing his place in history as an important founder of modern democracy.

PLACES NEARBY

With two Cotswolds A-listers, Chipping Campden (see page 96) and Broadway (see page 77), to the southeast (and practically on Evesham's doorstep), you'd be foolish to go in any other direction. If you've already been, travel southwest. Tewkesbury's (see page 223) not far away, and Cheltenham (see page 88) and Winchcombe (see page 233) are not far from there.

Fairford MAP REF 258 B4

Every July the Royal International Air Tattoo is held at RAF Fairford. But the town, located on the River Coln and the A417, is more than an airfield. It has a busy lowland feel not entirely characteristic of the Cotswolds.

Fairford's magnificent 'wool' church of St Mary deserves a place in any roll call of fine Cotswold churches. Rebuilt in the 1490s by John Tame and his son Edmund, the most influential of Fairford's medieval wool merchants and hardly altered since, the building's impressive fame is, however, often eclipsed by the renown of its virtually complete set of spectacular late medieval glass. Made between 1500 and 1515, they comprise the only surviving complete set in the country, and narrate the highlights of the Biblical story. They are most likely the work of Flanders craftsman Barnard Flower, whom Henry VIII commissioned to make the windows of the King's College Chapel in Cambridge and the Lady Chapel at Westminster Abbey. Flower probably didn't complete the massive undertaking alone, and almost certainly had help from English and Dutch craftsmen. The 28 windows tell many stories from the Old and New Testaments, culminating in the great west window that depicts Christ in Glory. Episodes from the early history of the Christian Church and its saints are also depicted. The great west window, which shows the Last Judgement, is particularly riveting and luminous. The amusing carved misericords – which include a drunkard and a woman beating her husband – underneath the choir stalls are not to be missed either.

The glass miraculously survived the Reformation, only for the west windows to be badly damaged in a storm in 1703. The windows were removed from the church and put into safe storage during World War II. The glass has been restored, repaired, partially renewed and cleaned through the centuries, but its survival as a set makes it unique.

Outside the church, don't miss the fascinating series of carved figures just below the roof parapet. The churchyard contains fine Cotswold tombs and monuments, some dating back to the 17th century. A favourite with visitors is more recent: a 1980 memorial with a stone sculpture of Tiddles, Fairford's much-loved church cat.

The church overlooks the green water meadows and the old mill by a picturesque bridge. From the church a pleasant circuit is possible and will bring you back to the main street. Most of the houses that line the street date from the 17th or 18th centuries. Along with the many inns, these houses serve as a reminder of Fairford's former role as a coaching town. John Keble, the 19th-century church reformer, was born at Keble House, on the north side of the main street at the east end of the town.

To the north you'll find the picturesque twin villages of Eastleach Turville and Eastleach Martin, which are separated by the River Leach, one of the Thames' many tributaries. The influence of the Tame family and the proximity of the river led Henry VIII's librarian, John Leland, to observe – dreadful pun alert – that 'Fairford never flourished afore the cumming of the Tames onto it.' Wool merchant John Tame, who built Fairford's church, became Fairford's lord of the manor. His son, Sir Edmund Tame, who was knighted by Henry VIII, is responsible for St Peter's at Rendcomb, 5 miles north of Cirencester (see page 105). His initials can be found there on some of the corbels and on an old glass pane in a nave window. The church tower at Barnsley probably also owes its existence to his patronage.

PLACES NEARBY

Uber-historic Cirencester (see page 105), once the second most important city in the country, is to the west. South Cerney and the activity-tastic Cotswold Water Park (see page 191) are slightly further south. The delightfully named Filkins (see below) and the excellent Cotswold Wildlife Park (see page 81) are to the northeast; Lechlade (see page 144) is to the east; gorgeous Bibury (see page 66) is north and shouldn't be missed either. You're in trouble here: too many choices.

Filkins MAP REF 258 B4

This quiet Cotswold village has a distinctly bypassed feel. Its cottages are distinguished for their solid craftsmanship rather than their beauty. Their story can be read in *Jubilee Boy*, an entertaining book by local resident George Swinford, which you can find on sale at the woollen mill (among other places). Swinford worked as a foreman on the estate belonging to statesman Sir Stafford Cripps, and also gave his name to Swinford Museum in the village. The last people to work some of the quarries in the Filkins area before George Swinford reopened them in 1929 were French POWs from the Napoleonic Wars.

The village is best known for its working woollen-weaving factory. It's one of the last, if not *the* last, in the Cotswolds – which is poignant when you think about how the whole constitution of the area owes its character to sheep. Cotswold Woollen Weavers keeps the flag flying, producing quality clothes on clattering old looms. The factory's located in an attractive old barn, a tangle of 18th-century buildings full of nooks and crannies. Visitors can watch all the processes of production, and while the enterprise is a serious and forward-thinking business concern with an online shop and an attractive website, it also takes time to pay tribute to the historical relevance of wool production with a permanent exhibition devoted to sheep and wool.

VISIT THE MUSEUM AND GALLERY

Cotswold Woollen Weavers
naturalbest.co.uk
GL7 3JJ | 01367 860660 | Open New Year–24 Dec Mon–Sat 10–6, Sun 2–6
This traditional 18th-century woollen mill is home to the Cotswold Woollen Weavers. Located in the village of Filkins, it houses a textile museum, design studio, shop and gallery. See traditionally woven cloth, interior textiles and traditionally made upholstered furniture, all hand-worked on site. Enjoy constantly changing collections inspired by the limestone landscape of the Cotswolds. Adjoining buildings contain more workshops devoted to other traditional crafts and there are occasional 'taster days' in stonemasonry.

PLACES NEARBY

A short distance east of Filkins, you'll find some interesting little villages. The Norman south doorway of the church at **Kencot** dates back to the 12th century, and is decorated with a carving of Sagittarius shooting an arrow into the mouth of a monster. The church at **Alvescot**, which is set in a quiet location to the north of the village, has a splendid 16th-century brass.

Gloucester MAP REF 260 C5

Gloucester is a town with a lot of history, and plenty of charms: it has an uber-magnificent cathedral, historic docks, remnants of Roman wall, and some great museums. If you're wondering why, with all this, it doesn't draw more tourists, it might have something to do with the large shopping arcades and a few other less appealing buildings – but all these things balance out. There is in fact quite a lot to see here, although with the exception of the obvious, magnificent cathedral, it has to be sought out (perhaps with the aid of a helpful travel guide...).

For many centuries, Gloucester was one of the most important cities in the kingdom. It was founded as Roman Glevum, a garrison town on the western edge of occupied England. It later became a 'colonia', a retirement community for legionnaires, who were rewarded after completing their service with a villa and a sinecure. In the 7th century, the Saxons established the monastery of St Peter in Gloucester. The town's current street plan takes after its Saxon incarnation, having changed significantly since the Roman period. Once Gloucester became the capital of a Saxon shire, Edward the Confessor held his winter court there. William I continued the tradition, and announced the creation of the Domesday Book, the great project of his reign, in the town. Soon after this announcement, work started on the Cathedral Church of

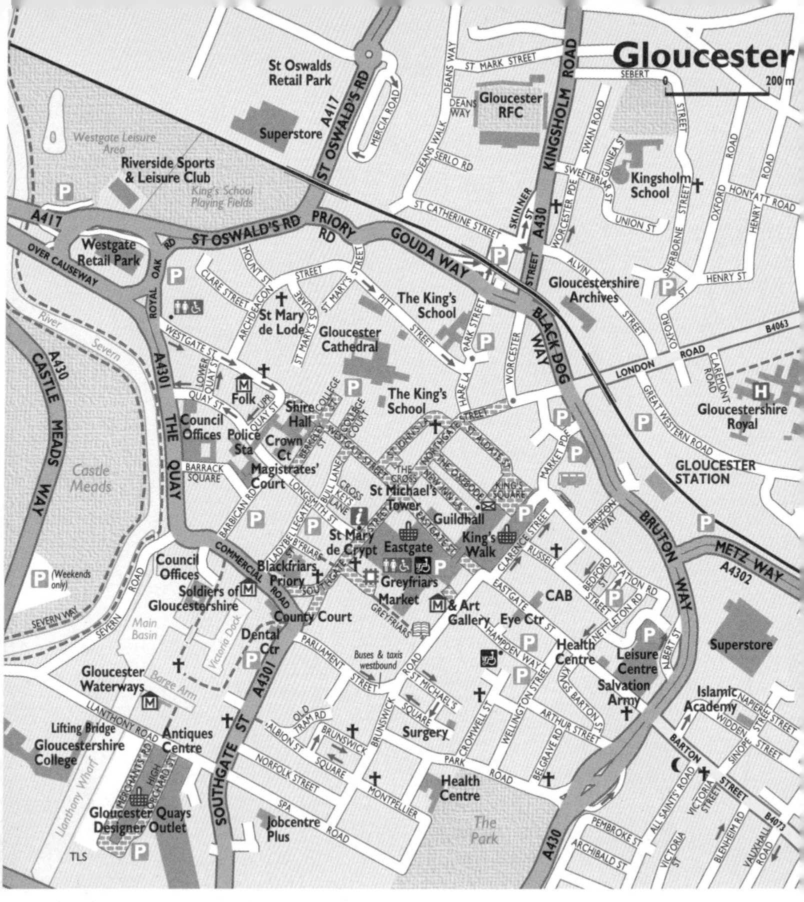

St Peter, the abbey church that was to become the city's chief landmark. In 1216, Henry III was crowned in Gloucester. He remains the only king of England proper not to have been crowned at Westminster. In 1327 the murdered Edward II was buried here, which turned Gloucester into a place of pilgrimage up until the Dissolution of the Monasteries.

Points of interest are scattered throughout the city, which makes an early visit to the tourist office in Southgate Street a good idea. St Michael's Tower stands by the site of the city's 13th-century stone cross, removed in 1751 'for the better conveniency of carriages'. It is also the meeting point of the city's four principal streets – the neatly named Westgate, Eastgate, Southgate and Northgate.

Gloucester Cathedral is just to the north of St Michael's Tower, and its own monumental tower is visible from afar. William I appointed Serlo, a Benedictine monk from Mont St Michel, as abbot. Serlo resuscitated the ailing Saxon abbey, and began its reconstruction during the reign of William II. It was consecrated in 1100 and completed in 1120, although additions were made over the following centuries. During the Dissolution

of the Monasteries the Abbey Church of St Peter was rededicated to the Holy and Invisible Trinity, becoming the cathedral church of the new diocese of Gloucester. It's an outstanding example of medieval ecclesiastical design that successfully blends Norman and Perpendicular influences.

The tower was built around 1450, and replaced an earlier, smaller tower and spire. It contains Great Peter, the last medieval Bourdon bell. The nave is lined with magnificent Norman arcading. The nave's vault dates back to 1242. Its equally antique roof was constructed from 110 oak trees from the Forest of Dean. The south transept is a very early example of the Perpendicular style, while the Norman crypt reflects the original Norman church above. The massive east window (from 1349), the beautifully carved 14th-century choir stalls, the late Perpendicular-style Lady chapel, the tomb of Edward II and the Norman chapter house are all worth a look. Indeed, you may have already given Gloucester Cathedral a look without even knowing it: the cloisters (famous for their magnificent fan vaulting) feature in two of the Harry Potter films. Houses from the 16th, 17th and 18th centuries surround the cathedral green. The cathedral also looks out on the 15th-century half-timbered Parliament Room where Richard II held Parliament (weren't expecting that, were you?) in 1378.

Gloucester's docks, another of the city's major historical attractions, have long been redundant. The area has been restored, however, and is worth perusing. Warehouses have been resurrected as offices, restaurants and museums, among them the Waterways Museum. In another warehouse you'll find the Gloucester Quays Antiques Centre, which has 100 tiny shops to browse. At the north end of the docks, the Old Custom House is home to the Soldiers of Gloucestershire Museum.

A walk through the city's main streets reveals Gloucester's rich history. The medieval New Inn sits on Northgate Street, a short way from St Michael's Tower. Designed to accommodate the growing number of visitors to the tomb of Edward II in the 15th century, the Inn is built around a beautiful galleried courtyard. On Southgate Street, the Church of St Mary de Crypt is a fine example of the Perpendicular style. It has an interestingly chequered past: the crypt once served as a tavern, and the church became an explosives factory during the Siege of Gloucester in 1643. Blackfriars, the finest surviving Dominican Friary in the country, has been restored. This religious institution also has a somewhat irreligious backstory – it was built on the site of a Norman military fortification.

◀ Gloucester Cathedral

Aficionados of museums will find several worth visiting, besides those located in the old docks. Visitors can see the remains of the city's Roman Wall under the City Museum. Eclectic Gloucester City Museum and Art Gallery on Brunswick Road contains Roman mosaics and the Birdlip Mirror, together with a natural history section with a freshwater aquarium and an excellent art collection. The Folk Museum is housed in half-timbered houses on Westgate Street. Not far from here is Ladybellegate House, the finest town house in Gloucester, notable for its fine rococo plasterwork.

Robinswood Hill Country Park, just on the outskirts to the south of Gloucester on a Cotswold outlier, offers an impressive view from its 651-foot (198m) height. Presumably the animals of the park's rare breeds farm enjoy the scenery. The old quarry on the hill's west side is a Site of Special Scientific Interest: its exposure of lower and middle lias rock is the finest inland example in the country.

TAKE IN SOME HISTORY

Gloucester Cathedral

gloucestercathedral.org.uk
College Green, GL1 2LX | 01452 528095 | Open daily 7.30–6; restricted access during Sunday services (7.40am, 8.00am, 10.15am and 3pm); guided tours Mon–Sat 10.30–4 (summer) and 10.45–3.15 (winter), Sun 12–2.30

Maintenance on Gloucester Cathedral keeps a team of stonemasons in full-time employment. Visitors can spot the building's Norman components or, with the aid of a guided tour, see where scenes from Harry Potter were filmed.

VISIT THE MUSEUMS AND GALLERIES

Soldiers of Gloucestershire Museum

glosters.org.uk
Custom House, Gloucester Docks, GL1 2HE | 01452 522682 | Open all year daily 10–4.30; closed Sun & Mon in winter

Soldiers of Gloucestershire tells the remarkable stories of those who have served in the regiments of Gloucestershire since 1694. Their courage, humour, sacrifice and moving individual acts of bravery are brought together in exciting and colourful exhibitions. The World War I trench exhibit allows visitors to feel and hear the deafening sound of guns, and engage with interactive displays. The Museum features memorabilia from the 18th, 19th and 20th centuries, including uniforms and medals.

Gloucester City Museum & Art Gallery

gloucester.gov.uk
Brunswick Road, GL1 1HP
01452 396131 | Open Tue–Sat 10–5; (until 4 Apr–Sep) closed mid-Dec to 1 Jan

The impressive range of artefacts includes the Rufus Sita tombstone; the amazing

Iron Age Birdlip mirror; one of the earliest backgammon sets in the world; dinosaur fossils; paintings by famous artists such as Gainsborough and Turner; full-sized dinosaurs; preserved wildlife from the city and the Gloucestershire countryside; beautiful antique furniture, glass, ceramics and silver; and hands-on displays, computer quizzes and activity workstations throughout the galleries. An exciting range of temporary exhibitions spotlights anything from contemporary art and textiles to dinosaurs and local history. The museum also hosts children's holiday activities and regular special events.

The Gloucester Waterways Museum

canalrivertrust.org.uk/gloucester-waterways-museum
Llanthony Warehouse, The Docks, GL1 2EH | 01452 318200 | Open all year daily 11–4 (weekends 10.30–4.30)

Based in Gloucester Docks, this museum takes up three floors of a seven-storey Victorian warehouse and tells the story of inland waterways and the history of Britain's water-based transport. The emphasis is on hands-on experience, including working models and engines, interactive displays, actual craft and computer interactions. A traditional butty narrowboat, one of the original World War II Dunkirk little ships and a working steam dredger are among the fleet of floating exhibits. Boat trips run daily in summer (but call ahead).

Gloucester Folk Museum

gloucester.gov.uk
99–103 Westgate Street, GL1 2PG
01452 396868 | Open all year, Sat, 10–3 (Mon–Sat in school holidays)

So what exactly does a folk museum cover? Local history, domestic life, crafts, trades and industries from 1500 to the present, the Siege of Gloucester, Victorian kitchen and laundry equipment – you might have an easier time outlining what it *doesn't* cover. The museum is partly housed in three floors of splendid Tudor and Jacobean timber-framed buildings, which date from the 16th and 17th centuries. New buildings contain the ironmonger's shop, as well as a wheelwright's and a carpenter's workshops. Brand new buildings contain education exhibits and the Folk Tearooms. The Toys and Childhood gallery lets you get hands-on with the toys, including a puppet theatre. Delve further into the history of childhood with the Victorian classroom. Throughout the year, the museum holds a wide range of exhibitions, hands-on activities, events, demonstrations and role-play sessions. The special events often take place in the museum's attractive cottage garden and courtyard, and often include live animals and outside games.

Gloucester Docks
gloucesterdocks.me.uk
The Docks
Following the opening of the Sharpness Canal in 1827, 14 warehouses were built here to store grain and other goods. Most of the warehouses have since been renovated, transformed into offices and the Gloucester Quays shopping mall. One now houses the Gloucester Waterways Museum. Despite the modernisation of the area, it's still a satisfying place to stroll and soak up some history.

ENTERTAIN THE FAMILY

House of the Tailor of Gloucester
tailor-of-gloucester.org.uk
9 College Court, GL1 2NJ
01452 422856
Beatrix Potter's *The Tailor of Gloucester* is set in this tiny shop, which Potter sketched while visiting the city. The shop sells ornaments, books and toys, as well as merchandise from other Potter classics like *Peter the Rabbit*. The building also contains a small museum.

GO SHOPPING

Gloucester Quays Antique Centre
gloucesterquays.co.uk/antiques-centre
99a High Orchard Street, Gloucester Quays, GL1 5SH
01452 338912 | Open Mon–Fri 10–5, Sat and BH 10–5, Sun 11–5
Don't miss your chance to rifle through period and 20th-century furniture, ceramics, glassware, gold, silver and antique jewellery, toys clocks, watches and so much more at Britain's largest provincial antiques market. This converted Victorian warehouse in the revamped historic dockland has three fascinating floors of shops and cabinets, representing 100 dealers.

WATCH A MATCH

Gloucester RFC
gloucesterrugby.co.uk
Kingsholm Road, GL1 3AX
Home to a leading rugby union club, Gloucester's Kingsholm is a notoriously raucous ground.

CATCH A PERFORMANCE

Three Choirs Festival
3choirs.org
GL1 2LX | Jul–Aug
Europe's oldest choral festival is held at the cathedrals of Hereford, Gloucester and Worcester on a rotating basis.

Guildhall Arts Centre
gloucesterguildhall.co.uk
23 Eastgate Street, GL1 1NS
01452 503050
The centre hosts live music, comedy, theatre, film, exhibitions and talks.

The Kings Theatre
kingstheatregloucester.co.uk
Kingsbarton Street, GL1 1QX
01452 300130

Picturedrome Theatre
theatregloucestershire.net
Barton Street, GL1 4EU
01452 560445

▲ Historic Docks, Gloucester

GO SKIING

Gloucester Ski & Snowboard Centre

gloucesterski.com

Robinswood Hill Dry Ski Slope, GL4 6EA | 01452 501438

Where Eddie 'The Eagle' Edwards learnt skills that led him to stardom.

PLAY A ROUND

Gloucester Golf Club

gloucestergolf.com

Matson Lane, Robinswood Hill, GL4 6EA | 01452 411331

Open daily all year

This undulating, wooded course is built around a hill with superb views over Gloucester. The formidable 12th hole consists of a drive straight up a hill, nicknamed 'Coronary Hill'.

EAT AND DRINK

The Coffee Shop

gloucestercathedral.org.uk

Gloucester Cathedral, GL1 2LX

01452 528095

Near the cloisters, this friendly place serves teas, coffee, soup and irresistible cakes, as well as its famous Pilgrim's Pie.

The Queens Head

queensheadlongford.co.uk
Tewkesbury Road, Longford,
GL2 9EJ | 01452 301882

This pretty, 250-year-old, half-timbered pub/restaurant is just out of town, and cannot be missed in summer when it is festooned with hanging baskets. Inside, a lovely old flagstone-floored locals' bar proffers a great range of real ales and ciders. The owners, at the helm since 1995, believe in giving their diners high-quality, freshly prepared modern British food that is great value for money. A couple of caveats: the dress code is smart casual, and the restaurant doesn't admit children under 12.

The Wharf House Restaurant with Rooms ®

thewharfhouse.co.uk
Over, GL2 8DB | 01452 332900

Profits from this restaurant in a former lockhouse (and its rooms) go towards the upkeep of 34 miles of canals in Herefordshire and Gloucestershire. Located on the River Severn, the restaurant is actually owned by the counties' canal trust. It really comes into its own when the weather allows diners to sit on the terrace overlooking the water. But with its wooden tables, parquet floor and fashionably neutral colour palette, it's still a pleasant space if you're dining indoors. The menu has modern influences, often continental.

PLACES NEARBY

Gloucester is so conveniently close to Cheltenham (see page 88) that the wise thing to do is make the latter your base, as it has better accommodation and dining options. From there, you can visit Gloucester for perhaps a day or an afternoon. Looking southeast, you'll find Painswick (see page 176), the self-proclaimed 'Queen of the Cotswolds'. Its fascinating churchyard and the spectacular hill fort on the Beacon are a short drive away, and well worth your time. If nature is your thing you mustn't miss Nature in Art at Twigworth, with its original approach to combining nature and art.

Nature in Art

natureinart.org.uk
Wallsworth Hall, A38 Twigworth,
GL2 9PA | 01452 731422
Open all year, Tue–Sun & BHs 10–5

Nature in Art is the world's first museum dedicated exclusively to art inspired by nature. Within the fine Georgian mansion, displays embrace two- and three-dimensional work in all mediums and styles, ranging from Picasso to Shepherd. Spanning 1,500 years, the collection contains work by 600 artists from more than 60 countries. As well as a temporary exhibition, you'll find watercolour landscapes, contemporary glass, works by Flemish masters, oriental art, bronze sculpture, ethnic art, textiles and even some modern abstract interpretations.

The Guitings MAP REF 262 A4/A5

The valley running east of Winchcombe, following the meandering course of the River Windrush towards Bourton, is sprinkled with some charming and idiosyncratic villages. There are two Guitings, for example – the intriguingly named **Temple Guiting** and the un-Cotswoldsishly named **Guiting Power**.

Temple Guiting takes its name from the Knights Templar, who owned the manor from the mid-12th century until 1308, when the order was violently disbanded. It's a pretty village among trees at the edge of a stream. The church retains fragmentary remains of its original Norman construction, while the stained glass is 16th-century and the tower, pulpit and windows are 18th-century. East of Temple Guiting, you'll find the Cotswold Farm Park. Gorgeous and friendly Guiting Power, a couple of miles to the south of Temple Guiting, is clustered around a small green, and is a perfect example of an English village.

The church to the south of the village, also once owned by the Knights Templar, has an exceptionally fine Norman south doorway. Sadly the interior is rather uninspiring. The foundations of a Saxon chapel have been discovered north of the existing church. Guiting Power hosts a small but significant annual music and arts festival in July with classical, jazz and folk performances by national and international artists.

MEET THE ANIMALS

Adam Henson's Cotswold Farm Park
cotswoldfarmpark.co.uk
GL54 5UG | 01451 850307
Open daily mid-Feb–late Dec 10.30–5 (closes 1 hr early in winter)

Meet over 50 breeding flocks and herds of rare farm animals, including the only living descendants of the famous Cotswold Lion – the breed of sheep that made the eponymous area famous and prosperous way back when. There are rabbits and guinea pigs to cuddle, lambs and goat kids to bottle feed, tractor and trailer-rides, a Touch Barn, a Maze Quest, birds of prey displays and safe, rustic-themed play areas both indoors and out. Lambing occurs until early May, followed by shearing and then milking demonstrations later in the season. The Farm Park was created by Adam Henson's father, Joe, initially to highlight the fact that dozens of rare breeds had become extinct since the beginning of the 20th century. The venture has gone from strength to strength since Adam became a TV personality and behind all the fun things to do there is still a serious message as they continue to run breeding programmes. There's also a 40-pitch camping and caravanning site with its own farm shop and cafe.

10 places to drink

- **Egypt Mill,** Nailsworth, egyptmill.com
- **The Hollow Bottom,** Guiting Power, hollowbottom.com
- **Howard Arms,** Ilmington, howardarms.com
- **The King's Arms Hotel,** Woodstock, kings-hotel-woodstock.co.uk
- **The Old Spot,** Dursley, oldspotinn.co.uk
- **Rose & Crown Inn,** Nympsfield, theroseandcrowninn.com
- **The Swan,** Southrop, theswanatsouthrop.co.uk
- **The Village Pub,** Barnsley, thevillagepub.co.uk
- **The Wheatsheaf Inn,** Northleach, cotswoldswheatsheaf.com
- **The Woolpack Inn,** Slad, thewoolpackslad.com

EAT AND DRINK

The Old Post Office

theoldpostoffice.biz
Guiting Power, GL54 5UR
01451 850701

A delightful tea room-cum-shop where you can browse the eclectic collection of furniture, interior decoration, gifts and greetings cards from around the world, then have a coffee and a large slab of homemade cake or a bacon buttie. Well-behaved dogs welcome.

PLACES NEARBY

The Guitings are, approximately, bang in the middle between historic Stow-on-the-Wold (see page 195), scene of the last battle in the English Civil War, spectacular Sudeley Castle (see page 217), which has even more stories to tell, and welcoming Winchcombe (see page 233). To the south, Northleach (see page 158) awaits. Longborough, just northeast of Temple Guiting, has a good place to eat.

The Cotswold Food Store & Café

cotswoldfoodstore.com
Near Longborough, GL56 0QZ
01451 830469

This shop and cafe is run by a family who know good food when they see (or eat) it. Most of the food is sourced from the Cotswolds. Savour homemade dishes and scrummy cakes in the cafe or on the terrace and then buy some fruit, pies, bread and cheese to make up your own picnic.

Hidcote Manor Garden MAP REF 261 F3

nationaltrust.org
Hidcote Bartrim, near Chipping Campden, Gloucestershire, GL55 6LR
01386 438333 | Open May–Oct daily, and most other weekends and selected days; closed Jan to mid-Feb; check website for details

Hidcote Manor Garden combines restraint with *joie de vivre*. The garden exemplifies the Arts and Crafts movement's landscaping incarnation: it has a well-defined ground plan, marked by dramatic paths; hedges in strong, straight lines and strict – though sometimes fanciful – topiary shapes. The garden has surprises at every turn.

It was created over 100 years ago by Lawrence Johnston who, with his mother Gertrude Winthrop, bought the property in 1907. At that time, the house was surrounded by nothing but fields and a few mature trees. Johnston read extensively, studying the work of leading garden designers, especially Gertrude Jekyll. He became a recognised horticulturist himself, and sponsored and took part in many plant-hunting expeditions to the Alps, Kenya and South Africa, building up a network of fellow plantsmen around the world with whom he exchanged specimens. As a result of these expeditions, over 40 new species were cultivated in the UK. Many of these bear Johnston's name. The Royal Horticultural Society awarded him three Awards of Garden Merit for his plant-hunting achievements. A yellow climbing rose Johnston bought from a breeder as an unnamed seedling was first dubbed a 'Hidcote Yellow', but later renamed 'Lawrence Johnston'. It now garlands the north wall of the Old Garden.

Clipped hedges of holly, beech, hornbeam and yew divide the garden into separate compartments – Johnston called it a 'garden of rooms' – each with a distinctive characteristic and colour theme. The use of tapestry hedging in the Circle close to the Old Garden was innovative, though mixed planting was commonplace in ancient hedgerows. Here the blend of different species, such as yew, beech and holly, creates an intriguingly mottled appearance. Unlike an evergreen hedge, this row varies its colour and characteristics by the season. To further reinforce the ground plan, the garden's two axes run uncompromisingly north–south and east–west, with a gazebo at their intersection. The hedges separating the garden rooms are tall, and thus there is no cheating – one has to enter each room to experience its particular explosion of colour, its sensuous planting and its compatible marriage of formal topiary shapes, blowsy, old-fashioned roses, rare shrubs and perennials.

In some cases, the sense of occasion and anticipation is heightened by the style of the entrance. One of the most formal areas, the Bathing Pool garden, has a massive topiary hedge. Shaped in the centre, with a steeply pitched, overhanging roof, it forms a truly triumphal arch. Its reflection in the circular pool increases the impact.

The Red Border is reached via a wide flight of stone steps, flanked by a pair of tall, narrow brick pavilions with incurved roofs topped by ball-shaped finials. Pots of red geraniums and agaves on the stone walls hint at the exciting colour profusion to come. The border is a flamboyant coming-together of red, purple, orange and bronze. The groundwork is laid with the purple-bronze foliage of *Heuchera* 'Palace Purple', which perfectly complements the 1946 blood-red *Floribunda Rosa* 'Frensham', the blazing reds of *Lobelia cardinalis* 'Will Scarlet' and 'Queen Victoria', *Canna indica* 'Roi Humbert' and, as always, the cherry-red verbena. A bright star in this border is the striking daylily *Hemerocallis fulva* 'Flore Pleno' with its orange-going-on-red petals the colours of leaping flames.

Inspired by designer and writer Vita Sackville-West's garden at Sissinghurst Castle in Kent, the White Garden has a billowing profusion of silver-leaved and white-flowering plants, their contrasting forms and textures linked by their uniformity of colour. The beds are bordered with low clipped hedges topped by topiary peacocks. Tall, erect spires of white acanthus tower above common wormwood, *Artemisia absinthium* 'Lambrook

◀ Hidcote Manor Garden

Silver', a glorious snow-white cistus, mop-headed phlox and shrub roses. Later in the season huge clumps of white dahlias hold centre stage.

One of the glories of summer in Hidcote Manor Garden is the flourish of old roses in the Rose Garden. Johnston gradually built up a collection of 18th- and 19th-century damask, gallica and moss roses, many of which were bred in France, and planted them in two long borders. These romantic and sweetly-scented roses bloom in one short-lived but exquisite midsummer burst.

'Mrs Winthrop's Garden', named after Johnston's mother, has a Mediterranean ambience and a largely blue, yellow and lime green colour theme. The edges of the garden room's brick paths and circular brick terrace are blurred by billowy hummocks of yellowy-green Lady's mantle (*Alchemilla mollis*) and blue geranium. Clusters of aconitum give the scheme height and structure, and terracotta pots of lemon verbena and aloe vera produce dramatic shape contrasts.

Closer to the garden boundaries, Johnston's planting became more cottagey – some would say jungle-like – with such delightful combinations as poppies, alliums and ferns. Azaleas, rhododendrons and rare and unusual trees are evidence of his worldwide plant quests.

Long views in the garden are scrupulously managed to enhance the wow factor of the garden's situation in the beautiful Vale of Evesham. At the end of the Long Walk, the tall iron gates are left open to frame the distant view. Another grass walk slopes up to the Stilt Garden, a wide avenue bordered by tall hornbeams on stilt-like trunks – surely evidence of a French influence.

In 1948 Johnston retired to Serre de la Madone, his property in the south of France, and the National Trust took over Hidcote Manor. It was the first gift they accepted solely because of the garden.

Fellow garden designer and passionate plantswoman Vita Sackville-West wrote of Lawrence Johnston's garden at Hidcote Manor, 'this place is a jungle of beauty. I cannot hope to describe it in words, for indeed it is an impossible thing to reproduce the shape, colour, depth and design of such a garden through the poor medium of prose.'

The Monarch's Way path runs to Hidcote. Follow it a short way from the car park and into the delightful Cotswold hamlet of Hidcote Bartrim, with its traditionally thatched stone cottages that were once home to Johnston's gardeners.

▸ Kiftsgate Court Gardens

GO ROUND THE GARDENS

Kiftsgate Court Gardens
kiftsgate.co.uk
GL55 6LN | 01386 438777
Open Apr & Sep, Sun, Mon & Wed 2–6, May–Jul Sat–Wed 12–6, Aug Sat–Wed 2–6

It's rare to find two spectacular gardens as close together as Kiftsgate and Hidcote Manor Gardens, but Heather Muir, who began work on the Kiftsgate gardens in 1920, was a close friend of Major Lawrence Johnston, the creator of Hidcote. Kiftsgate benefited from Johnston's plant-hunting expeditions to Japan and China. Kiftsgate sits atop the Cotswold Hills, and from the terrace there are spectacular views to the Malvern Hills. A splendid rose, 'Frühlingsgold', which blooms magnificently in June, guards the garden's edge. In springtime the White Sunk Garden is a mass of flowering bulbs. Among the white roses is *Rosa sericea*, 'Heather Muir', a single, early-flowering shrub that grows up to 12 feet in height. But the glory of the rose border is the striking *Rosa filipes* 'Kiftsgate', a white rose which, when last measured, was 80 feet by 90 feet with a height of 50 feet.

PLACES NEARBY

Chipping Campden (see page 96) is southwest of Hidcote, and little Ilmington (see page 140) is to the northeast. Mickleton, the northernmost village in Gloucestershire, is where you'll find the Three Ways House restaurant and hotel and its famous Pudding Club (see page 100), and is closer.

Hills & Commons

Cleeve Hill, the northern part of the Cotswold escarpment, offers superb views across the Severn Vale to Wales. Cleeve Cloud, the hill's 1,083 feet (333m) summit, is the highest point of the Cotswolds hills and the highest point in lowland England. This lonely, windswept plateau straddles the way between Cheltenham and Winchcombe. In a landscape that's relatively unmarked by modern forms of industrial development, the hill is distinctive for the radio towers, which are starkly visible across the area. Part of the hill is now occupied by a municipal golf course, but most of it remains ancient common, bright with gorse bushes on a carpet of coarse grass, studded with orchids and attracting birds and butterflies. A walk up Cleeve Common (see page 236) from Winchcombe is a fine thing. A walk that takes in the atmospheric Belas Knap long barrow (see page 239) as well becomes possibly the finest in the Cotswolds.

Leckhampton Hill offers spectacular views back across Cheltenham and the north end of the Cotswolds escarpment. Like many of the hills along the length of the Cotswold escarpment, Leckhampton attracted the attention of Iron Age locals, who built a hill fort upon it. It was similarly attractive to the Celtic La Tène people, who arrived from the continent from about 300 BC and built a long barrow here. More recently, Leckhampton's quarries provided much of the stone for Regency Cheltenham. Tramways ran from the limestone quarries directly to Gloucester Docks. Just below the lip on the west side of the hill you'll find local landmark the Devil's Chimney, a pinnacle of stone left behind by 18th-century quarriers and said to arise from Hell.

Crickley Hill, just south of Leckhampton, is in part a country park. It's a good place for family walking, with a number of trails of varying lengths. It too has earthwork remains of a fort used both in the Neolithic and Iron Ages. **Cooper's Hill**, southeast of Gloucester, is an almost sheer slope used for the annual cheese-rolling event (see page 54).

On the slopes near Brockworth, you'll find **Great Witcombe**. In the vicinity, near woodland, are the remains of a Roman villa.

Ilmington MAP REF 262 B3

Get out your hankies and bells, and grab a good stick. Yellow-hued Cotswold limestone houses with pretty, well-tended gardens set amid a tangle of intersecting lanes on the Ilmington Downs, the highest point in Warwickshire, give this agreeable village the mellow, rustic feel of a true Cotswolds

▲ Leckhampton Hill

settlement. Less immediately obvious, unless you stumble into the middle of a performance, is the village's strong Morris dancing tradition. The dances are often performed in the grounds of the delightful manor house, especially on the annual Gardens Day in June. During the summer months you'll find the Ilmington Morris Men dancing on Wednesday evenings in the surrounding villages. The group was formed in 1974. It performs up to 20 traditional 'Ilmington' dances that have been collected over the last hundred years, as well as other forms of the dance. There is evidence of Morris dancing having taken place in Ilmington since the 17th century, when dancers from Ilmington performed their sequences around a flag high up on Dover's Hill at Chipping Campden.

EAT AND DRINK

The Howard Arms

howardarms.com
Lower Green, CV36 4LT
01608 682226

A stunning 400-year-old Cotswold-stone inn on the picturesque village green of Ilmington, The Howard Arms is the starting point and finish line for a number of fabulous local walks, and is popular with ramblers. A detailed guide of walks can be bought at the bar for a small donation, with all monies going to the church funds. The flagstoned bar and open-plan dining room create a civilised, informal look without sacrificing period charm. A log fire burns for most of the year. Drinkers can choose from award-winning local ales, such as Wye Valley and Hook Norton, or a carefully selected list of over 30 wines by the glass. The inn's efforts to source seasonal ingredients and use local suppliers are equally solid.

PLACES NEARBY

Ilmington has the fantastic Hidcote Manor Garden to the west (see page 135), Stratford-upon-Avon (see page 198) a little way further to the north, and Shipston-on-Stour (see page 181) to the east.

Ilmington Manor MAP REF 262 B3

ngs.org.uk

CV36 4LA | 01608 682230 | Open for NGS or by appointment

Few who visit the lovely 3-acre gardens of Ilmington Manor today would guess that they are, for the most part, only 90 years old. When Mr and Mrs Spencer Flower came to this delightful village in 1919, the honey-coloured stone manor house, built by Sir Thomas Andrews around 1600, needed massive restoration, and a derelict orchard occupied the position of the present garden. With a flair for design and a clear idea of what they wanted, the Flowers restored and enlarged the manor house, planted many specimen trees and set about creating the interesting and beautiful flower- and topiary-filled gardens that we see today. Their grandson, Martin Taylor, owns the manor today. With his late wife Miranda, Taylor completed the restoration of the manor and its cottages, as well as gardens that have grown into a haven of peace and beauty in all seasons.

The Long Walk has six well-stocked herbaceous borders, which form the centrepiece of the main garden. To the right of the drive, which is lined with hornbeams, sits a little yew-hedge-bordered Pond Garden. The edges of the square pond are decorated with carved stone panels from India, and the surrounding paving is overgrown with many different varieties of scented thyme. The beds are filled with pink diascia, dianthus and other sun-lovers, while trailing sedums continue the patterns on the walls of the pool. This attractive area is bounded to the north and east by walls draped with clematis, a fine banksia rose and other aromatic climbers. It is a surprise to find *Buddleia crispa* here, as the Himalayan Butterfly Bush has a reputation for tenderness.

South of the house beyond the forecourt are three large walnut trees and a dovecote perched high above a neatly clipped hedge. Drifts of naturalised daffodils and brightly coloured crocuses enliven the area in spring.

To the west of the house are steps leading into the large formal Rose Garden, which is planted with old and modern shrub roses.

The so-called Cupid Garden – really more of an informal cottage garden – is one of the most colourful parts of Ilmington Manor. It features an enchanting mixture of roses, lavender and scented mock oranges. Peonies and hardy geraniums stand alongside clematis-clad walls. Nearby is Miranda's Buddha, a white garden walk with white camellias, white roses and hellebores.

Kelmscott MAP REF 258 C4

The fame of this small village is strongly linked to the 19th-century poet, artist and Arts and Crafts theorist William Morris. Morris is represented in carved relief on the facade of a terrace of cottages on the main street, seated in the shade of a tree, with his knapsack and hat at his side. Kelmscott Manor, on the edge of the village, was his home from 1871 until his death in 1896. He is buried in the local churchyard in a grave designed by Philip Webb, modelled on a Viking tomb.

This village came to mean much to him, and he named his private printing press in London after it. He wrote of it the following sentimental lines:

The wind's on the wold
And the night is a-cold,
And Thames runs chill
'Twixt mead and hill.
But kind and dear
Is the old house here
And my heart is warm
Midst winter's harm.

Ernest Gimson, an important member of the Arts and Crafts Movement, designed the Morris Memorial Hall, Kelmscott's village institute. The playwright, George Bernard Shaw, opened it in 1934 in the presence of British Prime Minister Ramsay MacDonald. The site was a gift from Lord Faringdon, while the stone was gifted by Sir Stafford Cripps, and came from the nearby quarry at Filkins (see page 123). Gimson died before the hall's completion.

TAKE IN SOME HISTORY

Kelmscott Manor
sal.org.uk/kelmscottmanor
Kelmscott, GL7 3HJ | 01367 252486
Open Apr–Oct Wed & Sat 11–5

Kelmscott Manor (limited public opening) was built in the late 16th century. Morris only rented it, but it now contains a fine collection of items associated with the man and with his craft – most notably those comparatively simple domestic artefacts that he strove to see reinvigorated through the Arts and Crafts Movement. The manor also contains pictures by Rossetti and Burne-Jones.

PLACES NEARBY

From here it's only a short distance west to Lechlade (see below). Over the Thames to the south is Buscot Park (see page 145), with Rembrandts and other works of art.

Lechlade on Thames MAP REF 258 B4

Lechlade sits at the confluence of the Coln, the Leach and the Thames rivers. At Lechlade, stone quarried at Taynton used to be loaded onto wagons, which would then set out for London. Among other things, such stone was used in the construction of St Paul's Cathedral. From 1789 the Thames was linked to the Severn via the Thames and Severn Canal. The canal started to the southeast, at Inglesham. There an old round house, built for the men who were responsible for the maintenance of certain lengths of the canal, still stands.

Inevitably, wherever there are rivers, there are bridges. Just south of the town, the A361 crosses the Thames via the old 18th-century, bow-backed Halfpenny (or ha'penny) tollbridge. To the east, the A417 crosses the Thames by means of the 18th-century St John's Bridge. A statue of Father Thames presides here. The Thames' highest lock also provides a fine view of the town.

Lechlade is built around its Market Square and its wool church. A collection of fine 17th- to 19th-century buildings look out over the square and the streets that radiate from it – Burford Street, High Street and St Johns Street. The church, with its distinctive spire, dates from the late 15th century. Most of the stone used to build it comes from the same Taynton quarries that later provided the stone for St Paul's. The church contains an east window from 1510 and a fine chancel roof. There's also a brass commemorating the wool merchant John Townsend. One balmy summer evening in 1815, the church inspired the Romantic poet Percy Shelley to write:

Thou too, aerial Pile! whose pinnacles
Point from one shrine like pyramids of fire.

The bustle of commercial river life has long ago faded in Lechlade, although pleasure craft still bring colour and movement to the river, and it is possible to hire small boats from the boatyard near the Ha'penny Bridge. The walk along the Thames, southwest from the Ha'penny Bridge, is very enjoyable. At Inglesham you'll find the pretty church of St John the Baptist, 30 feet (100m) from the river, which was saved from decay by William Morris.

TAKE IN SOME HISTORY

Buscot Park

buscot-park.com
Faringdon, Oxfordshire, SN7 8BU
01367 240932 | Open Apr–end Sep Wed–Fri, every other weekend 2–6

Buscot Park, a handsome 18th-century house, is just to the southeast of Lechlade. Its many works of art reflect the taste of the 1st Lord Faringdon. There's a well-known series of paintings by Burne-Jones in the saloon, and a trio of Rembrandts. The house is set in parkland, close to the village of Buscot. Buscot has an interesting church, and an 18th-century parsonage, now owned by the National Trust.

GO FISHING

Lechlade and Bushyleaze Trout Fisheries

lechladetrout.co.uk
Lechlade, GL7 3QQ | 01367 253266

Anglers can choose between a 9-acre lake and 250 yards of wild brown trout fishing on the River Leach.

LEARN A NEW SKILL

Southrop Manor

thyme.co.uk
Southrop, GL7 3NX | 01367 850174

The Manor offers cooking, growing, gardening, foraging, bread making, charcuterie and other artisanal skill courses.

EAT AND DRINK

The Trout Inn

thetroutinn.com
St John's Bridge, GL7 3HA
01367 252313

Workmen constructing a new bridge over the Thames in 1220 built themselves an almshouse to live in for the duration of the work. That almshouse became an inn in 1472 and its flagstone floors and beams now overflow into the old boathouse. The extensive menu features meat, fish and vegetarian options, pizzas, jacket potatoes and burgers. This family-friendly pub offers smaller portions for children, who also have their own separate menu. The large garden often hosts live jazz, an annual steam week and a beer festival, both in June, plus a riverfolk festival in July.

The Swan

theswanatsouthrop.co.uk
Southrop, GL7 3NU | 01367 850205

Overlooking the green, The Swan is clearly the village focal point. Summer ivy covers the external walls, while those in the stone-floored bar and restaurant are painted white, soft grey-blue or left unrendered. The first-class food is sourced locally where possible. A good real ale line-up includes Hook Norton Hooky, Bath Ales Gem and Sharp's Atlantic, with six red and six white wines by the glass.

PLACES NEARBY

Kelmscott Manor (see page 144), William Morris' former home, is east of Lechlade, while Fairford (see page 121) is west and the delightfully named Filkins (see page 123) are both to the north.

Malmesbury MAP REF 257 D4

Just a few miles south of Tetbury, on the southern edge of the Cotswolds, Malmesbury perches on a hilltop, one of the oldest continuously inhabited sites in Britain. The town is virtually encircled by the River Avon: a 2-mile walk taking in points of interest such as the Abbey House Gardens (see opposite).

Because of its strategic location between Oxford and Bristol, when the Civil War broke out Malmesbury changed hands several times with two direct assaults on the town itself, the first in 1643 when the Parliamentarians defeated the Royalists and then again in 1644 as the town had returned to the side of the King in the meantime. The west end of the Abbey is riddled with bullet holes where prisoners were executed.

The town centre is a blend of 17th- and 18th-century buildings overlooked by the imposing abbey (see below). At the heart of the town is the octagonal Market Cross. Thought to date from 1490, it was the location of the local farmers' market until the summer of 2015.

Malmesbury Abbey
malmesburyabbey.com
SN16 9BA | 01666 826666 | Open daily 9–5 (4 in winter)

Malmesbury's parish church since the Reformation, the present building is the third abbey to be built on this site, dating from 1180. The 12th-century south porch has some very intricate Romanesque carvings. Work continued and a 431-foot spire (taller than the one at Salisbury Cathedral) was built, which fell down in the late 15th century. In 1539 the abbey was closed at the Dissolution. The buildings were sold to William Stumpe, a merchant who used them for his cloth-weaving enterprise, and he gave the church to the town.

The abbey fell into disrepair and the tower fell down in 1550. It was the site of fierce fighting during the Civil War.

King Athelstan, the grandson of Alfred the Great, has his tomb in the abbey, but it is empty. The abbey was also the site of the first attempt at flight. In around 1010, one of the monks, Brother Eilmer, strapped some makeshift wings to his arms and jumped off a tower, not surprisingly breaking both legs in the process.

Abbey House Gardens
abbeyhousegardens.co.uk
SN16 9AS | 01666 822122| Open Mar–Oct daily 11–5.30
The 5-acre garden, right by the abbey, has a knot garden, laburnum tunnel and a riverside walk. The house itself dates from the 16th century (not open to the public) and is home to the Naked Gardeners who have been featured on TV. Each year they have a few 'Clothing Optional' days for visitors – watch out for the nettles!

Athelstan Museum
athelstanmuseum.org.uk
Cross Hayes, SN16 9BA | 01666 829258 | Open daily 10.30–4.30 (Sun 11.30–3.30 Nov–Mar)
The volunteer-run museum, located in the Town Hall, houses a collection of artefacts on the history of Malmesbury. The collections on display change regularly but include Malmesbury lace, a much sought-after fashion item in the 17th and 18th centuries, Saxon and Roman coins, an 18th-century fire engine, and some particularly uncomfortable 19th-century pennyfarthing bicycles.

Minchinhampton MAP REF 257 D3

Overlooking the Nailsworth valley on the fringe of the eponymous common, Minchinhampton easily goes unheeded. That just makes it the Cotswolds' best-hidden gem. By the 18th century it was one of the most important cloth towns of south Gloucestershire. Yet it was also a town of small traders, and as such it was unable to withstand the various crashes that periodically afflicted the industry. The town's importance ebbed, and Minchinhampton finally lapsed into rural calm. The church's truncated tower attests to the departure or subsidence of the wealthy patrons who might have replaced its decayed spire.

Minchinhampton remains an attractive wool town built around an old market square. Its 17th-century Market House, balanced on stone pillars, and the post office that resides in a former coaching inn are worth a look. There are also some excellent cafes. The church, just off the square, dates back to the 12th century. It contains a particularly fine set of brasses, while the 14th-century south transept contains a stately array of tombs and effigies.

Minchinhampton Common, 580 acres of National Trust-owned grassland, is a wide, windswept expanse of pasture, fringed with the villages of the Golden and Nailsworth valleys. If you circumnavigate the common you'll be rewarded with good views. Princess Anne lives up the road, at Gatcombe Park.

PLAY A ROUND

Minchinhampton Golf Club (Old Course)

old.minchinhamptongolfclub.co.uk
GL6 9AQ | 01453 832642
Open daily all year

This open grassland course, 600 feet above sea level, provides panoramic views. It's best described as an inland links course with no water or sand bunkers.

Minchinhampton Golf Club (New Course)

minchinhamptongolfclub.co.uk
GL6 9BE | 01453 833866
Open daily all year

Both courses offer scenic countryside and outstanding tests of golfers' skill. The Cherington is a testing inland links course, and The Avening is a parkland course, offering a different – but no less challenging – experience.

EAT AND DRINK

Burleigh Court Hotel

burleighcourthotel.co.uk
Burleigh, GL5 2PF | 01453 883804

Built at the outset of the 19th century, Burleigh Court is a three-storey, classic English country-house retreat, with an oak-panelled lounge bar and all the rest. The cooking takes a gentle country-house tone, using top-drawer ingredients and home-grown seasonal herbs and veg.

The Kitchen

thekitchen.co.uk
7 High Street, GL1 9BN | 01453 882655

Linger a while with a light lunch or snack perched in the bay window so you can watch the comings and goings. It is not unknown for cows to wander down off the common. The food is all freshly cooked and locally sourced and includes a good choice of vegetarian options (the cows can breathe a sigh of relief). They even serve proper afternoon teas with crustless cucumber sandwiches.

The Weighbridge Inn

weighbridgeinn.co.uk
Longfords, GL6 9AL | 01453 832520

Parts of this whitewashed free house date to the 17th century, when the original packhorse trail between Bristol and London passed by here. The inn has been carefully renovated and retains its original features, like exposed brick walls and open fires. It prides itself on its ales and ciders and the quality of its food. Everything is cooked from scratch, including its famous '2in1 pies'. One half contains your choice of one of seven fillings (such as pork, bacon or celery), while the other half has your choice of cauliflower cheese, broccoli mornay or root vegetables. The pies are cooked to order and are available for take away, or even to bake at home.

PLACES NEARBY

Minchinhampton Common

After the Common was granted to the people of Minchinhampton in the 16th century, any weaver was permitted to enclose land here and build a home. The bulwarks on the common are the remains of an Iron Age fort, and may have served as a base for Caratacus' resistance to the Romans. That wasn't the only time the common saw men rallying. George Whitefield, a Gloucester-born Methodist preacher, addressed a 20,000-strong congregation on Whitefield's Tump barrow in 1743. During World War I Australian airmen used the common as an airfield.

Minster Lovell MAP REF 258 C3

This village is indeed exceptionally Lovell-y. A fine old bridge spans the Windrush, and the main street is lined with buildings composed of Cotswold stone and thatch. Enjoy an entertaining introduction to the village at the Minster Lovell Heritage Centre, just over half a mile away from the main street on the Burford Road.

You can park at the far end of the main street and then walk down to the church, dedicated to St Kenelm. The church's beauty isn't terribly evident from the outside, but once you go in, the perfection of its design becomes obvious. It is welcoming and comforting, well-tended like a cared-for drawing room, yet uplifting and peaceful. Cruciform in shape, it was built in 1450 on the foundations of an earlier 12th-century church. The font is original, and the alabaster tomb probably belongs to William, the seventh Baron Lovell, who built the church. The church once had warm stained-glass windows, but unfortunately these have been lost to the centuries.

▼ The ruined hall at Minster Lovell

The romantic ruin of Minster Lovell Hall, which like the church was built by William Lovell, stands on the banks of the Windrush. Originally a fortified manor house on a grand scale, it was sold to Sir Thomas Coke. His descendants dismantled it in 1747, and the remains were used as farm buildings until the 1930s. Several legends are attached to Minster Lovell Hall. The strangest of these concerns Francis Lovell, a Yorkist who fled after the Battle of Bosworth and returned in 1487 to champion the cause of Lambert Simnel, pretender to the throne. Defeated at the Battle of Stoke, Lovell returned to the Hall and locked himself in a secret room, attended by a dog and a servant. Somehow, when the servant died, Lovell became trapped in the room and died there. In 1708, during work on the house, a skeleton was apparently discovered seated at a desk in a sealed room, with the skeleton of a dog at its feet. And if you believe that... A sturdy, round, medieval dovecote, which is also open to the public, can be found across the field, a short stroll from the hall.

TAKE IN SOME HISTORY

Minster Lovell Hall and Dovecote

english-heritage.org.uk

OX29 0RR | 0370 3331181

Open at any reasonable time, Dovecote exterior only

The extensive, picturesque ruins of Minster Lovell Hall are beautifully situated beside the River Windrush. Home of the ill-fated Lovell family, the ruins of the 15th-century house consist of a a fine hall, a tower and a complete dovecote. Although initially designed as a symbol of great wealth, after several changes of hands the Hall was abandoned – then dismantled and demolished – in the 18th century.

VISIT THE HERITAGE CENTRE

Minster Lovell Heritage Centre

minsterlovell.com

130 Burford Road, OX29 0RB

01993 775262 | Open Mon–Fri 10–1, 2–5, Sat by appointment only

The Heritage Centre is a small private collection situated on the outskirts of the village in one room of a busy picture-framing workshop. Owner Graham Kew has devoted a lot of time and energy keeping the history of Minster Lovell alive. Ask him to sing you the ballad of the 'Mistletoe Bough', or ask to see the Minster Lovell Jewel.

EAT AND DRINK

Old Swan & Minster Mill ❁

oldswanandminstermill.com

Old Minster, OX29 0RN | 01993 774441

In a wonderful English setting, the Old Swan is a smart country pub with plenty of rustic charm and a serious approach to food. It's very cosy on the inside, with lots of spaces to tuck yourself away in. There's real ale on tap.

There's also a local flavour to the menu, a refreshing lack of pretension, and even ingredients grown in the Old Swan's own kitchen garden. At lunchtime there's a range of tip-top ploughman's, or there's always the option of settling down for three courses. The garden is a gem. The more modishly done-out Minster Mill is next door.

PLACES NEARBY

The biggest nearby settlement is Witney (see page 242), which is famous for its blankets (you're there already, right?). The pretty village of **Crawley**, with its river bridge and old blanket mill, is also close by, and can be reached via a pleasant walk along the river. Just to the south of Minster Lovell lie the Charterville Allotments, the subject of a 19th-century social experiment. Chartists purchased the 300 acres and offered them as smallholdings to poor families, along with £30 and a pig.

Moreton-in-Marsh MAP REF 262 B4

The Cotswolds is big on evocatively named villages, and this is another of them. But though the name might call to mind the image of a romantic hamlet perched precariously in the middle of a bog, Moreton is actually a roadside town strung along the Fosse Way in the Evenlode Valley. The market town's historic importance derives from the fact that it has the immediate area's sole railway station. It arrived in 1843, and lines now extend to London.

Moreton is a place for wandering, particularly on a Tuesday when the market swings into action. Presiding over the market, Redesdale Market Hall may *look* Tudor, but it was actually built in 1887. The 16th-century Curfew Tower on the corner of Oxford Street, with its bell from 1633, was used as recently as 1860. Beneath the tower is the town lock-up and a board listing the 1905 market tolls. The small but fascinating Wellington Aviation Museum is on Broadway Road, just outside the town.

Some of the villages near Moreton are worth visiting. Bourton-on-the-Hill climbs the road to Broadway, and has a nice pub and a handsome church. The Bourton House Gardens are open to visitors, while the house's 16th-century tithe barn provides refreshments.

Sezincote House is Bourton's near neighbour. Samuel Pepys Cockerell built the extraordinary, early 19th-century, Indian-style house for his brother Charles. Together with its Mughal-influenced gardens, the house is worth at least strolling by. Charles Cockerell is buried in the attractive church in Longborough, the neighbouring village.

GO ROUND THE GARDENS

Sezincote House
sezincote.co.uk
Near Moreton-in-Marsh, GL56 9AW | House open May–Sep Thu, Fri 2.30–5.30; Garden open Jan–Nov Thu, Fri & Mon 2–6 or dusk if earlier; children allowed in the garden, but not allowed in the house without special permission. Groups by appointment only

This wonderfully incongruous Indian-style house was the inspiration for the outrageously ornate Brighton Pavilion. The Mughal style of India's Rajasthan region inspired the house's architecture. Sezincote's charming Garden of Paradise features waterfalls, trees of unusual size and a temple to the Hindu sun god.

Bourton House Gardens
bourtonhouse.com
Bourton-on-the-Hill, GL56 9AE 01386 700754 | Open Apr–Oct Wed–Fri 10–5

An ebullient riot of colour spreads across interlinked sections of garden. The garden abuts a 16th-century tithe barn and a grand house (not open to the public). The house and gardens featured in a major Japanese TV series, so both get an unusual amount of attention from fans.

GET ACTIVE

Rob Ireland Activity Days
robireland.co.uk
Barton-on-the-Heath, GL56 0PH 01608 651748

Former sporting champion Rob Ireland will organise activity days for groups, with options including quad biking, archery, paintball and clay pigeon shooting.

GO FISHING

Lemington Lakes
lemingtonlakes.co.uk
Todenham Road, Moreton-in-Marsh, GL56 9NP | 01608 650872

Set in 75 acres, Lemington offers course fishing and big carp.

SADDLE UP

Durham's Farm Riding School & Livery Yard
cotswoldriding.com
Chastleton, Moreton-in-Marsh, GL56 0SZ | 07811 339162

Durham's offers picnic rides and more, and has horses and ponies suitable for all levels of rider.

EAT AND DRINK

Manor House Hotel ®®
cotswold-inns-hotels.co.uk/manor
High Street, GL56 0LJ
01608 650501

Period character rubs along nicely with contemporary tastes in this mellow yellow Cotswold-stone classic. The Manor House comes from blue-blooded stock: Henry VIII bequeathed the house to the Dean and Chapter of Westminster in 1539. Careful renovation and updating have brought it squarely into the 21st century while retaining original features – a priest hole, for one. The Mulberry Restaurant focuses on highly refined country-house cooking in the modern British mould.

Redesdale Arms

redesdalearms.com
High Street, GL56 0AW
01608 650308

This fine old Cotswold-stone inn has been a part of the bustling, picture-postcard-pretty Moreton scene for centuries. Today it successfully blends venerable wood panelling, thick oak floorboards and exposed stone walls with a more relaxed contemporary style, achieved with the use of tobacco-hued sofas, modern art and muted colour schemes. There are two dining rooms, one in a rear conservatory, the other overlooking the high street. Its please-all menus combine quality, local and seasonal produce, simplicity and flavour.

10 gardens to visit

- **Hidcote Manor Garden,** page 135
- **Painswick Rococo Gardens,** page 177
- **Matara Gardens of Wellbeing,** page 232
- **Stanway House,** page 193
- **Snowshill Manor & Garden,** page 187
- **Kiftsgate Court Gardens,** page 139
- **Batsford Arboretum,** see overleaf
- **Rousham House & Garden,** page 180
- **Sezincote House & Garden,** see left
- **Misarden Park Gardens,** page 95

The White Hart Royal Hotel

whitehartroyal.co.uk
High Street, GL56 0BA
01608 650731

The 17th-century former coaching inn in the centre of Moreton looks a picture in summer, with its Cotswold-stone walls festooned with hanging baskets. Since every building from this era *must* have sheltered either Cromwell or Charles I at some point, let it be noted that the King holed up here for a night in 1644 after the Battle of Marston Moor. Refurbishment has been respectful of all that history, delivering spaces that have original charm alongside a few gently contemporary touches. The Courtyard restaurant – outside tables are a fair-weather treat – is a linen-free zone, the darkwood tables and bold colours creating a smart-casual space that will do for a special occasion or for when no excuse is needed. The menu takes a modern approach to cooking.

PLACES NEARBY

Batsford, to the northwest of Moreton, is an estate village. Its Victorian church contains some excellent monuments, while Batsford Park has an arboretum and a falconry centre. **Chastleton House**, a National Trust property to the southeast of Moreton, is one of the finest Jacobean houses in the country.

The **Four Shire Stone**, just to the east of Moreton, is a striking 18th-century monolith surmounted by a sundial and a ball. It marks the original meeting point of the counties of Gloucestershire, Oxfordshire, Warwickshire and Worcestershire. However, the boundaries have changed over the years and it no longer borders Worcestershire.

Batsford Arboretum
batsarb.co.uk
Batsford Park, Moreton-in-Marsh, GL56 9QB | 01386 701441
Open daily 9–6
Charity-run Batsford is home to one of the finest botanical collections in the country. Its position on a south-facing slope means you see the tree and plant collections from an unusual angle, as well as the great views of the Evenlode Valley beyond. Despite extending over 56 acres, Batsford is an intimate and even a romantic place, with interest all year round. There's a garden shop (with different opening hours) and a cafe, too.

Cotswold Falconry Centre
cotswold-falconry.co.uk
Batsford Park, GL56 9AB
01386 701043 | Open daily mid-Feb to mid-Nov
Conveniently located by the Batsford Arboretum, the Cotswold Falconry Centre gives daily demonstrations in the art of falconry. There are over 150 eagles, hawks, owls and falcons in residence. The emphasis here is on breeding and conservation, and 2013 marked the centre's 25th anniversary.

Chastleton House
nationaltrust.org.uk
Near Moreton-in-Marsh, GL56 0SU
01608 674981 | Open most of Mar–early Nov Wed–Sun 1–4, end Nov to mid-Dec Sat–Sun 11–3
A prosperous wool merchant built Jacobean Chastleton House between 1607 and 1612 to show off his wealth and power. The same increasingly impoverished family owned Chastleton until 1991, and the house remained pretty much unchanged for nearly 400 years. This gloriously unspoilt setting has an intriguing air of timelessness. There's not even a tea shop. Gasp. However, Chastleton is very much on the map now as it played host to the BBC's production of *Wolf Hall*.

The Greedy Goose
thegreedygoosemoreton.co.uk
Salford Hill, GL56 0SP
01608 646551
The interior of The Greedy Goose, all intriguingly patterned walls, swathes of polished wood flooring, elegant striped-fabric chairs and much else point to the talents of an interior design pro. A large, part-covered patio also reflects professional design input. In the bar North Cotswold Brewery Windrush Ale, Cotswold Best and Shagweaver monopolise the real ale pumps. The menu favours 'modern, fresh and hearty' dishes.

▲ A view over Nailsworth

Nailsworth MAP REF 257 D3

The small, characterful mill town of Nailsworth is set amid steep wooded slopes. It has a growing reputation for three things. First among these is football – not something readily associated with the Cotswolds, where the only league team is Cheltenham Town. The Forest Green Rovers, a Football Conference team, are owned by radical eco-energy tycoon and classic Stroud Valleys-type-person Dale Vince OBE. He's banned meat from the football ground – a world first for the sport – and plans to make the club fully sustainable, organic pitch and all. He also owns Rodborough Fort on Rodborough Common. If the Rovers ever get promoted, Nailsworth will be the smallest town ever to have League football.

Secondly, talking of food, 'Nelly' has a growing reputation for culinary excellence – a reputation backed by some sensational restaurants and cafes. Thirdly, Nailsworth has an impressive amount of alluring independent shops – it's becoming something of a shopping destination. It's an interesting place, still on the tourist path less trodden – if only just. The town should be proud of still having a town crier – even if most people might not be able to work out what he's going on about. It was also home to poet W H Davies (1871–1940), AKA Supertramp, who penned the famous words: 'What is this life if, full of care, we have no time to stand and stare?'

Just outside the town you'll find the fascinating Dunkirk Mill, which features both a massive overshot waterwheel and a well-presented history of the local textile industry.

VISIT THE GALLERY

Ruskin Mill College Gallery

rmt.org
Old Bristol Road, Nailsworth
GL6 0LA | 01453 837500
Open daily 10–4

When visiting this inspiring Arts and Crafts centre, make time to enjoy tea and organic cake in tranquil green, watery surroundings. Take a stroll round the gardens and ponds, and let yourself be captivated by a local storyteller, whose tales aim to please both children and adults. Come back in the evening for folk music (see the website's Events section).

GET INDUSTRIAL

Dunkirk Mill Centre

stroud-textile.org.uk
Just off the A46 near Nailsworth, GL5 5HH | 01453 766273
Open Apr–Sep some weekends and Wed. Check website for details

If you've an interest in the industrial, this is a great opportunity to see a massive working water wheel powering rare and historic textile machinery. The wheel – 12 feet wide and 13 feet in diameter – was installed in the mill in 1855. It's quite a sight in action, as are the large working model pair of fulling stocks and other industrial-cloth making rarities. There's no on-site public parking (except for disabled visitors), so drive to the car park behind Egypt Mill, just off the A46 on the edge of Nailsworth, and follow the cycle trail to the Mill Centre. It's a lovely walk, too.

TAKE OFF

Bristol and Gloucester Gliding Club

bggc.co.uk
Nympsfield, GL10 3TX
01453 860342

The Gliding Club offers trial lessons, instruction and taster courses for motor-less glider planes.

SADDLE UP

Barton End Stables

bartonendstables.co.uk
Barton End, GL6 0QF | 01453 834915

Lessons are available for riders five and older and riders with disabilities are catered for at this indoor/outdoor school.

WATCH A MATCH

Forest Green Rovers

forestgreenroversfc.com
The New Lawn, Another Way, Nailsworth, GL6 0FG
01453 834860 | Season Aug–May

Watch a game of football at one of the most unique clubs in the land – and definitely the greenest.

EAT AND DRINK

The Britannia

food-club.com
Cossack Square, GL6 0DG | 01453 832501

Occupying a delightful position on the south side of Nailsworth's Cossack Square, The Britannia is a stone-built, 17th-century building. The interior is bright and uncluttered, while outside you'll find a pretty garden with plenty of tables, chairs and parasols for sunny days. The menu offers an interesting blend of modern British and continental food, made with ingredients bought from both local suppliers and London's Smithfield Market. There are also great wines on offer.

The Canteen
thecanteennailsworth.co.uk
Day's Mill, GL6 0DU | 01453 836172
This distinctive cafe sells good-value coffee, cakes and light lunches. They cook with fresh, local ingredients from around Nailsworth and Stroud, creating great-tasting food that shows off those ingredients well. The decor is fun rustic chic and there is a small courtyard outside.

Hobbs House Bakery
hobbshousebakery.co.uk
4 George Street, GL6 0AG | 01453 839396
This may set ladies' hearts fluttering but the TV duo, the Fabulous Baker Brothers, have been known to be seen at the location of their family-run bakery. Established in the 1920s, the sixth generation of bakers is now on hand to continue the tradition of baking fine bread and we defy you to be able to walk past the shop without being drawn in by the irresistible smell. Be decadent and have a prosecco cream tea for a change. 'Come in and discover the meaning of loaf'!

Number 28
28 Fountain Street, GL6 0BL | 01453 298545
An unassuming exterior gives way to a small but welcoming cafe, where you can chow down on colourful, healthy food. The tapas are excellent value, and they also have a massive range of teas. The leather armchairs and eclectic bookshelf entice you to stay long after your meal has finished. At weekends they have a BYOB policy.

Wild Garlic Restaurant and Rooms ❁❁
wild-garlic.co.uk
3 Cossack Square, GL6 0DB | 01453 832615
So prolific is wild garlic around these parts that, not only have the owners named their stylish restaurant with rooms after it, but in 2015 they inaugurated a competitive garlic-hunting event as a red-letter day in the Nailsworth calendar. Chef-proprietor Matthew Beardshall and his enthusiastic staff make everything in-house. The brasserie-style menu of this small-yet-perfectly-formed modern restaurant changes monthly to reflect the seasons and to make the best use of the regional larder.

William's Food Hall & Oyster Bar
williamsfoodhall.co.uk
3 Fountain Street, GL6 0BL | 01453 832240
William's is a multi-award-winning delicatessen at the heart of the town, so try not to

get sidetracked by all the goodies that are on sale – an outstanding range of fruit, vegetables, cheeses, charcuterie, terrines and seafood – as you make your way to the few tables at the back or the nearby oyster bar. It's the perfect place to sit back and enjoy a glass of wine and a plate of deliciously prepared food. Named as one of Rick Stein's Food Heroes, luminaries such as Dame Judi Dench have been known to pop in.

PLACES NEARBY

The drive up the 'W' to visit cute little Minchinhampton (see page 147) is quite an experience. The drive back down offers the best possible view of Nailsworth. Head the other way out of town, via Horsley, for a meal in the Rose & Crown in Nympsfield.

Just outside the town, you can appreciate the massive overshot waterwheel at Dunkirk Mill (see page 156) at the same time as taking in a well-presented exhibit on the history of the local textile industry that made this region what it is today. Take a drive to see curious little **Avening**. Handsome Tetbury (see page 219) is a bit further east.

Rose & Crown Inn
The Cross, Nympsfield, GL10 3TU
01453 860240
Occupying a central position in the village, this 400-year-old coaching inn could well be the highest pub in the Cotswolds. Its close proximity to the Cotswold Way makes it a popular stop for hikers and bikers. Inside, the inn's character is preserved with natural stone, wood panelling, a lovely open fire and local Stroud Organic and Wickwar Cotswold Way real ales. In the galleried restaurant, the owners offer fresh, homemade food cooked to order. In the large garden, children will enjoy the playground area, which has a swing, slides and a climbing bridge.

Northleach MAP REF 258 A3

An important wool town in the Middle Ages, Northleach still just about manages to take you back to that period. The antique feeling comes from the fact that one of the finest wool churches in the Cotswolds overlooks the market square. This mighty fine example of the English Perpendicular style, the most striking building in town, dates from the 15th century. Its magnificent south porch is one of the finest in the country. The interior is quite stark, but beautifully proportioned. The church contains the grandest collection of monumental brasses in the Cotswolds, commemorating the medieval wool merchants who brought prosperity to Northleach and passed some of it along to the church.

▲ Church of St Peter and St Paul, Northleach

The A40 road, which replaces the old coaching route that ran through the town, fortunately bypasses Northleach. The Abbey of St Peter in Gloucester established Northleach Borough in 1226. The annual rents were one shilling (5p) for a burgage plot, 6d (2.5p) for a market stall and 1d for a cottage. These medieval property boundaries can still be traced. The High Street features an interesting mixture of houses of all periods, which reflects the burgage plots that belonged to the merchants of yore. Burgage plots were created to enable the maximum number of shops to line the main street. These plots were usually subdivided as time advanced and the population swelled – hence the jumble of buildings from different eras. Unusually for the area, some of these are half-timbered.

The Mechanical Music Museum occupies one of these buildings just east of the market place, in what was a school. This is a fascinating shop, but it's also a collection of clocks and mechanical instruments from all over Europe, ranging from barrel organs to pianolas. The tour guides give frequent, entertaining demonstrations of many of these instruments, and some of the restored items are for sale.

There are two sets of almshouses – one at Mill End, another at East End. At the western end of the town the High Street meets the Roman Fosse Way. On the other side of the road, you'll see an 18th-century building that was originally a prison.

Sir William Blackburn built it according to the ideas of the philanthropist Sir George Onesiphorus Paul, a member of an eminent family of Woodchester clothiers.

ENTERTAIN THE FAMILY

Mechanical Music Museum

mechanicalmusic.co.uk
The Oak House, High Street, GL54 3ET | 01451 860181
Open all year daily 10–5 (last tour 4)

The museum holds a fascinating collection of antique clocks, musical boxes, automata and mechanical musical instruments. These are restored and maintained in the world-famous workshops, displayed in a period setting, presented as a live entertainment, and played during regular tours. Visitors can play coin-operated instruments in an exhibition dedicated to the purpose.

SEE A LOCAL CHURCH

Church of St Peter and St Paul

Mill End, just west of the town centre, GL54 3HG

The church at Northleach is a monument to the 15th-century glory days of this sleepy little town, when Northleach wool was the country's finest and the town's merchants among the country's wealthiest. One of these merchants, John Fortey, raised the nave roof and added a lofty clerestory that fills the church with light. It includes an immense Perpendicular window above the chancel arch – a fine example of a feature that is special to Cotswold 'wool' churches. Fortey's contribution is commemorated in one of the church's fine collection of brasses. Other merchants of the time also provided funds to enrich their church. The Lady chapel and the elegant stone pulpit also date from this period, as does the pinnacled two-storey south porch: be sure to look up at the vaulting inside.

EAT AND DRINK

The Wheatsheaf Inn

cotswoldswheatsheaf.com
West End, GL54 3EZ | 01451 860244

A beautiful Cotswold-stone 17th-century inn on the square of the pretty former wool town of Northleach, The Wheatsheaf is everything anyone could wish for. With flagstone floors, beams, log fires and a vibrant, smartened-up feel throughout, it's perfect for sampling some seriously good food or chilling out in the bar with the papers after enjoying a bracing walk. Monthly menus evolve with the season.

PLACES NEARBY

Hampnett is a short drive (or walk) northwest of Northleach. It has an interesting Norman church, with carved birds on the chancel arch and Victorian stencilling, the idea of the vicar of the time, but disliked by the villagers, who fortunately failed to raise funds to whitewash over them.

Oxford MAP REF 259 E4

Oxford is both an inspiring (or perhaps, to some, an overwhelming) citywide temple of learning and a place with long associations with privilege and elitism. Some 26 UK prime ministers have studied at Oxford, including David Cameron. It looks like a film set, and there's an inescapable atmosphere of wizened oldness. It also gets really really busy with tourists, so judge the time of your visit carefully.

Both Oxford's glories and its bad points make the handsome home of one of the world's best and oldest universities one of the most deeply *English* places in existence. The country's essence seeps from the walls. Heritage and pomp intermingle here with student Rag Weeks and the minutiae of daily life in a cosmopolitan setting. Oxford is simultaneously a mildly bizarre and eccentric anachronism and a modern city getting on with its business.

Lying just under 60 miles northwest of London, situated amid low hills at the meeting point of the River Thames and the River Cherwell, Oxford is in some ways a typical market town. What distinguishes it from the many others like it in England is of course its ancient university. Oxford consists of some 38 colleges and six private halls, which are spread throughout the city itself. Students from England and abroad compete fiercely for admission. While they may value the university's excellent contemporary academic reputation and the valuable connections they might make as Oxford students, many are also drawn by the sheer gravity of tradition. To attend Oxford is to follow famous footsteps along hallowed halls. The buildings themselves are ancient and beautiful. Many students feel that to study at Oxford is a privilege, a pleasure, and an affirmation.

▾ New College

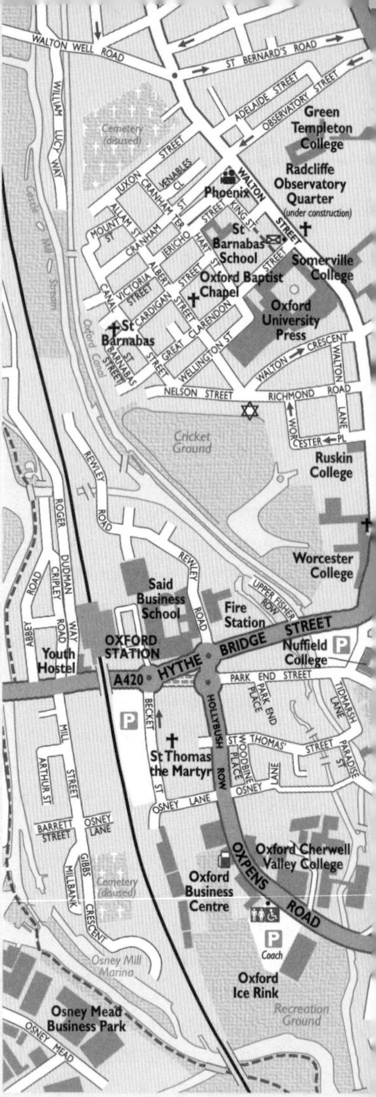

Oxford's mellow ambience of well-aged gentility feeds on its blend of architecture and setting. The architecture of the colleges ranges from Merton's early Gothic edifice to St Catherine's bracing modernism. The sprawl of riverside meadows and parkland attracts cyclists, punters, rowers, and less athletically minded visitors with an eye for scenery.

Although the city's origins are lost in time, Oxford has been an established town since the 9th century. Its life as a centre of education began in 1167, when students who had been expelled from Paris settled in the town under the patronage of Henry II. The university's colleges exert a palpable influence without entirely dominating city life. Beneath the mantle of Oxford the University, Oxford the city still lives and breathes – although if you stay long enough, you gradually detect a frisson of tension between 'gown' and 'town'. Still, while today's students are noted for their boisterous post-exam antics, we can be thankful that things have calmed down over the years – in 1355, the St Scholastica's Day town/gown riot left 63 scholars and about 30 locals dead.

Beautiful, honey-coloured buildings populate the 'city of dreaming spires', among them the Museum of the History of Science, the Pitt Rivers Museum and the Ashmolean. The Ashmolean is England's oldest public museum. Founded in 1683, it houses a huge collection of priceless art and antiquities. The famous and lovely Bodleian Library and Sheldonian Theatre nestle nearby in an enclave of mainly 17th-century buildings.

There's plenty to see in Oxford even if you're not an architecture buff. The lively covered market has been trading

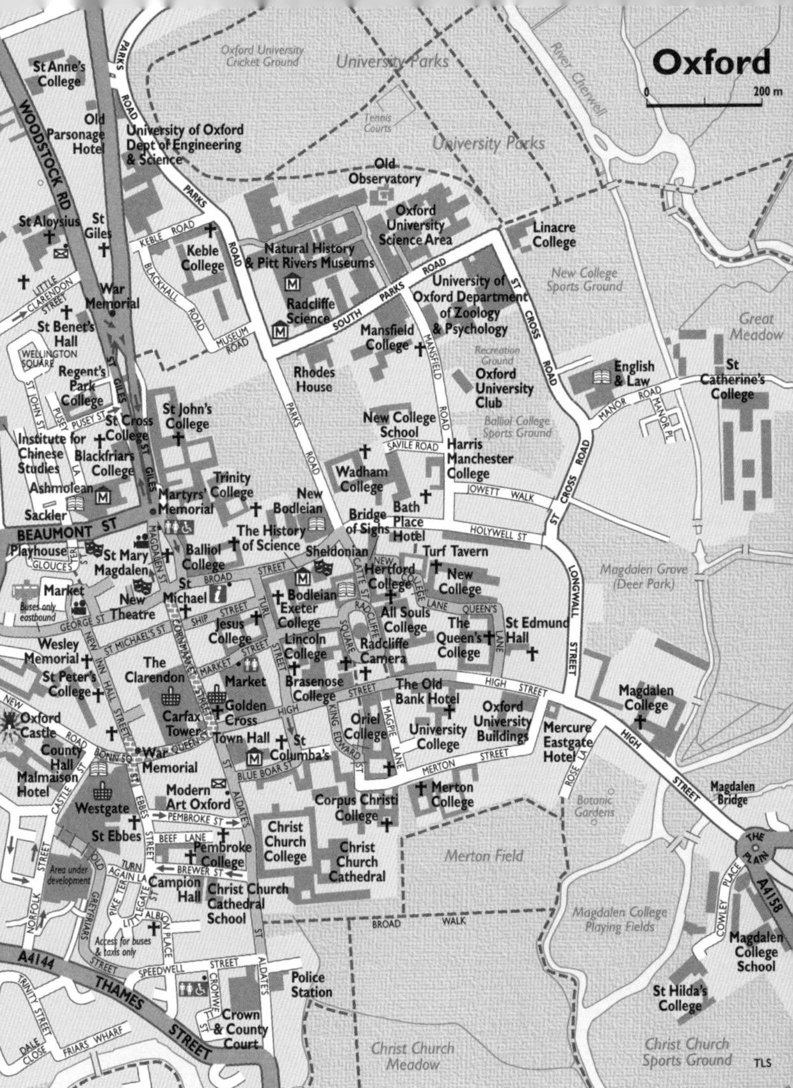

since 1773, making it one of Britain's oldest surviving markets. The town holds its main farmers' market at Gloucester Green every first and third Thursday of the month. Oxford was also the site of great automobile manufacturing. The Morris Oxford and the T-series MG sports car were created here.

If you plan on parking a car, consider using one of the five park-and-rides located on the outskirts of the city – central parking is very expensive. The best way to explore the town is undoubtedly on foot, with serendipity as a guide and frequent stops at coffee shops for on-going refreshment. A range of organised tours can reduce the aimless wandering from your free-range exploration. Do whatever floats your boat, as long as you nourish a healthy curiosity about and enthusiasm for one of the finest and most attractive cities in England.

SEE THE VIEWS OVER THE CITY

It's a good idea to get your bearings from the rooftops at the beginning of a visit to Oxford. You can climb the tower of the city's oldest building, St Michael's Church in Cornmarket Street. Alternatively, you could survey the city from Carfax Tower, a remnant of the 14th-century St Martin's Church. The tower is situated at the city's focal point, the busy crossroads known as Carfax. Another excellent vantage point can be found at the University Church of St Mary the Virgin on the High Street, which dates from 1280. Climb the 90-foot tower to access the external viewing gallery. This parish church also serves the university, and for a time was also the university's reference library and the venue for its degree ceremonies. Less pleasantly, it also served as a courtroom for the trials of bishops Latimer, Ridley and Cranmer between 1555 and 1556. They were found guilty of heresy, and were burned at the stake in Broad Street. A hundred metres away, you'll find the Martyrs' Memorial commemorating the event.

TAKE IN SOME HISTORY

St Edmund Hall

seh.ox.ac.uk
College of Oxford University, OX1 4AR | 01865 279000
Open daily 10–4, but check for occasional closures

This college of Oxford University retains its distinctive ancient title of Hall. St Edmund dates back to the 13th century, before most of the other colleges had been founded, and its premises include the only surviving medieval academic hall in Oxford. By virtue of its longevity, St Edmund has an unusual array of buildings: a Norman crypt, a 17th-century dining hall, a chapel, a quadrangle and 18th- and 20th-century contributions.

Christ Church

chch.ox.ac.uk
St Aldate's, OX1 1DP | 01865 276492
Opening times are complicated – check ahead

Founded in 1524, this is Oxford's largest and most-visited college. It has both the biggest quadrangle in Oxford and England's smallest cathedral. Christ Church Cathedral, which predates the college, serves as its chapel. Within the great hall, you'll find features familiar from the *Alice in Wonderland* stories. That's because former Christ Church don Charles Dodgson (1832–98) is better known as Lewis Carroll. Christ Church's Ante Hall was the inspiration for Hogwarts' great hall in the Harry Potter movies.

Christ Church Picture Gallery is the only public gallery owned by a single college in either Oxford or Cambridge. Its collection of 300 paintings includes Italian Old Masters – among them Tintoretto, Leonardo da Vinci, Michelangelo and Carracci.

Other Historic Colleges

Merton College (founded 1264) has peaceful gardens and the 14th-century Mob Quad, Oxford's oldest quadrangle. New College, which despite its name was founded in 1379, is famous for its hall, cloister and chapel, as well as its gardens, which are enclosed by the old city wall. Peep into St John's College, founded 1555, to see its arcaded Canterbury Quad. Queens College (founded 1341) features buildings by Nicholas Hawksmoor. Farther out in Parks Road you'll find Keble College (1870), a relative newcomer whose elaborate red-brick buildings are a Victorian tour de force.

Radcliffe Square

These university buildings form an eye-catching architectural group. The Sheldonian Theatre (built between 1664 and 1668) was the first major architectural work by Sir Christopher Wren, who was Professor of Astronomy at the time. The interior assumes the shape of a Roman theatre, and its grand ceremonial hall is used for university functions and concerts. High above, the cupola provides panoramic views of Oxford.

Close by, the Bodleian Library is one of six copyright libraries in the UK. As such it is entitled to receive a copy of every book published in the country. The circular domed Radcliffe Camera, designed by

▲ Radcliffe Camera

James Gibbs and built in 1737–49, is a reading room for the library.

Oxford Castle Unlocked

oxfordcastleunlocked.co.uk
44–46 Oxford Castle, OX1 1AY
01865 260666 | Open all year daily 10–5.30 (last tour 4.20)

For the first time in 1,000 years, the secrets of Oxford Castle will be 'unlocked', revealing episodes of violence, executions, great escapes, betrayal and even romance. Walk through these ancient buildings and experience the stories that connect the real people of the past to these extraordinary events. Take one of the weekend 'Ghost Trails' tours, which start from here.

VISIT THE MUSEUMS AND GALLERIES

Oxford University Museum of Natural History

oum.ox.ac.uk
Parks Road, OX1 3PW
01865 272950 | Open daily 10–5

Oxford's Museum of Natural History was built between 1855 and 1860 to satisfy the growing, increasingly professionalised academic interest in biology, botany, archaeology, zoology, entomology and related fields. The museum reflects Oxford University's position as a 19th-century centre of learning, with displays of early dinosaur discoveries and the most complete remains of a dodo in the world. Although visitors to the Pitt Rivers Museum must pass through the Museum of Natural History to enter it, the two should not be confused.

Ashmolean Museum of Art & Archaeology
see highlight panel opposite

Museum of the History of Science
mhs.ox.ac.uk
Broad Street, OX1 3AZ
01865 277280 | Open Tue–Sun 12–5
Got history overload yet? This special little place may get you reinvigorated. The first purpose-built museum in Britain, it contains the world's finest collection of early scientific instruments, including tools used in astronomy, navigation, surveying, physics and chemistry. The museum holds various events and exhibitions throughout the year.

Pitt Rivers Museum
see highlight panel overleaf

Museum of Oxford
museumofoxford.org.uk
Town Hall, St Aldate's, OX1 1BX
01865 252334 | Open Mon–Sat 10–5
This museum tells the story of Oxford and its people from prehistoric times to the present, from woolly mammoths to Morris Motors. A virtual high-speed bike ride takes you around the city with Oxford characters from history telling you their story. There's plenty of child-focused content as well.

Modern Art Oxford
modernartoxford.org.uk
30 Pembroke Street, OX1 1BP
01865 722733 | Open Tue–Sat 11–6, Sun 12–5
Founded in 1966 and currently funded by Arts Council England, this stylish gallery occupies a former brewery. It has changing exhibitions of contemporary art from Britain and beyond, as well as talks, live music and children's activities. There's also a shop and a cafe selling very good cakes.

GO BY RIVER

The Rivers Thames & Cherwell
These waterways slice through the remarkably verdant land close to central Oxford. The tree-lined Cherwell (pronounced charwell) is the place for punting, and provides almost rural views of Magdalen College (pronounced mordlin), one of Oxford's richest and most spacious colleges. Magdalen was founded in 1458, and was set in its own deer

Ashmolean Museum of Art & Archaeology MAP REF 259 E4

ashmolean.org

Beaumont Street, OX1 2PH | 01865 278000 | Open all year Tue–Sun 10–5, BH Mon 10–5

Opened in 1683, the Ashmolean is the oldest museum in the country. It contains Oxford University's priceless collections and displays many historically important art pieces and artefacts, including work from Ancient Greece through to the 20th century. The museum has undergone a massive redevelopment, including the building of 39 new galleries, an education centre, conservation studios and a walkway.

Pitt Rivers Museum MAP REF 259 E4

prm.ox.ac.uk
South Parks Road, OX1 3PP | 01865 270927 | Open all year Tue–Sun & BH Mon 10–4.30, Mon 12–4.30

The collections held at this museum (founded in 1884) are internationally acclaimed, and somewhat unusually organised. The museum contains objects from different cultures of the world and various periods, all grouped by type or purpose. Highlights include a striking 36-foot-high totem pole, a monkey-skull that boys from a headhunting tribe used to imitate adults, like a modern child might play with a toy kitchen, and a bottle that supposedly contains a witch who would be released if the bottle broke. There are regular talks and tours and even Object Handling on Saturday mornings.

park – walks through which are really stunning. University rowing crews train on the Thames (also known here as the Isis). Stroll through the Oxford Botanic Garden, founded in 1621, the oldest garden of its kind in Britain. Travelling thus, you can reach Christ Church Meadow and the confluence of the rivers on foot – or you could rent a punt or rowing boat from Magdalen Bridge or the Cherwell Boathouse in Bardwell Road and reach it by water.

SEE THE HISTORIC CHURCHES

The University Church of St Mary the Virgin

university-church.ox.ac.uk
High Street, OX1 4BJ
01865 279111 | Open Sep–Jun Mon–Sat 9–5, Sun 12–5, Jul–Aug Mon–Sat 9–6, Sun 12–6

St Mary the Virgin serves as both a parish church and the University Church. In the Middle Ages it was the centre of university life. The steeple, one of the finest in England, dates back to the early 14th century. Much of the exterior fabric of the church has been enriched with decoration from later centuries. One particularly notable example of such enrichment, the 1637 baroque south porch, reflects the exuberance of its time.

The chancel retains its original oak stalls and misericords. Memorials to past worthies – clerical, academic and civic – abound throughout the church. Few are more evocative than the slab recently erected on the north wall, close to the screen. It lists the martyrs of different religious persuasions who have been associated with the church over the centuries. The trials of Bishops Latimer, Ridley and Cranmer took place in the nave in 1555–6. In 1744, John Wesley preached his famous sermon attacking the sloth of the unreformed university here. Later, in 1833, John Keble and John Henry Newman began their Anglo-Catholic crusade from the same pulpit.

Oxford Oratory Church of St Aloysius Gonzaga

oxfordoratory.org.uk
25 Woodstock Road, OX2 6HA
01865 315800 | Open Mon–Fri 7am–7pm, Sat 8–7pm, Sun 7.45–12.30pm, 5–7.30

Jesuits built the Church of St Aloysius in 1875, and it became the principal Roman Catholic church in Oxford. Cardinal John Newman, the founder of the Oratory in England, had planned to establish an Oratory in Oxford in 1866, but his plans came to nothing, and the Oxford Oratory was finally established here in 1990. The building has a wide and spacious interior. Its equally wide apse has many Gothic features, fine lancet windows and a prominent rose window.

St Mary Magdalen

stmarymagdalenoxford.org.uk
c/o St Mary Magdalen Vicarage, 15 Beaumont Street, OX1 2NA

This 13th-century church is just outside the old city walls. It has two particular points of interest: it's as wide as it is long, and it's home to the city's largest Anglo-Catholic congregation. The church is also adjacent to a memorial to the Protestant martyrs. The Martyrs' Memorial was devised in 1841 by a Low Church group to commemorate the three martyrs, Bishops Latimer, Ridley and Cranmer.

St Michael at the North Gate
smng.org.uk
cnr Ship Street & Cornmarket Street, OX1 3EY | 01865 240940
Open daily 10.30–5 (10.30–4 in winter)
As its name implies, this church originally formed part of the town gate on the northern route out of the city, and was once connected to the ancient walls that protected the city and its inhabitants. Only a few traces of the northern wall remain, but the Saxon tower attached to St Michael's provides a vivid reminder of said tower's role in medieval times as a prison. At street level, a crudely blocked doorway indicates the exit used by Latimer, Ridley and Cranmer as they were taken to be burnt at the stake in the adjacent Broad Street. The site of the martyrdom is marked in the street there. Built in the first half of the 11th century, the tower is also significant as the oldest church tower in Oxfordshire. The church as it stands today is mainly in the Perpendicular style, except for the fine Early English chancel with lancet windows at the east end. This is a church of town rather than gown, and it contains many memorials to non-academic Oxford worthies.

Wesley Memorial Church
wesleymem.org.uk
New Inn Hall Street, opposite St Michael's Street, OX1 2DH
Perhaps surprisingly, the Methodist Wesley Memorial Church gives Oxford one of its most elegant spires. Built in 1878 in a conventional Gothic style, Wesley Memorial has a spacious interior. The design of its aisles is typical of Methodist churches of the period, but overall the design is grounded in Church of England aesthetic principles. The first Oxford meeting house Wesley himself preached in was opposite the present church, now 32–34 New Inn Hall Street. Its importance is signified by a plaque on the wall.

GO TO THE MOVIES

Phoenix Picturehouse
picturehouses.co.uk
57 Walton Street, OX2 6AE
0871 9025736
Opened in 1913, the Phoenix shows independent and classic films. There's a small but well-formed bar offering wines, spirits and beers. It's ideal for those post-film debates. The cinema also screens live broadcasts by Stratford-upon-Avon's famous Royal

Shakespeare Company and hosts Q&A sessions with filmmakers of various kinds.

EXPLORE BY BIKE

The Carter Company
the-carter-company.com
01296 631671
Why not try a 'luxury self-guided' cycling holiday in Oxford and the Cotswolds?

TAKE A BOAT TRIP

Blakes Holiday Boating
blakes.co.uk
0844 8567060
Take a narrowboat along the Oxford & Midlands Canal, or down the Thames to Lechlade.

GO SHOPPING

The Covered Market
oxford-coveredmarket.co.uk
Market Street, OX1 3DZ | Open Mon–Sat 8–5.30, Sun 10–4
Oxford's legendary covered market has been developing since 1773. Today it houses a wide variety of stalls. You'll find jewellers, butchers and chocolatiers, as well as clothing and footwear dealers, delicatessens and giftshops.

Alice's Shop
aliceinwonderlandshop.co.uk
83 St Aldates, OX1 1RA
01865 723793 | Open Jul–Aug daily 9.30–6.30, Sep–Jun 10.30–5 (Sat 9.30–6)
This is the original Old Sheep Shop featured in Lewis Carroll's *Through the Looking-Glass*. The real-life Alice Liddell also used to buy her sweets here. Predictably, it stocks a wide range of Alice-themed gifts. The shop is keen to promote Wonderlust generally, and happy to direct you to other Oxford sources of Alice-interest. The Alice's Day festival in July celebrates the birth of the *Alice in Wonderland* stories with city-wide events that actually last over two days. Local historian and guide Mark Davies conducts *Alice in Wonderland* tours; see website for details.

Blackwell's
bookshop.blackwell.co.uk
48–51 Broad Street, OX1 3BQ
01865 792792 | Open Mon 9–5, Tue 9.30–6, Wed–Sat 9–6
Blackwell's extensive Oxford empire spans four floors and three shops. This incarnation is a renowned and well-stocked academic bookshop, but you can also check out the Art and Poster Shop at No. 27 and the Music Shop at No. 53.

▼ The Covered Market

WALK THE RIDGEWAY NATIONAL TRAIL

nationaltrail.co.uk/ridgeway
The National Trails Office, Signal Court, OX29 4TL | 01865 810224

The fantastic Ridgeway National Trail is a chalk ridge once used by prehistoric man. As such it is perhaps Britain's oldest road. It's 87 miles long, stretching from Overton Hill near Avebury to Ivinghoe Beacon in the Chilterns.

EAT AND DRINK

Gee's Restaurant

gees-restaurant.co.uk
61 Banbury Road, OX2 6PE
01865 553540

Combine this impressive Victorian conservatory with an unpretentious, clear-headed approach to culinary matters that includes a dedication to well-sourced ingredients and it is easy to see why Gee's has been satiating the good people of Oxford for three decades. The restaurant's luminous, handsome, Grade II listed frame contains thriving potted olive trees, garden-style furniture, and a tiled floor. The food is based on excellent produce served up with style. Weekend brunches and inexpensive lunch deals

▼ All Souls College

remain popular, as does the Med-influenced modern brasserie cooking.

Cotswold Lodge Hotel ◉
cotswoldlodgehotel.co.uk
66a Banbury Road, OX2 6JP
01865 512121
This stately Victorian villa is replete with period style, all high ceilings, sweeping staircases and expansive bay windows, but a light contemporary facelift has leavened the 19th-century chintz. Dining takes place in its Restaurant 66A (that's the address on the busy Banbury Road), an understated space with darkwood floors and tables. The kitchen deals in contemporary food with clear European accents.

The Magdalen Arms
magdalenarms.com
243 Iffley Road, OX4 1SJ
01865 243159
Just a short stroll from Oxford city centre, this bustling pub is run by the team behind Waterloo's hugely influential Anchor & Hope gastro-boozer. There is a similar boho feel to the place. Its dark red walls, vintage furniture and the nose-to-tail menu will be familiar to anybody who knows the pub's London sibling. Real ales are complemented by a vibrant modern wine list.

Malmaison Oxford ◉
malmaison.com
Oxford Castle, 3 New Road, OX1 1AY | 01865 268400
Who would have thought it? The city's former prison now has people turning up at its doors wanting to be let in. Reincarnated as a classy hotel by the boutique Malmaison chain, sybaritic bedrooms have been installed in the cells. Cast-iron staircases and arched doorways are an atmospheric reminder of its past, but Malmaison's mood is now pure 21st-century seduction, dressed up in shades of chocolate brown and aubergine. The moodily lit brasserie in the old basement canteen eschews the traditional porridge, serving French classics as well as a please-all repertoire of simple modern dishes, all based on good-quality materials.

The Oxford Kitchen ◉◉
theoxfordkitchen.co.uk
215 Banbury Road, OX2 7HQ
01865 511149
Rubbing shoulders with high-end boutiques and stylish delis along the Banbury Road, The Oxford Kitchen is a switched-on modern venue that is establishing itself as a foodie landmark. Inside, you'll find a pared-back decor of tiled and blond wood floors, industrial pendant lamps above darkwood booths, and exposed brick walls punctuated by colourful prints of Warhol's soup cans, and the welcome from smartly uniformed staff is warm. The kitchen cooks to a broadly modern British template that has clear roots in classic French thinking.

The Oxford Retreat

theoxfordretreat.com
1–2 Hythe Bridge Street, OX1 2EW
01865 250309

Smack beside the River Isis, the decked, tree-shaded waterside garden at this imposing gabled pub is best enjoyed after a day exploring the city of dreaming spires. Relax sipping cocktails or a pint of London Pride, then order from the sharing-inspired global pub menu. In winter, retreat inside and cosy up around the log fire.

The Punter

thepunteroxford.co.uk
7 South Street, Osney Island, OX2 0BE | 01865 248832

Seek out this rustic-cool pub on Osney Island, in the heart of the city – it enjoys a magnificent and tranquil spot beside the River Thames. The decor is eclectic and interesting, with mismatched tables and chairs and artwork on whitewashed walls. Come for a relaxing pint by the river or refuel on something tempting from the daily menu.

The Rickety Press

therickety press.com
67 Cranham Street, OX2 6DE
01865 424581

The Rickety Press is in the heart of historic Jericho. Deceptively spacious, there's a large conservatory restaurant, a snug and a bar serving real ales, wine, coffees and teas, while the spicy aroma of mulled wine fills the winter air.

The Rusty Bicycle

therustybicycle.com
28 Magdalen Road, OX4 1RB
01865 435298

You can't miss the hanging sign for this quirky suburban pub – look for a 1950s grocer's bike swinging high above Magdalen Road's pavement. Inside the design is decidedly eccentric and Edwardian. This is a community pub in a very cosmopolitan part of the city, with the ambition of catering for all-comers. The plan appears to work well, with grand beers from owners Arkell's Brewery and carefully chosen guests coupled with a menu that is both traditional and eclectic.

The Turf Tavern

turftavern-oxford.co.uk
4 Bath Place off Holywell Street, OX1 3SU | 01865 243235

The Turf Tavern is a jewel of a pub, and it's consequently one of Oxford's most popular. It is certainly one of the city's oldest pubs, with some 13th-century foundations and a 17th-century low-beamed front bar. It's not easy to find, but if anything the tangled approach through hidden alleyways adds to the Turf's allure. Previously called the Spotted Cow, it became the Turf in 1842, probably in deference to its gambling clientele. It's also had brushes with literature, film and politics. Three beer gardens help when its busy, but the 11 real ales and reasonably priced pub grub keep the students, locals and visitors flowing in.

PLACES NEARBY

The most obvious way to head into the Cotswolds proper from Oxford would be on the A40, which soon calls in at Witney (see page 242) then Burford (see page 78), with the Cotswold Wildlife Park (see page 81) nearby. Though heading northwest to Woodstock and Blenheim Palace (see page 246) is another very attractive option.

St Mary the Virgin

iffley.co.uk
Church Way, Iffley, 2 miles south of the centre of Oxford, off the A4158, OX4 4EJ

St Mary's is a magnificent building. It's rightly called an almost perfect specimen of a Norman church, with unusually rich decoration both inside and out. Built between 1170 and 1180, it was the gift of the St Remy family, rich patrons who held the manor of Iffley in the second half of the 12th century.

St Mary's consists of a large, aisleless nave and a chancel, with a massive battlemented tower in the centre. The west front contains a superb doorway, richly carved with chevron and beakhead mouldings. The south door is equally splendid, and the carvings are excellent, with elaborate capitals. Inside, the principal features are the great Norman arches supporting the central tower, ornamented with zigzag carving and shafts of black marble.

The Fishes

fishesoxford.co.uk
North Hinksey, OX2 0NA
01865 249796

A short walk from Oxford city centre, this attractive tile-hung pub stands in three acres of tranquil wooded grounds running down to Seacourt Stream, with a decking area and a children's playground. Providing plenty of shade, these grounds are ideal for barbecues and picnics, which can be ordered at the bar, or choose from the seasonal menus of modern British dishes.

The Green Dragon Inn

green-dragon-inn.co.uk
Cockleford, Cowley, GL53 9NW
01242 870271

With a pretty rose- and creeper-covered Cotswold-stone facade, this building was recorded as an inn in 1675. However, it was 1710 before Robert Jones, a churchwarden, became the first landlord, splitting his time between pew and pump for the next 31 years. In summer the secluded patio garden overlooking a lake is an obvious spot to head for, and lunchtime meals can be served here. Step inside the stone-flagged Mouse Bar and you will notice that each piece of English oak furniture features a carved mouse, the trademark of Robert Thompson, the Mouseman of Kilburn. The menu here is extensive and there are good wines to boot. Children are catered for with a range of favourites.

Painswick MAP REF 257 D2

Perched regally on the steep slopes of Painswick Valley, the 'Queen of the Cotswolds', as Painswick rather bumptiously calls itself, is a hive of activity. The village's energy and buildings collect in the network of lanes surrounding the church. Painswick is the most Dickensian of the Cotswold villages, and due to the character of the local stone, its overall colour is more likely to remind you of ivory than honey. Like other important towns around here, Painswick's prosperity reached its peak in the 17th and 18th centuries, when denizens harnessed the stream to work mills producing wool cloth. The purity of Painswick's water also meant that cloth dyeing became an important local industry. The fine houses built by the era's wealthy wool merchants give the village its character.

But Painswick's most striking feature is its church's graceful 17th-century spire. The church itself was mainly built in the 15th century, and contains some interesting monuments. But despite these attractions, the church*yard* is actually better known. Clipped colonnades of yew have graced it since 1792. The colonnades are made up of 99 trees. Many attempts have been made to plant a final tree to bring the number to a round 100, but try as the gardeners might, that final tree simply will not take. Supposedly this is due to the intervention of the Devil

▾ The Cotswold Way, Painswick Beacon

himself, who always kills off the hundredth – perhaps out of a deep loathing for symmetrical landscape design? Rather like the Rollright Stones (see page 103), the trees are nigh-on impossible to count. Some have become intertwined with others, complicating the issue. The courtyard is also distinguished by its 17th- and 18th-century table tombs. Many were carved by local mason John Bryan and his two sons.

The Clypping Ceremony at Painswick church has nothing to do with pruning the famous yew trees. The name derives from the Old English word 'clyppan', meaning to embrace. The ceremony takes place on the nearest Sunday to 19 September, in association with the Feast of the Nativity of St Mary. In the afternoon, the children involved in the ceremony join hands to form a circle around the church. They approach the church and retreat from it three times, singing a traditional hymn. Painswick residents also bake a special cake. Known as 'puppy dog pie', it contains a small china dog – a reminder, perhaps, of the obscure pagan origins of the festivity.

A stroll around the heart of the town can be rewarding. Along Bisley Street, the original main street and the oldest part of Painswick, you'll find the Little Fleece. This National Trust rental property used to be a bookshop and is a largely 17th-century house, which was itself built onto the 15th-century Fleece Inn.

The area around Painswick has strong associations with the Arts and Crafts Movement. Morris & Co designed the Congregational Church's window, while Sidney Barnsley designed both the Gyde Almshouses and the public baths. These traditions are carried on today by the Gloucestershire Guild of Craftsmen, based in Cheltenham and the longest-established craft guild in Britain. Painswick is well known for things that go 'bump in the night'. Even King Charles I haunts a local stately B&B.

Just outside the town on the Gloucester road, you'll find Painswick Rococo Garden. The landscaped 18th-century garden wraps around Painswick House and is utterly charming, particularly in early spring when snowdrops flower in abundance.

GO ROUND THE GARDENS

Painswick Rococo Garden
rococogarden.org.uk
GL6 6TH | 01452 813204
Open 10 Jan–Oct daily 11–5
This beautiful Rococo garden is the only one of its kind to survive intact. Ponds, woodland walks, a maze, a kitchen garden and herbaceous borders are all set in a Cotswold valley that's famous for its early spring snowdrops. Check website for details of special events.

SADDLE UP

Cotswold Trail Riding
cotswoldtrailriding.co.uk
Ongers Farm, Brookthorpe
01452 813344
Hacks from one hour to all day, plus children's activity days.

EAT AND DRINK

The Falcon Inn
falconpainswick.co.uk
New Street, GL6 6UN
01452 814222
This small hotel, restaurant and pub, opposite the church with its iconic 99 yew trees, dates from 1554 – but spent over 200 years as a courthouse. Expect a good choice of local real ales, including Hook Norton, Wye Valley HPA and various guest ales. Lunch and dinner menus are varied, offering something for everyone.

PLACES NEARBY

Nearby **Painswick Beacon** is the site of both an Iron Age fort known as **Kimsbury Camp** and a golf course. From here you can catch massive views across the plain to Gloucester.

The neighbouring villages of **Slad** (see page 215) and **Sheepscombe** (see page 216) are noted for their associations with *Cider With Rosie* author Laurie Lee.

The Butchers Arms
butchers-arms.co.uk
Sheepscombe, GL6 7RH
01452 812113
Tucked into the western scarp of the Cotswolds and reached via narrow winding lanes, pretty Sheepscombe radiates all of the mellow, sedate, bucolic charm you'd expect from such a haven. The village pub, dating from 1670 and a favourite haunt of *Cider With Rosie* author Laurie Lee, lives up to such expectations and then some. Views from the gardens are idyllic while within is all you'd hope for: log fires, rustic furnishings, village chatter backed up by local beers from Prescotts of Cheltenham Brewery. Walkers, riders and locals all beat a path to the door beneath the pub's famous carved sign showing a butcher supping a pint of ale with a pig tied to his leg. The pub takes its name from its association with Henry VIII's Royal Deer Park, which was located nearby, when deer carcasses were hung in what is now the bar. The food here includes locally sourced meats, including beef from Beech Farm. To drink, there's a cracking range of ales, and a traditional farmhouse scrumpy cider.

Prinknash MAP REF 257 D2

Close to Painswick on the sheltered slopes beneath Cranham Woods, Benedictine Prinknash (pronounced 'Prinish') is one of Britain's few working abbeys. Despite looking like a huge cinema, the building just about succeeds in blending in with its surroundings. This is a testament to the use of good local materials, in this case stone from the quarries around Guiting. The building has a 16th-century foundation and has been put to a variety of purposes over the centuries. It started as a hunting lodge for the abbots of Gloucester, and then became a manor house and chapel. Prince Rupert used it as his headquarters during the Siege of Gloucester. Horace Walpole celebrated its location in 1774, describing Prinknash as 'commanding Elysium'. The last private owner, a Catholic, invited the monks to leave their home on Caldey Island, off the Welsh coast, and relocate to Prinknash. Additional building work began in 1939.

The abbey is worth visiting for its gardens and the views it affords. The nearby Bird and Deer Park, set in 9 acres of parkland, is well stocked with birds, goats and deer.

ENTERTAIN THE FAMILY

The Bird and Deer Park
thebirdpark.com
Prinknash, GL4 8EX
01452 812727 | Open daily Mar–Oct 10–5, Nov–Feb 10–4

The park is a sure-fire kid-pleaser, with peacocks, less-well-known (but equally attention-grabbing) birds, bats, donkeys and fallow deer. Visitors can feed the birds or take advantage of the beautiful riverside setting's great walking trails and picnic spots. The park is punctuated by follies like a Gypsy Caravan. They have special events at Christmas, Halloween and Easter, and a few less-seasonal events, including a Teddy Bears Picnic.

PLACES NEARBY

Prinknash isn't far from Gloucester (see page 124). Appealing Painswick (see page 176) is to the south. The Great Witcombe Roman Villa, some lovely walkable woods and **Cooper's Hill** – of cheese rolling fame – are to the northeast.

Great Witcombe Roman Villa
english-heritage.org.uk
Off A46, 1.5 mile south of reservoir in Witcombe Park, GL3 4TW
0370 333 1181 | Access during reasonable daylight hours

The remains of this large villa, built around AD 250, include a bathhouse complex and the shrine of a water spirit.

The Rissingtons MAP REF 258 B2, 262 B5

The three Rissingtons lie southeast of Bourton-on-the-Water. Around its attractive village green, **Great Rissington** has a handsome 17th-century manor house and a church with some interesting memorials. **Little Rissington**, on the slope of the Windrush Valley, has an RAF base. The church, set some way away from the village itself, has an RAF cemetery. The village overlooks former gravel pits, which have now been transformed into sanctuaries for birds.

Wyck Rissington is the loveliest of the three. Its 17th- and 18th-century cottages cluster around a wide green and village pond. From the 18th century, it formed part of the Wyck Hill estate. In the 1930s the depression forced landowners to sell off the village.

Like several near the Fosse Way, the church is dedicated to St Laurence, who was martyred in Rome in AD 257. The church contains some fine 14th-century stained glass, and Flemish wooden plaques dating from the 16th century. Cheltenham-born composer Gustav Holst was the organist here in 1892, when he was 17. Wyck Rissington is thus a stop on the Gustav Holst Way ramblers' route.

PLACES NEARBY

Bourton-on-the-Water (see page 70) and its myriad delights are close by. Stow-on-the-Wold (see page 195) lies to the north.

Rousham House MAP REF 263 E5

rousham.org

OX25 4QU | 01869 347110 | Gardens open daily 10–dusk (last entry 4.30)

Since the 1630s, members of the same family have owned this imposing, almost fortress-like Jacobean mansion. Acquiring a nice bit of turf was all the rage (for rich people) on the eve of the English Civil War, and this plot on the curve of the River Cherwell hit the spot for staunch Royalist Sir Robert Dormer. The gardens, designed to complement the house and blend effortlessly into the Oxfordshire countryside, have changed little since landscape architect William Kent designed them a little more than a century later. As the only classical landscape gardens to have survived almost unaltered, they have acquired a unique place in the history of horticultural design.

Charles Bridgeman, a royal gardener, laid down the original plan for the gardens in the 1720s. It was Kent, however, who created an Augustan landscape, with features that evoke not only the glories of Renaissance Italy but also the splendour of ancient Rome. Kent was a Yorkshireman who'd studied art in London and then moved to Italy and painted frescoes for ten years. He envisaged this garden as a landscape painting, and his design for it used painting techniques to maximum effect.

He used water from springs in the hill above to create cascades, rills and ornamental pools: simple features that formed romantic cameos within the classical framework. One curvaceous rill runs through a stone channel linking the Cold Bath and the so-called Venus's Vale. Other rills, sparkling and light-catching, feed into ornamental pools.

PLACES NEARBY

To the northeast of Rousham you'll find little **Lower Heyford**. The historic Holt Hotel, founded in 1475 as a coaching inn, sits at the crossroads of the A4260 Oxford Road and the B4030.

Shipston-on-Stour MAP REF 262 C3

As the name might imply, the small market town of Shipston (its name derives from 'Scepwaeisctune', the Old English for Sheep Wash Town) was once an important centre of the wool trade. After the demand for local wool began to decline in the 19th century, Shipston continued to prosper thanks to its position. The strategic location that had enabled it to succeed as a market town made it an important stop for coaches. Many of the inns in the High Street date from that time. A branch line from the horse-drawn tramway linking Moreton-in-Marsh with Stratford-on-Avon opened in 1836. This line converted to steam power in 1889.

PLACES NEARBY

A number of places around Shipston are worth a visit. To the northwest is Ilmington (see page 140), a delightful scattered village with a fine manor house. Ilmington's church contains work by Robert Thompson, a celebrated early 20th-century furniture maker and craftsman whose signature was always a wooden mouse. The attractive village of **Honington**, to the north, can be approached via a minor road which leads over a pleasing five-arched bridge.

Just north of Honington you'll find the well-manicured village of **Tredington**, complete with its parish church and fine 15th-century spire. Spot the fossilised remains of a creature like an ichthyosaurus (a fish lizard) in the porch floor. **Cherington**, to the south of Shipston, is home to attractive 18th- and 19th-century houses made of local stone.

Church of St Lawrence

Church Lane, Oxhill, northeast of Shipston-on-Stour, CV37 0QR

Both the nave and chancel of St Lawrence's are 12th-century, and the north porch protects the original, beautifully carved Norman north doorway. The porch and the sturdy little tower were built in the 15th century. On the south side of the church there's another beautiful Norman doorway. Above it, look for the row of strange carved heads. Inside, there is a 12th-century font with carvings of Adam and Eve in two of its 16 panels; the other 14 have trees, flowers and decorative patterns. A gravestone in the churchyard commemorates Myrtilla, 'negro slave to Mr Thomas Beauchamp of Nevis. Buried Jan ye 6th 1705'.

Whatcote St Peter
Rectory Lane, east of the A429, south of the A422, CV36 5EB
Whatcote is a tiny hamlet located at the junction of two Roman roads, deep in rural Warwickshire. The village's small size and remote location make it all the more surprising that its church was hit by a bomb during World War II. It did a great deal of damage, but the church was restored in 1947. You can still see many features of the old church, including the 12th-century doorway on the north side of the nave. A tall medieval cross with an 18th-century sundial at its top stands in the churchyard. In the 17th century the church had the same rector, John Davenport, for more than 70 years. He died in 1668 at the age of 101.

The Red Lion
redlion-longcompton.co.uk
Main Street, Long Compton, CV36 5JS | 01608 684221
The nearby Rollright Stones and their stories about kings and witches will give you plenty to ponder while you sip a pint of real ale at The Red Lion's bar. Built in 1748 as a coaching inn, the Grade II listed freehouse has a traditional old-world atmosphere with oak beams and inglenook fireplaces, but there's also a contemporary vibe. The bill of fare is amped-up pub food, with the emphasis on eye-catching presentations and unimpeachable raw materials. Daily specials are chalked on the board to supplement the frequently changing menu. There's a good children's menu, too.

Shipton-under-Wychwood MAP REF 258 C2

Formerly neighbour to Bruern Abbey, and once located at the centre of the Wychwood Forest, Shipton was built in the Evenlode Valley around a large village green. At the lower end of the green you'll find St Mary's, a late 13th-century church. A fine octagonal spire grows out of its tower. Within the church are a 14th-century effigy of a woman and a delightful Tudor monument of a family group at prayer.

The uniquely named Shaven Crown Hotel, housed in a handsome stone building close to the green, can trace its history back to 1384. At one time the Cistercian monks of formerly nearby Bruern Abbey ran the hotel. Bruern was founded in the reign of King Stephen and dissolved in 1536. Nothing now remains of it. In contrast the Shaven Crown survived to have the dubious honour of once hosting English Fascist leader Sir Oswald Mosley during World War II. He was arrested during the course of his visit, though, so perhaps the Shaven Crown did have the last laugh.

On the green of Shipton-under-Wychwood, close to the Shaven Crown, stands a 1878 memorial for 17 parishioners.

They died when a ship named the *Cospatrick* caught fire off Cape Town on its way to New Zealand in 1874. Tragically, of the 477 *Cospatrick* passengers presumably aiming to start a new life in the colonies, only three survived.

Although Wychwood Forest once covered a large area between Stanton Harcourt and Taynton, there is almost nothing left of it. A project to restore some of its original landscape and habitats is under way. The Normans favoured Wychwood as a hunting ground, and the forest was well known for its deer. Most English kings prior to Charles I hunted here, and the citizens of Burford were entitled to do so as well. In later centuries, many of the vicinity's notable estate parks, such as Blenheim and Cornbury, were carved out of Wynchwood. A National Nature Reserve stands in the centre of what remains of the forest, just 2 miles east of Shipton.

SEE A LOCAL CHURCH

St Mary's Church

Church Street, just east of the main road through Shipton, far side of the village green, OX7 6BP

The size and grandeur of St Mary's reflects the fact that Shipton parish used to include Ramsden and Leafield, villages that now have Victorian churches of their own. Shipton's largely 13th-century church stands between the Old Prebendal House and the village green. The tower and broach spire are typically Early English, and have some fine detailing.

Inside, the church is quite plain, with aisles on both sides of the nave and late Norman capitals in the chancel arch. Most of the windows are from the 13th and 14th centuries. Several of the monuments commemorate the Reade family, who were squires here for 200 years. There's a 15th-century pulpit and font.

EAT AND DRINK

The Shaven Crown Hotel

theshavencrown.co.uk

High Street, OX7 6BA

01993 830500

The monks of Bruern Abbey built this 14th-century

▼ The Shaven Crown Hotel

coaching inn as a hospice for the poor. Following the Dissolution of the Monasteries, Elizabeth I used it as a hunting lodge. She gave it to the village in 1580, and it became the Crown Inn. Thus it stayed until 1930, when it passed into private ownership and a brewery with a sense of humour changed the name in homage to the familiar monastic tonsure. The Inn is full of original architectural features, like the great hall. Light meals and real ales are served in the bar, while the restaurant offers modern English dishes.

PLACES NEARBY

Shipton-under-Wychwood has Burford (see page 78), with its attractive inns and charming pubs, to its south; Chipping Norton (see page 101), the highest town in Oxford, to the north; the Rissingtons – Great, Little and Wyck – (see page 179) due west; and popular Bourton-on-the-Water (see page 70) a short way beyond these. Bourton can also be reached by walking along the Oxfordshire Way, or head the other way to Ascott-under-Wychwood and Charlbury (see page 84).

The Slaughters MAP REF 262 B5

Let's start with the names. Upper and Lower Slaughter have the reputation of being two of the prettiest Cotswolds villages, which is saying something in a region full of villages you'd happily retire to. Their repute is well justified, but it *is* rather at odds with their names, which suggest a rather different form of coming here to die. So when did the two mass slaughters the names allude to take place? They didn't. 'Slaughter' merely means muddy in Old English – and the villages are no longer even that muddy. If you were hoping for gore and feel a touch disappointed, perhaps take solace in the fact that Lower Slaughter especially has an unmistakable *Midsomer Murders* vibe.

Lower Slaughter is about a half-mile walk from Upper Slaughter and a mile from Bourton-on-the-Water. A number of footbridges span the River Eye, and a 19th-century corn mill with a working waterwheel and steam chimney makes good use of it. Copse Hill Road, one of the most photographed streets in the Cotswolds, was voted Britain's Most Romantic Street in a Google Street View poll. After bringing yet another photo of Copse Hill Road into the world, visitors can head on up to the Victorian flourmill museum.

Upper Slaughter has less instant appeal and tourist infrastructure, but the village is arguably more appealing for that. It's the more pastoral of the two, partly clustered around its fine 17th-century manor (now a hotel) and 12th-century church. The church contains a monument to F E Witts, 19th-century rector, lord of the manor and writer of *Diary of a Cotswold Parson*. The scene beyond the church is absurdly picturesque – the forded River Eye bubbles below some wonderful stone cottages in the shade of an oak tree.

VISIT THE MUSEUM

Old Mill Museum
oldmill-lowerslaughter.com
Mill Lane, Lower Slaughter, GL54 2HX | 01451 820052 | Open Mar–Oct daily 10–6, Nov–Feb 10–dark
This interesting museum demonstrates the mechanics of a Victorian flourmill with its working waterwheel and steam chimney. The collection includes one of only three unused millstones left in the country. There's also a gift and craft shop, and a riverside tea room that offers free tastings of their award-winning organic ice cream in summer.

EAT AND DRINK

Lords of the Manor ®®®
lordsofthemanor.com
Upper Slaughter, GL54 2JD
01451 820243
This former rectory was built in the 17th century. Standing in eight acres of lushly landscaped grounds, complete with lake, it's a wonderfully relaxed place. Head chef Richard Picard-Edwards combines elements of French classical cooking with more contemporary ideas to create a menu that suits the style of the hotel.

Lower Slaughter Manor ®®®
lowerslaughter.co.uk
Lower Slaughter, GL54 2HP
01451 820456
This 17th-century stone manor house, set in pretty gardens, dates from the time of the Commonwealth, but despite the weight of centuries it's a superbly relaxing place to be. There are plenty of elegant public rooms for lounging, and the rooms are colourful without being excessively cluttered. The kitchen delivers modern and creative dishes via tasting and table d'hôte menus.

PLACES NEARBY

Bourton-on-the-Water (see page 70) is the natural itinerary-accompaniment to the Slaughters. Visit them all and you'll sample three classic Cotswolds villages, each with a very different flavour. Further west, **Naunton** is a handsome, quiet place, tucked into a valley.

Slimbridge Wetland Centre MAP REF 256 B2

The Wetland Centre at Slimbridge is the brainchild of the late Sir Peter Scott, artist and naturalist. Established in 1946 as the Severn Wildfowl Trust, the salt marshes around the Gloucester and Sharpness Canal and the River Severn have now become home to one of the largest collections of waterfowl in the world, ranging from swans and geese to flamingos and cranes. Slimbridge is the winter home of Bewick's swans, which migrate every year from Siberia, and whooper swans, which come mainly from Iceland. Swans mate for life, and some pairs have been coming to Slimbridge for more than 21 years. The Trust operates an adoption scheme to help ensure their future. Excellent viewing facilities are available and in winter, towers and hides provide remarkable views of migrating birds. There are also displays of wildlife art and many other attractions.

The village of Slimbridge itself is well worth a visit. It boasts a 14th-century church, which is a very fine example of the Early English style. The Rectory, behind the church, stands on the site of the old Manor House. Maurice of Berkeley, a scion of the great Berkeley dynasty, left from here to fight at the Battle of Bannockburn in 1314.

Slimbridge may have been the birthplace of William Tyndale, who first translated the Bible into English, but North Nibley (see page 254) also contends for the title – and they've stolen a march on Slimbridge by putting up a monument to Tyndale, which is surely cheating. (Though we should point out that this monument manoeuvre also worked for Riverside, Iowa, which claimed the coveted 'birthplace of Captain Kirk' title over America's many potential Riversides with the aid of a strategic *Enterprise* statue and a very confident plaque in the public square.)

▼ Mute swans, Slimbridge Wetland Centre

MEET THE WILDLIFE

Slimbridge Wetland Centre

wwt.org.uk

GL2 7BT | 01453 891900

Open all year daily 9.30–5.30 (winter till 5)

Slimbridge is home to perhaps the world's largest collection of swans, geese, ducks and flamingos. This internationally renowned reserve shows visitors an astounding array of wildlife, from water voles to waders, otters and dragonflies. Facilities include a tropical house, a summer trail, a discovery hide, a children's outdoor play area, a shop and a restaurant. You could also try a canoe safari.

PLACES NEARBY

Frampton on Severn (see page 216), which is two miles north of Slimbridge, is an extensive village, said to have the largest village green (22 acres) in England. The restored church contains a rare lead Norman font.

Snowshill Manor & Garden MAP REF 262 A4

nationaltrust.org.uk

WR12 7JU | 01386 852410 | Open Apr–Jun & Sep–Oct Wed–Sun 12–5; Jul & Aug Wed–Mon 11.30–4.30; guided tours only Sat & Sun in Nov

Charles Wade was the sort of entertainingly eccentric and brilliantly left-field friend you'd be glad to have, but who you'd simultaneously rather didn't ever actually pop round to your house. Wade was a wealthy sugar plantation owner, and Snowshill Manor once belonged to him. His family motto was 'Let nothing perish', and Wade embodied it. He spent his life and his inheritance amassing a spectacular collection of everyday and extraordinary objects from across the globe, buying objects because of their colour, craftsmanship and design and restoring this golden-yellow Tudor-era manor house to display them.

Laid out theatrically according to Wade's wishes, Snowshill Manor is literally packed to the rafters with 22,000 or so unusual objects – ranging from bicycles to musical instruments, clocks, Chinese lacquer cabinets, farm implements, works of art, tiny toys, suits of Samurai armour and more. Having filled the manor house with his finds, Wade had to live without any comforts or conveniences in the old Priest's House out in the lovely terraced garden, and to sleep in an old Tudor bed.

The fame of Snowshill Manor rightly travelled far and wide. Eminent people – John Buchan, John Betjeman and J B Priestley among them – were frequent visitors. Queen Mary had a look around, and apparently said that the finest thing in the house was Wade himself.

Snowshill Manor is one of the most astonishing and absorbing museums it's possible to imagine. Its wildly diverse collection has something to interest all but the most hardened detractors of museums. But the interest of the place extends beyond the house itself. Wade was an architect, and a devotee of the Arts and Crafts ideals popularised by William Morris. In 1919 he commissioned another like-minded architect, M H Baillie Scott, to transform grounds he called 'a wilderness of chaos'. Chaos became a series of terraces, the Armillary Court, a notable shrubbery, the Well Garden and the kitchen gardens. In short, the Manor is surrounded by an intriguing terraced hillside garden designed in the Arts and Crafts style.

Like Hidcote Manor Garden (see page 135), the Snowshill Manor gardens were built as a series of interconnecting 'rooms'. Snowshill's rooms provide spectacular views over some of the most beautiful countryside in Gloucestershire. A beautiful double border to the left of the terrace garden combines bright red Oriental and yellow Welsh poppies. Artfully trained climbers conquer the other wall, while the bold lines of espaliered figs stand out in tempting fashion.

Charles Wade had a special love of the colour blue. The seats and woodwork throughout the gardens at Snowshill are painted with a particular shade now known as 'Wade' blue – a powdery dark blue with a touch of turquoise. This blue harmonises well with the Cotswold stone walls, and is a particularly attractive colour in a landscape setting. It also provides a sympathetic foil for the mauves and purples the gardens use to good effect. In adopting this 'signature' colour for the garden furniture, Wade acted in accordance with his feeling that no shade of green paint could possibly match the magnificent hues of nature.

A spring rising under the manor house feeds a garden fountain and several small basins and pools. As you climb the steps near the shrubbery, the path is overhung with weeping white mulberries. The atmosphere of the Victorian romantic garden is strong.

For almost two decades, the garden at Snowshill has been managed without the use of any chemicals. The gardeners rely on wildlife to maintain a perfect natural balance. They use natural feeds composed of seaweed extract, blood, fish and bone. Snowshill's home-grown compost has an added special ingredient: dove excrement from the dovecote. The judicious planting of nectar-rich species, including alliums, asters, echium, marigolds, mignonette and sedums, attracts bees and other beneficial insects into the garden. In turn, they earn their keep by feeding on aphids and other pests. Sloe, hawthorn, elderberry and spindleberry, guelder rose, wild roses, dogwood and field maple are planted along visitors' route to the manor. These British natural shrubs produce early blossoms, nuts or fruits, or provide habitat for birds and small mammals. Visitors to the garden who might be unaware of these specific planting plans are nonetheless almost certain to notice the joyous variety of bird songs and the friendly hum of the bees as they wander through the grounds.

Today, the National Trust owns and operates Snowshill. The trust displays Wade's eccentric collections and maintains the charming country gardens to its usual high standard.

PLACES NEARBY

Pronounced, according to some, 'Snowzzle', or even 'Snozzle', charming and comparatively remote **Snowshill** village is gorgeous, as is the nearby lavender farm with its tea room and gift shop. Parts of the movie *Bridget Jones' Diary* were shot here.

A circuit of Stanway, Snowshill and Stanton makes for an excellent walk, allowing you to take in three handsome but different Cotswolds villages. Portions of the walk consist of a testing hill climb, so seek out or avoid it according to your level of fondness for that sort of thing.

The Sodburys MAP REF 256 B5/C5

What an Old Sodbury! There's something childishly pleasing about the names of the three Sodburys – Old, Little and Chipping. The three villages are all scattered around narrow lanes down the Cotswold escarpment, though their remote character has more in common with the vale than the nearby Edge.

Handsome **Chipping Sodbury** (Chipping means 'market') is the newest of the trio, established as a market town in 1227. J K Rowling, author of the Harry Potter books, was born here rather more recently. The main – market – street is extraordinarily wide and the clock tower, the location of a twice-monthly farmers' market (second and fourth Saturdays of the month), is worth a glance. The houses on Hatters Lane are Tudor.

Old Sodbury, the original (as the 'Old' suggests), has an impressively elderly church and an atmospheric (if you can ignore the noisy A46) Bronze-to-Iron Age encampment above the town.

Little Sodbury is the most interesting of the three Sodburys. Small as it is, this village has a rich history. Gloucestershire-born scholar William Tyndale (*c*.1494–1536), the translator of the Bible into English, came to its manor house in 1521 as tutor and chaplain (you can see the Tyndale Monument at North Nibley, page 254). A few years later, Henry VIII and Anne Boleyn stayed in the house, which has a wonderful 15th-century great hall. The church, the only one dedicated to St Adeline, an obscure saint who may have originated from Normandy, originally stood next to the manor house. Urgent repair work necessitated moving the church to its present site. It was built in Victorian times on the site of an earlier church, of which only the pulpit (where Tyndale would have preached) remains.

The Somerset, or Hawkesbury, Monument was erected near the Sodburys in 1846 to commemorate Lord Edward Somerset, one of the Badminton Beauforts. He served at the Battle of Waterloo with exceptional gallantry, and the government of his day gave him their thanks.

PLACES NEARBY

Horton, to the north, was originally a Norman hall. It later became a manor house, and the National Trust owns its court, though it's currently closed to the public. **Hawkesbury Upton**, nearby on the Cotswold Edge, has the Somerset Monument. If you're going south along the A46, **Marshfield** is worth turning off for and looking about (especially if it's Boxing Day, see page 54). There's a broad, handsome high street, and if you could delete all the cars then just looking at it would probably take you back in time. Also look out for the Marshfield farm shop, which has excellent ice-cream.

South Cerney MAP REF 257 F3

South Cerney, 3 miles southeast of Cirencester, is situated on the banks of the Churn. You'll find rows of attractive cottages here along Silver Street and Church Lane. The church has a Norman south doorway, above which are sculptures reflecting Heaven and Hell. Within, you'll find the remains of a 12th-century crucifix, one of the earliest surviving examples of wood carving in the country. The old Thames and Severn Canal passes just to the north of the village, and walks along the tow-path are possible. The village is best known nowadays for the series of flooded gravel pits that make up the Cotswold Water Park.

Broadly speaking these man-made lakes fall into two sections, one between Cricklade and Kemble (where South Cerney is situated), the other between Fairford and Lechlade. The park provides facilities for nature lovers, birders and sports people alike. The eight nature reserves and the wetlands collectively attract over 20,000 wildfowl, and birdlife gets particularly hopping in the winter. The various activities coexist happily on 150 lakes.

GET OUTDOORS

Cotswold Water Park
waterpark.org
GL7 5TL | 01793 752413
There are excellent birdwatching sites here, and visitors get a chance to see winter waterbirds, redwings, lapwings, grebe, plovers and more, as well as the chance to meet other locals – otters, water voles, dragonflies, fritillaries, orchids, birds, bats and even beavers. If you'd rather be active, the park offers you a choice of many activities, from angling to archery, cycling, climbing, sailing, kayaking, walking and wakeboarding.

WALK THE HIGH ROPES

Head 4 Heights
head4heights.net
GL7 6DF | 01285 770007
A range of climbing, jumping and swinging and obstacle activities.

TAKE OFF

Ballooning In The Cotswolds
ballooninginthecotswolds.co.uk
Cotswold Water Park
GL5 3EX | 01453 753221
see page 72

EXPLORE BY BIKE

Go-By-Cycle
go-by-cycle.co.uk
Tall Trees Water Lane,
Somerford Keynes, GL7 6DS
01285 862152
This husband-and-wife operation offers all-terrain bikes, as well as plenty of child-friendly options (including tricycles) and tandems for a great family day out.

SADDLE UP

South Cerney Riding School
southcerneyridingschool.co.uk
Cerney Wick Farm, Cerney Wick,
GL7 5QH | 01793 750151
The school provides tuition for students from 18 months up, and caters for people with disabilities. They also offer 1- to 2-hour rides for riders of all ages and abilities on Cotswold Water Park bridleways.

10 quintessential Cotswolds names

- **Bishop's Itchington**
- **Bourton-on-the-Water,** page 70
- **Broughton Poggs**
- **Little Sodbury,** page 189
- **Old Sodbury,** page 189
- **Ozleworth,** page 253
- **Stow-on-the-Wold,** page 195
- **Upper Slaughter,** page 184
- **Waterley Bottom**
- **Wotton-under-Edge,** page 252

PLACES NEARBY

Cirencester (see page 105) is to the north and **Cricklade** to the south. Little Cricklade's Latin motto *in loco delicioso* means 'a delightful place' and few would disagree. Dating back to the 12th century, the historical high street is still a treat today.

To the east are the Ampneys, villages set in flat countryside, with their historical churches. **Down Ampney** is also the birthplace of composer Ralph Vaughan Williams, who gave the village's name to one of his best-known hymns. There's a small exhibition about the composer inside the church.

Stanton MAP REF 261 E3

Though its somewhat unpromising name means 'stony farm', little, attention-dodging Stanton is perhaps the fairest of all Cotswolds villages. It has a fine collection of farmhouses and cottages. Most of them were built during the 17th century, the golden period of Cotswold vernacular architecture. A village of quite ridiculous perfection, Stanton seems almost to have been preserved in aspic. As such it's regularly used as the backdrop for period films.

Stanton owes its peculiar 'frozen-in-time' quality to the man who bought much of the village before World War I, the architect Sir Philip Stott. Stott was originally from Oldham in Lancashire, but having moved to Stanton Court he was determined to restore the town. Stott's restoration introduced modern conveniences, but also ensured by covenant that the more unsightly features of the 20th century could never disfigure the village.

Stanton is a place to stroll around, after you've made use of the car park around the corner of Broadway road. The church, St Michael's, is delightful and well worth a visit, particularly for its spectacular gargoyles. Elsewhere, look out for Stott lanterns and a medieval cross in the middle of the village. At the far end of the village is Shenberrow Hill, well worth investigating for its Iron Age earthworks and magnificent views.

SEE A LOCAL CHURCH

St Michael & All Angels
Church Lane, WR12 7NF

St Michael's has a handsomely slender spire, a number of 12th-century features in the north arcade and two pulpits – one 14th-century, one Jacobean. It also has some 15th-century stained glass, which came from Hailes Abbey near Winchcombe.

GET CRAFTY

Stanton Guildhouse Trust's Arts Events
stantonguildhouse.org.uk
WR12 7NE | 01386 584357

The Trust runs workshops in wood turning, pottery, furniture restoration, watercolouring, printmaking, stained and kiln-fired glass blowing and even patchworking and quilting. It also holds literary readings, musical evenings, art exhibitions and motivational speaking sessions. Book early.

SADDLE UP
Cotswolds Riding
cotswoldsriding.co.uk
WR12 7NE | 01386 584250
Lessons for all levels of rider, including ponies for children.

PLACES NEARBY
Stanway, and with it the arresting facade of Stanway House, are only up the road (and only further down this page, by happy alphabetic coincidence), and should be combined with your Stanton visit. Both golden Broadway (see page 77) and Winchcombe (see page 233) are fairly nearby too.

Stanway House MAP REF 261 E4

stanwayfountain.co.uk
Stanway, GL54 5PQ | 01386 584469 | Open Jun–Aug Tue & Thu 2–5

Not unlike nearby Snowshill Manor, Stanway's creatively named Stanway House has attracted and enchanted a surprising amount of famous people, especially writers. The nearby cricket pitch is the first clue. *Peter Pan* author J M Barrie (1860–1937) fell in love with Stanway and especially Stanway House. He holidayed at the house repeatedly, and donated the cricket pavilion. There Barrie entertained the likes of Sir Arthur Conan Doyle and H G Wells.

The Tracys, a family who'd owned land in the region since the Conquest, constructed the Jacobean building between 1590 and 1630. Two Mercian magnates gave the property to the Abbey of Tewkesbury as its first endowment. During the Dissolution of the Monasteries, Stanway changed hands for the only time in 1,270 years, when Richard Tracy obtained the lease of the property with the assistance of Thomas Cromwell. Current owner, Lord Neidpath, lives in the house, and although it contains many items of interest and value, a less fossilised atmosphere than Stanway's is hard to imagine.

Approaching the house, you pass the magnificent 14th-century tithe barn built by the Abbey. You also pass the charming, jewel-like gatehouse, which dates from around 1630. Splendid gables and magnificent tall windows give light to the Great Hall and dominate Stanway's facade. Beyond the screens passage, the hall still possesses an unmistakable Elizabethan atmosphere. There's a raised dais at one end, and at the other a minstrels' gallery above the screen – though it's now been

▲ Stanway House

made into a bedroom. The Audit Room has a rent table from 1780, where the estate still receives payment in person from its tenants.

The old water gardens have been superbly restored. Pride of place goes to the fountain, the tallest in Britain, which rises to over 300 feet. The old brewhouse has been revived. The coppers are built over log fires, making this one of the few log-fired breweries in the country. Stanway produces several beers. Stanney, the most popular, is available in local pubs.

For a long time the arresting 17th-century gatehouse, the only part of the house you can really see from the road, was thought to be the work of Inigo Jones. That theory's been superseded by the belief that it's the work of Timothy Strong, a mason from the Barringtons whose family worked with Sir Christopher Wren on St Paul's Cathedral. Either way the glow of the stone is breathtaking, particularly at sunset.

Visitors can reach Stanway House via the B4077 Stow road. Coming this way, they'll pass the striking *St George and Dragon* bronze war memorial by Alexander Fisher. It rests on a plinth by Sir Philip Stott, 'saviour' of nearby Stanton. The local church, with its Jacobean pulpit, is next to the house. The name 'Stanway' is a reference to the old Salt Way trading route.

PLACES NEARBY

Stanton (see page 192), the prettiest village in the Cotswolds, is just up the road, and should be combined with your Stanton visit. Happily both handsome Broadway (see page 77) and welcoming Winchcombe (see page 233) are fairly nearby too.

Stow-on-the-Wold MAP REF 262 B5

There's something curiously satisfying about a place name that helps explain a town's geography, and the Cotswolds has a few of these. Stow is indeed up on the wolds, making it the highest town in the Cotswolds. It's also situated at the meeting point of seven roads and lies on the Roman Fosse Way, midway between Bourton and Moreton. Stow's an interesting, historical place, nowadays known for its antiques and twice-yearly gypsy horse fair. The amount of visitors it attracts is perhaps surprising, but as ever, acerbic newspaper critic A A Gill took things too far when he called it 'catastrophically ghastly'.

Stow's heart is its old market square, for Stow's formative period was spent as a busy market town. The square, surrounded by attractive pubs, coaching inns, shops and restaurants, is not typical of the Cotswolds – its even, rectangular shape is more reminiscent of an Italian piazza, sans arcades. Perhaps Stow's exposed position on the wolds dictated its shape, to protect market traders from the wind? A number of walled alleys or 'tures' lead into the square. It's thought these once directed sheep towards the market place. Gloriously, old stocks remain in a corner of the square, while in the centre stands the Victorian St Edward's Hall. Its bombastic situation and massive presence tend to overpower the more modest lines of the other buildings. The medieval market cross, just to the south of the Hall, was placed in its prominent location so that it might appeal to the religious conscience of traders as they engaged in their dealings.

The imposing Norman church of St Edward overlooks the square. In 1646 it played host to 1,000 Royalist prisoners after the final bloody battle of the Civil War, which was fought near neighbouring Donnington. The church's north door is picturesquely framed by a pair of tree trunks, while just outside the churchyard, on Church Street, you'll find Stow's 16th-century school (now a Masonic hall). Antiques lovers will enjoy browsing the offerings crammed into Durham House Antiques on Sheep Street. The Porch House (formerly the Royalist pub), at the junction of Park Street and Digbeth Street (which runs southeast from the square), claims to be the oldest pub in the country. It might not be all talk: unlike the many other claimants for this title, remains of wooden beams have been discovered in the Royalist, and tests prove these beams were in place a thousand years ago.

There are a number of villages in the vicinity of Stow that are worth visiting. Broadwell is a 45-minute walk (or a short drive) to the north. It's built around a large green with a ford, and overlooked by a fine pub, The Fox. The Swells, Lower and

Upper, are to the west. In Lower Swell, beside the River Dikler, the unusual design of Spa Cottages persists as a reminder of the chalybeate spring – that's water containing iron salts to the rest of us – that was discovered here in 1807. Investors hoped that this discovery would encourage visitors to come and take the waters, according to the fashion of the time, but the project foundered. At the tiny rural hamlet of Upper Swell, the road crosses a narrow 18th-century bridge near a mill, complete with a 19th-century wheel.

GO SHOPPING

Stow-on-the-Wold Farmers' Market
fresh-n-local.co.uk
The Square, GL54 1BL
Second Thu of each month, 9–1

EAT AND DRINK

The Bell at Stow
thebellatstow.com
Park Street, GL54 1AJ
01451 870916

This ivy-clad stone pub in lovely Stow offers a warm welcome to all, including dogs. Open-plan with flagstone floors, beamed ceilings and log fires, it's a relaxed setting to enjoy a pint of Young's Special or one of the 10 wines sold by the glass. Seafood dominates the daily-changing specials boards.

Number Four at Stow Hotel & Restaurant 🏵🏵
hotelnumberfour.co.uk
Fosseway, GL54 1JX | 01451 830297

This stylish boutique hotel operates in a building dating from the 17th century. Number Four is one of those places that gets everything pitch perfect, from the opulent contemporary look to the sort of prescient service that anticipates guests' needs. In the oldest part of the house, light and modern cooking is served in characterful, beamed and painted-wood-panelled Cutler's Restaurant. Head chef Brian Cutler uses local, seasonal produce from a well-chosen network of suppliers to good effect in well-executed dishes.

The Porch House 🏵🏵
porch-house.co.uk
Digbeth Street, GL54 1BN
01451 870048

Claiming to be the oldest inn in England, the original building in the centre of pretty Stow-on-the-Wold has been dated to AD 947, when it is believed to have been a hospice built by the order of Aethelmar, Duke of Cornwall, on land belonging to Evesham Abbey. From then on, every century has done its bit to create the atmospheric construction that exists today. A 21st-century refurbishment has matched the undoubted period charm with a rustic-chic contemporary finish, and it's looking good. There's a relaxed feel about the place, especially in the bar, which dispenses a range of real ales, including several from the pub's brewery owners Brakspear. The kitchen turns out some impressive modern British dishes, served in the bar, conservatory and dining room.

Wyck Hill House Hotel & Spa ◎◎
wyckhillhousehotel.co.uk
Burford Road, GL54 1HY
01451 831936

Visitors' first sight of this old Cotswolds property, set in 100 acres of fabulous grounds with lovely views of the Windrush Valley, gives them some high expectations. These are met by Wyck Hill's antique-furnished lounges, its oak-panelled bar and a glitzy spa. On the food front, there's a classy restaurant with a conservatory surveying the estate, where light floods in on cream-painted tongue and groove walls, and plushly-upholstered seats at white-linen tables on bare floorboards. It's a suitably elegant backdrop for meals with a contemporary British tone and a fondness for regional produce.

PLACES NEARBY

If you are looking to keep children entertained, Adam Henson's Cotswold Farm Park (see page 133) to the west of Stow, near Temple Guiting, is a must. Created by Cotswold farmer Joe Henson, the farm has a fascinating collection of rare British breeds, which it aims to help protect.

Little **Adlestrop**, known as Tedestrop in the Domesday Book, is comparatively remote. You'll find it off the A436, between Stow-on-the-Wold and The Greedy Goose pub, near Salford. It's a one-shop village, best known for a poem of the same name by war poet Edward Thomas:

Yes, I remember Adlestrop –
The name, because
one afternoon
Of heat the express-train drew
up there
Unwontedly. It was late June.

The steam hissed. Someone
cleared his throat.
No one left and no one came
On the bare platform. What I saw
Was Adlestrop – only the name

And willows, willow-herb,
and grass,
And meadowsweet, and
haycocks dry,
No whit less still and lonely fair
Than the high cloudlets
in the sky.

And for that minute a
blackbird sang
Close by, and round him, mistier,
Farther and farther,
all the birds
Of Oxfordshire and
Gloucestershire.

Thomas never actually set foot in Adlestrop, just observing the station from the train. The sign now adorns a bus shelter, the station having long gone. Thomas never saw his poem in print as he was killed in action in France in 1917.

Stratford-upon-Avon MAP REF 262 B2

'I am a stranger here in Gloucestershire: These high wild hills and rough uneven ways draws out our miles, and makes them wearisome.'

Richard II

If William Shakespeare's only reference to the Cotswolds in his world-famous plays is anything much to go on, he was not an enthusiastic hill-walker. Shakespeare may be from the Cotswolds, but the historic market town that bore him reveals little about the bard's early career. His birth and baptism are recorded, but other than the fact that 'he had been in his younger years a schoolmaster in the country' (John Aubrey, 1681), he remains a vague personage until he materialises in London, virtually a fully fledged poet and playwright. He spent much of his life in Stratford, providing it with more than enough justification to celebrate his association with the town tastefully, authoritatively as well as lucractively. Well, and why not?

There is no better place to start exploring Stratford than the fine 16th-century building where Shakespeare was born. It's located on what was then and is now a busy thoroughfare. Just on the edge of the town centre you'll find the Church of the Holy Trinity. It's worth visiting in its own right for its delightful architecture, but most visitors come to pay their respects to Shakespeare, who lies buried here. Not far away sits the thatched farmhouse cottage where Shakespeare's wife Anne Hathaway grew up. The cottage is at Shottery, on the town's outskirts, and has often been described as the most romantic in England. It remained in the possession of Hathaway descendants until the late 19th century, and still contains numerous items belonging to the family.

It's likely that Stratford would have made an enticing destination even in an alternate universe where there never was a Shakespeare. It's quite a delight to stroll along the streets, inescapably imbued with Shakespeariana, taking in the splendours of medieval craftsmanship and the aura of 16th- and 17th-century England. Among the town's finest buildings are the aforementioned house in which Shakespeare was born,

Thomas Nash's House on Chapel Street (owned by the first husband of Shakespeare's grand-daughter), and Hall's Croft in the Old Town (named after Dr John Hall, who married one of Shakespeare's daughters). Stratford's most ornate home, Harvard House, is a splendid example of an Elizabethan town house. Rebuilt in 1596, Harvard House is Stratford's most striking Elizabethan townhouse. At Wilmcote, 5 miles north of Stratford, you'll find Mary Arden's House, the site of the Shakespeare Countryside Museum. Mary Arden, Shakespeare's mother, lived in this timbered farmhouse before marrying John Shakespeare and moving to Stratford.

Stratford is internationally renowned as the home of the Royal Shakespeare Company, long recognised as Europe's – and indeed the world's – leading classical theatre corporation. Its annual repertoire of superb theatre productions features a mix of classical plays by Shakespeare, his contemporaries, and other classical playwrights, modern drama and musicals. The RSC also specially commissions many new plays. Some of the most distinguished actors and directors in the world perform with the company.

A successful campaign to bring theatre to Stratford began in 1875, with a donation of land from Charles Flower. Little did Flower know that Stratford would one day be a titan in the field. The world-famous company was founded in Stratford in 1879, with the opening of the Shakespeare Memorial Theatre. That theatre was destroyed by fire, and a replacement was built in 1932. The art deco building, by Elisabeth Scott, was Britain's first important public structure to be designed by a female architect. In later decades, the RSC spread its wings far and wide, occupying London's Aldwych theatre in 1960 and a studio theatre (the Warehouse) in 1977. Between 1982 and 2002, it took space in the Barbican and, more recently, the Roundhouse in Camden.

The company expanded its Stratford home as well. In 1974 the RSC opened a studio theatre, The Other Place, and in 1986 it opened the Swan. The company has recently opened the new 1,000-seat Royal Shakespeare Theatre.

Even with all this on the go (not to mention the falderal involved in filming performances for distribution and sending companies touring around the world), the RSC still resists sliding into any kind of complacency. The company consistently manages to present not simply performances that set the industry standard, but also productions that redefine their texts and advance the field of theatre. Sir Anthony Quayle, Sir Peter Hall and Sir Trevor Nunn have been among the RSC's artistic directors.

You might be fooled into thinking otherwise at times, but there is more to Stratford than Shakespeare. Famous for its literary associations, Stratford bustles with culture and history. But there are also superb shops and restaurants, as well as a vibrant Friday market. You could try your luck at the horses at the exciting Stratford Races, take a tour of the city on an open-top bus, make a visit to a butterfly farm or spend the afternoon on a boat trip on the River Avon. The medieval bridge that spans the Avon greatly contributed to the town's early economic prosperity. It still provides a link between the town and the surrounding countryside.

▾ The River Avon

TAKE IN SOME HISTORY

Shakespeare's Birthplace

see highlight panel opposite

Anne Hathaway's Cottage

see highlight panel overleaf

Harvard House

shakespeare.org.uk
High Street, CV37 6AU | 01789 338534 | Open mid-Mar to Oct daily 10–5, Nov to mid-Mar 11–4
This ornate timbered house was once the home of Katherine Rogers, mother of clergyman John Harvard (1607–38), who emigrated to Massachusetts in the US shortly before his death. His generous bequests to the newly founded US college at Cambridge led to its being named after him. Harvard University now own the house (open at the time of writing but may close some time in 2016).

Hall's Croft

shakespeare.org.uk
Old Town, CV37 6BG
01789 338533 | Open mid-Mar to Oct daily 10–5, Nov to mid-Mar 11–4
This elegant 17th-century house belonged to Susanna, Shakespeare's eldest daughter, and her husband, Dr John Hall. It is an impressive building, with many exquisite furnishings and paintings from the period and an intriguing exhibition on early medicine. The gardens are pretty and relaxing, and there's also a cafe.

Nash's House & New Place

shakespeare.org.uk
Chapel Street, CV37 6EP
01789 292325 | Closed at time of writing but reopens Apr 2016
Nash's House is the elegant home that Shakespeare's granddaughter lived in and is named after her first husband, Thomas Nash. It's been preserved and restored in keeping with the period: the ground floor is furnished as it would have been in the late 15th century.

New Place is the site of the house Shakespeare retired to and where he subsequently died in 1616. A new exhibition in Nash House will feature rare artefacts relating to his life at New Place.

10 famous Cotswolders

- **WWII British Prime Minister Sir Winston Churchill**
- **World-famous playwright William Shakespeare**
- ***Cider With Rosie* author Laurie Lee**
- **Polar explorer Edward Wilson**
- **Harry Potter author J K Rowling**
- **King Alfred the Great** (born in Oxfordshire)
- **Influential poet John Betjeman**
- **Prince Charles** (lives near Tetbury)
- **Princess Anne** (lives near Minchinhampton)
- **Composer Gustav Holst**

Shakespeare's Birthplace

MAP REF 262 B2

shakespeare.org.uk
Henley Street, CV37 6QW | 01789 201845 | Open Jun–Aug daily 9–5.30, Apr–May & Sep–Oct 9–5, Nov–Mar 10–4

This is the house where the world's most famous playwright was born and grew up. Here, you can discover the fascinating story of Shakespeare's life, and see it brought to life by the costumed guides. Enjoy the famous *Beyond Words* exhibition, and see Shakespeare Aloud!'s live performances in the garden.

Anne Hathaway's Cottage

MAP REF 262 B2

shakespeare.org.uk
Cottage Lane, Shottery, CV37 9HH | 01789 338532 | Open Jun–Aug daily 9–5.30, Apr–May & Sep–Oct 9–5, Nov–Mar 10–4

Shakespeare's wife once lived in this pretty thatched cottage, and it stayed in the Hathaway family until the 19th century. Much of the original family furniture remains. You can get here by walking along the country lane from Hall's Croft, which might help you avoid the traffic.

VISIT THE MUSEUM

Mary Arden's Farm and the Shakespeare Countryside Museum

shakespeare.org.uk
Wilmcote, CV37 9UN
01789 338535 | Open mid-Mar to early Nov 10–5

The childhood home of Shakespeare's mother is 3 miles north of town. The Shakespeare Countryside Museum surrounds the cottage. It has displays about life and work on a Tudor farm, a working blacksmith's and falconers. Walk here along the towpath of the Stratford-upon-Avon Canal, or take the train one stop beyond Stratford.

MEET THE BUTTERFLIES

Stratford Butterfly Farm

butterflyfarm.co.uk
Swan's Nest Lane, CV37 7LS | 01789 299288 | Open daily 10–6 (Mar & Oct 10–5.30, Nov–Feb 10–5)

Hundreds of the world's most spectacular and colourful butterflies populate the lush tropical landscape of the UK's largest live butterfly and insect exhibit, flitting above splashing waterfalls and fish-filled pools. See the strange and fascinating Insect City: a bustling metropolis of ants, stick insects, beetles and other insects. Arachnoland features big spiders, scorpions and other troublesome terrors.

CATCH A PERFORMANCE

Royal Shakespeare Company

see highlight panel overleaf

SEE A LOCAL CHURCH

Holy Trinity Church

stratford-upon-avon.org
Old Town, beside the River Avon, CV37 6BG | 01789 266316
Open Mar & Oct Mon–Sat 9–5, Sun 12.30–5, Apr–Sep Mon–Sat 8.30–6, Sun 12.30–5, Nov–Feb Mon–Sat 9–4, Sun 12.30–5

There's no escaping the Shakespeare industry in Stratford. Yet the church escapes the heaviest crowds of tourists, saved by the fact that it's a short walk away from the town centre. Shakespeare is buried in the chancel. His memorial, commissioned by his widow in 1616, was said to have been his best likeness.

The church itself is outstanding, and would be celebrated even without the Shakespeare connection. Its origins are pre-Norman, but the present building dates from the 13th century and after. It is a large building, full of light, with a central tower crowned by a tall and beautiful spire erected in 1763. The architect G F Bodley deftly restored the church in the 19th century. The organ case he designed sits splendidly above the crossing arch in the centre of the church.

The church contains many memorials and other items of interest, and Clopton Chapel is particularly full of these. The early 17th-century tomb of George Carew and his wife Joyce Clopton is one of the chapel's finest monuments.

In the chancel, look out for 26 misericords. These date from about 1450, and include some famous examples.

CELEBRATE SHAKESPEARE'S BIRTHDAY

shakespeareliveshere.co.uk
Nearest weekend to April 23

Shakespeare was not born on 23 April. That was the date of his baptism, and therefore the date on which his birthday is celebrated with a weekend of events around the town.

GO TO THE MOVIES

Stratford Picturehouse
picturehouses.co.uk
Windsor Street CV37 6NL
0871 9025741

This comfortable, modern two-screen cinema shows the latest releases.

BOOK BEAUTY TREATMENTS

Wildmoor Spa & Health Club
wildmoorspa.com
Alcester Road, CV37 9RJ
01789 299666

After a cultural session in Shakespeare's home town, you may feel the need for a bit of pampering. Individual treatments and day sessions are available at this sleek, modern spa and health club, based around an old farmhouse on the edge of town.

PLAY A ROUND

Stratford-on-Avon Golf Club
stratfordgolf.co.uk
Tiddington Road, CV37 7BA
01789 205749
Contact club for opening times

EXPLORE BY BIKE

The Carter Company
the-carter-company.com
01296 631671

Why not try a 'luxury self-guided' cycling holiday in Oxford and the Cotswolds?

EAT AND DRINK

The Arden Hotel ❁❁
theardenhotelstratford.com
Waterside, CV37 6BA
01789 298682

Directly facing the theatre complex of the world-renowned Royal Shakespeare Company, The Arden has been coping with the tides of business generated by the Swan of Avon for many a long year. Overseas tourists and school parties of A-level students alike have trooped through its dining room, though these days a modern brasserie with big picture windows looking out over the river is the order of the day. Outdoor tables and a champagne bar play their parts in rising to the occasion, as does the enterprising contemporary cooking on offer.

The Billesley Manor Hotel ❁
thehotelcollection.co.uk
Billesley, Alcester, B49 6NF
01789 279955

Billesley Manor is a charming, refined, mellow-stone Elizabethan mansion, sitting in 11 acres of preened grounds in deepest Shakespeare country, which also contain a century-old topiary garden and fountain. A further attraction for those on the Shakespeare trail is a

Royal Shakespeare Company

MAP REF 262 B2

rsc.org.uk

Waterside, CV37 6BB | 01789 403493

The Royal Shakespeare Company (RSC) maintains Stratford's theatrical traditions, presenting both Shakespeare's plays and other works. The principal theatre, the Royal Shakespeare, was designed in cinema-style in the 1930s. Both the Royal Shakespeare and its smaller sister theatre, the Swan, re-opened in early 2011 after being comprehensively redesigned. Venues built to house the company during these works, such as the hexagonal Courtyard Theatre, will reopen in 2016 as The Other Place. Visit the website to see what's on and when. You can also take a guided tour behind the scenes. To rub shoulders with thespians, visit The Dirty Duck. This 16th-century watering hole near the theatre complex is a favourite with RSC actors.

library reputedly used by the literary legend himself, but for those with culinary rather than literary matters in mind, the classic oak-panelled Stuart Restaurant is a more relevant venue. It is the quintessential English country-house setting – all plushly upholstered comfort and formal service – and the kitchen has no intention of rocking this particular boat, sending out classically inspired dishes with a nod to modern trends and presentation and a keen eye on the use of seasonal ingredients.

The Falcon Hotel ◉
sjhotels.co.uk
Chapel Street, CV37 6HA
01789 279953
Beyond the impressive black-and-white, half-timbered facade of this 16th-century former residence lie oak-beamed public areas with leaded windows, while to the rear are modern bedrooms. While hardly necessary to mention that Stratford was Shakespeare's birthplace, it does serve to introduce Will's Place, the hotel's opulent dining room, where the menu, although short, has enough modern British dishes to satisfy most tastes. Traditional afternoon tea is served in the courtyard garden throughout the spring and summer.

Macdonald Alveston Manor ◉
macdonald-hotels.co.uk
Clopton Bridge, CV37 7HP
01789 205478
Happily, historic Alveston Manor – set in primped grounds rich with the scent of closely mown lawns – hasn't lost all its Tudor-house charm in its hotel makeover. The story that its cedar tree was the backdrop for the debut performance of *A Midsummer Night's Dream* will excite those drawn to the area in pursuit of things Shakespearean. It's also just a short walk from the Royal Shakespeare theatre. The Manor Restaurant's traditional charms – original gnarled oak beams, timbers and mullioned windows – don't let the side down. Traditional service from table-side trays is the vehicle for the subtly modernised British dishes that emerge from a classically rooted kitchen.

Mercure Stratford-upon-Avon Shakespeare Hotel ◉
mecure.com
Chapel Street, CV37 6ER
01789 294997
From the outside, this link in the Mercure chain is all you'd hope for given the location. The historic, black-and-white timbered building is a real looker. Inside matches it: a contemporary finish blends nicely with the original features, including old beams. When it comes to dining, the hotel bursts its moorings and fast-forwards a few centuries for Marco's New York Italian cooking, in a room with well-upholstered chairs at clothed tables, as well as a swish bar and terrace dining.

The One Elm
theoneelmstratford.co.uk
1 Guild Street, CV37 6QZ
01789 404919
Named after the elm tree marking the boundary of Stratford-on-Avon, the One Elm occupies a prime location in the town centre conveniently near the river and the theatre. Opening at 9.30am for coffee and breakfast, there's an informal, almost continental feel about the place, especially in the stylish front lounge area with its wood floor, brightly painted walls, squashy leather sofas and low tables displaying the day's newspapers. Beyond the central, open-to-view kitchen is the more formal dining area. The upstairs seating area has an even grander feel. The menu consists of eclectic modern pub food, while the secluded terrace gives you a feeling of being abroad.

Hallmark Hotel The Welcombe ⊛⊛
hallmarkhotels.co.uk
Warwick Road, CV37 0NR
01789 295252
If not exactly the Palace of Versailles, the formal garden out front of this splendid Victorian house is mightily impressive and brings a stately presence to the Jacobean-style property. With 157 acres of grounds all to itself, there's plenty of space to wander (or take your wedding photos), and lots of opportunities within for pampering in the spa. The restaurant matches the setting with its grandeur, with period features such as oak panels and huge windows looking out over the grounds combining with plush decor (swagged curtains, patterned carpet and formally laid tables). The menu offers a contemporary take on classic country-house cuisine.

PLACES NEARBY

From Stratford you'll need to head south or risk leaving the Cotswolds. Why would you want to do that? The most obvious things to head for are Bredon Hill (see page 76) – especially if you fancy stretching your legs – and uber-elegant Chipping Campden (see page 96). You could also call in at Hidcote garden (see page 135) to see some serious flower power.

▼ Statue of the Jester in Henley Street

St Nicholas' Church, Loxley

Wellesbourne Road, CV35 9JP

Loxley's church is a study in contrasts. It sits on a sloping site in a wildflower-speckled churchyard, but it also has less than pastoral a battlemented tower from the 13th century. The church's origins are far earlier than that. Parts of the building are Saxon, and date from about AD 950. Much of the church was rebuilt in the 18th century. The large windows in the nave, with their clear glass, and many of the internal fixtures and fittings date from this restoration. There are many excellent monuments to the rich wool merchants who poured their wealth into the creation of the building.

St James the Great

Church Road, Snitterfield, CV37 0LG

William Shakespeare's family came from Snitterfield, and his grandfather Richard was a churchwarden. His Uncle Henry had a farm in the village, but had a poor reputation with regard to the church. He was fined for 'dressing inappropriately' and was eventually excommunicated for non-payment of his church tithes.

Much of the church of St James the Great was built during the 13th and 14th centuries. The tower was built in at least two phases, its construction having been interrupted by England's first wave of the bothersome Black Death (1348–9). One of the most interesting features of the church is its 14th-century font. Like others in Warwickshire, the font has carved heads round the base of the bowl. Time has weathered and chipped at these faces, giving their expressions an enigmatic quality. Centuries after they were first carved, they are nevertheless still commanding.

The church has several literary connections. Poet Richard Jago was a curate here in the 18th century, and was buried in a vault in the church in 1781. His poems have perhaps not weathered as well as the faces on the font. They include a long account of the Battle of Edgehill, which took place nearby.

The Old Quaker Meeting House

Halford Road, Ettington, CV37 7TH (the approach path is hard to find from the road – look for a modest notice board), several hundred yards south of the parish church | Usually only open on Sundays, but can be opened on request

Built between 1681 and 1684, this tiny meeting house – in common with most Quaker meeting houses – is anything but ostentatious. It's a very simple, single-storey building, with an exterior of local stone and a plain slate roof. It's just as modest inside. It stands in a peaceful garden that also serves as a Quaker burial ground.

Stroud & the Five Valleys

MAP REF 257 D2

Stroud is the sort of place where rainbow trousers don't get a second glance, and people just assume that you can probably juggle – or failing that, at least ride a unicycle across a wire while playing Bach on the violin. Really? Just a backwards somersault then. Stroud, partly because of its size and industrial heritage, doesn't have the instant visual appeal of Painswick or Tetbury. But get to know it, and you'll find a place full of individualism, traditionalism, wholesomeness and resurgent folk culture. It's the sort of place where words like 'organic' are the norm rather than the exception. It's full of independent shops, cafes and galleries, and has one of the largest farmers' market in the country. It's been only half-jokingly nicknamed the Covent Garden of the Cotswolds. More places should be like Stroud.

The Cotswold Edge runs north–south for around 90 miles, unbroken expect for one large, convoluted dent. The landscape here is the natural place for a settlement, sitting as it does at

▾ Stroud from Selsley Common

▲ Stroudwater canal

the head of five valleys. Stroud became the centre of the wool industry from the 15th century, as cloth supplanted fleece in importance. During the 18th century the valleys bristled with mills, powered by the rivers on the bottoms of the valleys. This is perhaps the one place in the Cotswolds where you can really see industrialisation of sorts. There were once 150 mills running simultaneously in the Five Valleys, before decline set in as the industry moved away to Yorkshire.

Today Stroud spreads over the Cotswold slopes like a cloth. It has no great beauty, but it is nonetheless a place of independent spirits – and independent shops. This bustling town is centred in the area around the High Street. Close by, you will find the Shambles, the former meat market, and the Tudor Town Hall. The handsome 19th-century Subscription Rooms on nearby George Street are now home to the Tourist Information Centre. The Museum in the Park, situated next to the Stratford Park Leisure Centre, offers an excellent insight into the history of the area. Among other items, it displays a collection of early lawnmowers – Edwin Beard Budding, the inventor of the lawnmower, was from this valley.

Southwest of Stroud lie **Selsley Common** and Selsley. Selsley's church is of particular interest – it has stained glass by William Morris, Philip Webb, Dante Gabriel Rossetti, Edward Burne-Jones and Ford Madox Brown. A little farther west, near Stonehouse, you'll find one of the area's pre-industrial legacies. The 13th-century **Frocester Tithe Barn** is one of the finest of its type in England.

To the east of Stroud is hill-hugging **Chalford**. Its houses cling to its steep lanes and line the terraces and shelves of the north slope of the valley. The Chalford Community Store maintains the tradition of door-to-door deliveries from the local shop. Some of the paths are too steep and narrow for any form of modern transport to be practical, and so a woman named Anna and two donkeys, Chester and Teddy, do the rounds. A legacy of the Industrial Revolution, Chalford's houses were built by the clothiers and merchants who made their fortune during the 18th and 19th centuries, and by weavers working first from home and later in the mills that still line the Thames and Severn Canal. Chalford's two churches contain work produced by members of the Arts and Crafts Movement.

There are some good walks to be had along the **Stroudwater Canal**. Once the more successful part of the Thames and Severn Canal system, Stroudwater functioned until 1941, and is now being restored. The Thames and Severn Canal system was one of those great Georgian enterprises that were magnificent in conception but almost redundant by the time of their realisation. The canal system, completed in 1789, was intended to facilitate trade between two rivers that were important commercial waterways. The project was plagued by problems related to the number of locks, the size of the 2.17-mile Sapperton Tunnel, and even a shortage of water – which you'd have thought would be the one thing they'd have plenty of. Other, better canals and the arrival of the railways put paid to it, and the last recorded journey was made in 1911. The two temple-like tunnel portals are visible at Coates and Daneway, where the pubs, built for the boatmen, still function. A stroll along the old canal is recommended, as is a visit to the village of **Sapperton**, the home of Ernest Gimson and the Barnsley brothers, of Arts and Crafts Movement fame.

Just to the north of Chalford is gorgeous little **Bisley** village, with pubs and a church with a dramatic spire. The churchyard contains a unique 'Poor Soul's Light' – a 13th-century structure that contained candles lit during masses for the poor.

Woodchester, south of Stroud, is the site of a Roman villa with a magnificent Orpheus mosaic buried in the churchyard – which, frustratingly, can't be viewed. Woodchester Mansion lies south of Woodchester, on the road to Dursley. The house, abandoned by its builders in the mid-1870s before it could be completed, is a fascinating place to visit. It is preserved in the state of construction at which it was abandoned.

Rodborough Common, just to the southwest of Stroud, links to Minchinhampton Common (see page 148). A good place for walking, the common is also the site of Rodborough Fort, which local dyer George Hawker built as a pleasure-house in 1764. It was rebuilt in Victorian style in 1870.

VISIT THE MUSEUM

Museum in the Park

museuminthepark.org.uk
Stratford Park, Stroud, GL5 4AF
01453 763394 | Open Apr–Sep Tue–Fri 10–5, Sat–Sun 11–5, Oct–Mar Tue–Fri 10–4, Sat–Sun 11–4; closed Mon (except Aug, BH)

In his 1897 will, William Cowle included a bequest of £4000 to provide a museum for Stroud. Housed on two floors of a Grade II 17th-century wool merchant's mansion, it celebrates the rich history of the Stroud area. It also has a gift shop and cafe.

LOOK FOR GHOSTS

Woodchester Mansion

woodchestermansion.org.uk
Nympsfield, GL10 3TS | 01453 861541 | Open Tue–Sun 11–5 (last entry 4)

Woodchester Mansion is a 19th-century Victorian-Gothic masterpiece, mysteriously abandoned mid-construction in 1873 – the most popular theory is that the site was so haunted that the workers dropped tools (which can still be seen) and legged it. Hidden in a secluded valley, this Grade I listed building has been saved from dereliction – frozen in time, but never to be completed. The carvings in Woodchester Mansion are among the finest of their kind in the world. Entrance to the car park is on the B4066 (Stroud–Dursley road) five miles south of Stroud, at a junction with a minor road leading to Nympsfield. Beware – putting the postcode in your satnav won't take you here.

GO WALKING

There's excellent walking around here, with five valleys to choose from, atmospheric woodlands and big views from the hilltops. Laurie Lee's Slad Valley, Sapperton and the Golden Valley are all great destinations, as are the Jurassic grasslands of Selsley, Minchinhampton Common (see page 148) and Rodborough Common (see page 213). The two commons are close enough to be enjoyed in one walk and offer endless big views into the valleys, though you needn't bother with climbing hills if you don't fancy it.

EAT AND DRINK

Bear of Rodborough Hotel

cotswold-inns-hotels.co.uk
Rodborough Common, GL5 5DE
01453 878522

This 17th-century former alehouse takes its name from the bear-baiting that used to take place near by. It's located amidst the rolling grassland of Rodborough Common where cattle roam free in the summer. A stone-walled dining room called the Library is more of a *trompe l'oeil* design feature than actual rows of volumes, but it has superb views and a menu of thoroughgoing British modernism.

The Bell at Sapperton

bellsapperton.co.uk
GL7 6LE | 01285 760298

Built of mellow Cotswold stone and set in an idyllic village close to Cirencester Park, the

300-year-old Bell attracts local walkers, families, drinkers, diners and horse riders. On warmer days, the secluded rear courtyard and landscaped front garden are lovely venues for alfresco dining. The Bell attracts discerning folk for its Butcombe, Hook Norton, Otter and Stroud ales, and its innovative, homemade pub food, served in four cosy dining areas, each with its own individual character.

The Ram Inn

South Woodchester, GL5 5EL
01453 873329

Originally a farm, this 17th-century Cotswold-stone inn became an alehouse in 1811 and is still full of historic little gems. In winter seek the warmth of the huge fireplace, but in other seasons head for the terrace and admire the splendid views. Children have their own menu.

Stroud Brewery

stroudbrewery.co.uk
Unit 11, Pheonix Works (off Hope Mill Lane), London Road, Thrupp, GL5 2BU | 01453 887122

The popular Stroud Brewery's distinctive, award-winning beverages are excellent value, and the process of their manufacture is diligently ethical and eco-minded. The beer-making waste gets eaten by lucky local pigs and cows. Their very own bar is open Thursday to Saturday evenings and also for Sunday brunch. They're developing a cult following.

Woodruffs Organic Cafe

woodruffsorganiccafe.co.uk
High Street, Stroud, GL5 1AJ
01453 759195

Organic and seasonal food makes up the menu here. Their fare is mainly vegetarian (and they'll cater for more specific diets, too), but with several fish dishes on offer, the selection of meals is very enticing indeed – and it all looks so healthy.

PLACES NEARBY

This side of the Cotswolds has fewer of the must-see villages and sights, but Bisley, Slad (both below) and Sheepscombe (see page 216) are ideal for exploring places without crowds. Frampton on Severn (see page 216) is worthy of a visit, as is St Augustine's Farm in Arlingham (see page 216).

Bisley

Perched at the top of a wooded valley, delightful Bisley is an undiscovered Cotswold secret, despite the fact that novel writer Jilly Cooper lives here. Queen Elizabeth I once spent time here too. As with most of these sorts of places there's not much to actually do, other than amble about the historic village, go 'ooh' a bit then visit the pub for lunch. But there aren't many better places to do that than here.

Slad

Made famous by Laurie Lee, there's little more to Slad than his much loved Woolpack pub and perhaps an over-the-wall look at the houses Lee was brought up in and the one he lived in as an adult. It's still strikingly similar to the way Lee lovingly described it in *Cider With Rosie*.

Sheepscombe

No name could be more Cotswolds than Sheepscombe, alluding to the region's famous industry and landscape in one go. On the edge of the Slad Valley hidden among beech woods, you won't see a single tourist here. Again it's pretty enough for a short visit without there being a great deal to do, though the village pub, the Butchers Arms, is worth going to (see page 178).

The Bear Inn

bisleybear.co.uk
George Street, Bisley, GL6 7BD
01452 770265

There has been a pub here for almost 400 years. Stories and legends abound and there is even a priest hole halfway up the inglenook fireplace. The pub's original character and charm is still evident, from the friendly bar serving pints of Butcombe beer to the dining room where food is traditional and comforting.

St Augustine's Farm

staugustinesfarm.co.uk
Arlingham, GL2 7JR | 01452 740277
Open most days end Mar to mid-Sep 11–5 (Fri–Sun term time)

This 50-acre organic farm is a great place to take the kids. They can hand-feed farm animals, play traditional games in the barn, run free in the toddler play area or, if they're a little older, run free in the wide, safe green spaces. There's also a picnic area.

Frampton on Severn

The village lies close to the banks of the River Severn and is believed to have the longest village green in the country, an impressive 22 acres. Part of the green is a Site of Special Scientific Interest. A walk through the old part of the village reveals a mix of Tudor and Georgian houses which are close to the Gloucester–Sharpness canal. A stroll along here is a grand way to watch narrow boats pootling along. In the southwest corner of the village stands the church, which was consecrated in 1315. Its ancient lead font, just one of six identical Romanesque fonts remaining in the country, predates the church.

Frampton Court Estate

framptoncourtestate.co.uk
GL2 7EP | 01452 740698 | Manor gardens open Mon & Fri afternoons end Apr–early Aug; house and barn tours by appointment only

The estate comprises a 16th-century timber-framed manor house and splendid 18th-century Frampton Court with its eccentric orangery. The Wool Barn dominates the farmyard at the manor. The Clifford family have had the stewardship of the estate since the 11th century.

Sudeley Castle MAP REF 261 D4

sudeleycastle.co.uk
Near Winchcombe, GL54 5JD | 01242 602308
Open mid-Mar to early Nov daily 10–5

Despite a castle not being a very Cotswolds type of thing – the region's not really a place of grand gestures and aggressive buildings, tending more towards the cosy and twee – you may find this to be one of the highlights of the Cotswolds. Set in deeply wooded countryside and beautifully sited beneath the Cotswold escarpment, Sudeley Castle incorporates the remains of a magnificent medieval mansion. It also has some spectacularly colourful ornamental gardens.

During its Tudor and Elizabethan heyday, Sudeley was a place of eminence. Henry VIII is believed to have visited with Anne Boleyn in 1535. His last wife, Catherine Parr, eventually married the ambitious Sir Thomas Seymour, Lord High Admiral of England, in 1547 and moved to Sudeley. She died here after childbirth, and was buried in the chapel. Strangely this then seemed to be forgotten about, as her coffin was 'discovered' there again in 1782, and opened – souvenirs including locks of her hair and a tooth are still on display today.

The ill-fated Lady Jane Grey was among the large retinue that the Queen Dowager brought to Sudeley. Jane was later imprisoned in the Tower of London and beheaded, and still later portrayed by Helena Bonham-Carter in the inevitable biopic, opposite that fetching chap who played Westley in *The Princess Bride*. Win some, lose some. Queen Elizabeth I was to visit the castle on three occasions.

King Charles I found refuge here during the Civil War, when his nephew Prince Rupert established his headquarters at the Castle. It was damaged during a battle, and on Cromwell's post-war orders was left neglected and derelict for nearly 200 years. King George III was among those sightseers who came to admire the castle's romantic ruins.

After this long period of neglect, brothers William and John Dent, from a rich family of Worcester glovers, bought Sudeley in 1830. After their deaths their cousin, John Coucher Dent, inherited the castle. His wife Emma devoted her life to the enrichment of Sudeley. The original mellow stone of the banqueting hall, the tithe barn and the dungeon tower remained; the rest of the house was restored with the help of architect Sir George Gilbert Scott, who designed the beautiful tomb of Catherine Parr – over 300 years after her death – in the church. Conducted tours of the still privately owned castle reveal a remarkable collection of furniture and paintings. All are displayed with a delightful studied nonchalance. Visitors enter the castle apartments through the Rent Room, where an agent would have once collected the tenants' payments, or the North Hall, formerly the guardroom. This room displays a fine portrait of Charles I by Van Dyck. *Allegory of the Tudor Succession*, a remarkable painting by Lucas de Heere, hangs in the Queen's Bedroom. Blatantly political, it shows Queen Elizabeth I surrounded by the goddesses of peace and plenty. In marked contrast, her predecessor Queen Mary is depicted with her husband, Philip II of Spain, and Mars, the Roman god of war.

Among Sudeley's relics of Queen Catherine Parr are her prayer book and a love letter to Seymour, accepting his proposal of marriage. Civil War armour discovered during excavations and a fascinating letter from Charles I to the freeholders of Cornwall are also displayed.

Sudeley Castle's gardens were laid out during the 19th-century restoration. The Queen's Garden is famous for its rose collection; and the fine terraces offer spectacular views over the ancient trees in the Home Park. There are exhibitions, a gift shop and a plant centre.

PLACES NEARBY

Inviting Winchcombe (see page 233) is the perfect place to base yourself if your visit is any kind of hiking holiday. Even if it's not, consider a hike up Cleeve Common (see page 236) and/or Belas Knap (see page 239). If you're tired of walking spend the day on the Gloucestershire Warwickshire steam railway (see page 237). While you are waiting for the train, have a drink in the 1950s-style coffee shop where you can learn about the history of the railway line in the Discovery Coach.

Sudeley Castle

see highlight panel on page 217

Tetbury MAP REF 257 D4

Tetbury should be more famous, but it's still not really on the tourist buses' radars. It's an unreasonably handsome, small, tranquil, charming market town set among the broader slopes of the southern Cotswolds. By the 18th century, Tetbury was one of the most important cloth market towns of south Gloucestershire. Its main streets radiate from the still-impressive market square. The square is dominated by the 17th-century Town Hall or Market House, which rests on three rows of tubby Etruscan pillars – though it was reduced by one storey in 1817. The excellently named Snooty Fox Hotel (the artist formerly known as the White Hart), also on the square, was rebuilt by the designer of Westonbirt House with the aim of providing for attendees of the Beaufort Hunt.

The road next to the Snooty Fox leads to Chipping Steps and the site of the old livestock market (Chipping derives from the Old English 'ceapen' for a market). The old market is surrounded by some handsome 18th- and 19th-century houses, and near the Old Priory. The road continues down to Millennium Green – the scene of the annual Woolsack Races on Spring Bank Holiday Monday – at the foot of Gumstock Hill.

South from the square, along Church Street, you'll find the magnificent parish church of St Mary the Virgin, which was rebuilt in Gothic style in the late 18th century. The spire, the fourth highest in England, is 186 feet tall. The interior, lit by Perpendicular-style windows, is coolly elegant, with rows of box pews presided over by panelled galleries and two splendid chandeliers. The church is the home of the Tetbury Heritage Display.

At the western end of Long Street, which runs west out of Market Square, Tetbury has an unusual museum. The Tetbury Police Museum & Courtroom is housed in the cells of the Old Court House. It displays police memorabilia, such as uniforms on loan from Gloucestershire Constabulary.

GET OUTDOORS

Westonbirt Arboretum
see highlight panel overleaf

TAKE OFF

Ballooning In The Cotswolds
see page 72

EAT AND DRINK

Calcot Manor @@
calcotmanor.co.uk
Calcot, GL8 8YJ | 01666 890391
Set in 220 acres of prime Cotswolds countryside, Calcot Manor left behind its seven-

Westonbirt Arboretum MAP REF 257 D4

forestry.gov.uk
Westonbirt, GL8 8QS | 0300 067 4890 | Open Mar–Sep daily 9–8, Oct–Feb 9–5

The Victorian-era National Arboretum boasts more than 15,000 trees (of around 2,500 species) from Britain, China, North America, Japan, Chile and other temperate climates. Thriving specimens populate the Arboretum's 600 acres and line much of its 17 miles of footpaths. Its extensive collection of Japanese maples makes it particularly stunning in autumn, but it's wondrous at any time of year, including the magnificent displays of rhododendrons and azaleas in the spring. The magical Enchanted Christmas illuminated trails enliven the lead up to Christmas. Westonbirt House, which used to be part of the estate but is now a school, sits across the road from the Arboretum entrance. It was designed by Lewis Vulliamy. Vulliamy also designed the Snooty Fox in Tetbury and Dorchester House (demolished to make way for the hotel of the same name) in London.

centuries-old origins as a lowly farmhouse long ago. Nowadays it's a design-led, boutique-style country-house hotel, offering luxurious rooms and a state-of-the-art spa. The Conservatory Restaurant looks to the Mediterranean for inspiration, and local suppliers furnish the produce for its skilfully wrought modern menu.

The Close Hotel ®®
theclose-hotel.com
8 Long Street, Tetbury, GL8 8AQ
01666 502272
Although it's situated in the town, The Close Hotel has the feel of a country-house hotel. It's a handsome pile dating from the 16th century, and within there are period details and a finish of refined, contemporary elegance. There are two dining options in the form of a brasserie and fine-dining restaurant. Any sense of old-school solidity has been avoided by painting the wall panels in a fashionable shade of blue/grey and by keeping the tables free of heavy linen. The modern British menu strikes the right balance in this setting, with the dishes showing craft and creativity.

Gumstool Inn
calcotmanor.co.uk
Calcot Manor, near Tetbury, GL8 8YJ | 01666 890391
This stylish country inn, a stone farmhouse built by Cistercian monks in the 14th century, is now a popular free house. Part of Calcot Manor Hotel, the buzzy and comfortable Gumstool Inn has a real country-pub atmosphere. It stocks a good selection of ales, such as Butcombe Bitter, and local ciders, including Ashton Press. Gumstool offers an excellent choice of wines by the glass or bottle. The food here is top-notch gastro-pub fare, and there is a pronounced use of local suppliers. In the summer, grab a table on the pretty, flower-filled sun terrace, while indoor winter evenings are warmed with cosy log fires. Booking is recommended.

Hare & Hounds Hotel ®®
cotswold-inns-hotels.co.uk
Westonbirt, GL8 8QL
01666 881000
The handsome Cotswold-stone house cuts quite a dash as a country-house hotel, and the Beaufort Restaurant really puts it on the map. The vaulted hammer-beamed ceiling and stone mullioned windows overlooking the garden strike an elegant pose, while the well-designed chairs and smartly laid tables suggest this place is not stuck in the past. The menu is a roll call of modern British dishes that show adroit technical skills and impressive flavours.

The Priory Inn
theprioryinn.co.uk
London Road, Tetbury, GL8 8JJ
01666 502251
An enormous 'walk-around' open log fire greets visitors to this thriving gastro-pub and

hotel, parts of which date from the 16th century, when it was a stable block and grooms' cottages for the neighbouring priory. The beers are from microbreweries such as Uley and Cotswold Lion. White wine and sparkling rosé spring from a vineyard at Malmesbury and damson brandy, sloe gin and quince liqueur are made on the banks of the River Severn. Fresh ingredients come from sources based strictly within 30 miles of the inn and meals are served in the traditional, bare-boarded, beamed bar or the more contemporary lounge and restaurant. Children have the opportunity to create personalised wood-fired pizzas. The Early May Bank Holiday beer and cider festival is rightly popular.

10 places to sleep

- **Barnsley House,** Barnsley, barnsleyhouse.com
- **Bibury Court Hotel,** Bibury, biburycourt.com
- **Calcot Manor Hotel,** near Tetbury, calcotmanor.co.uk
- **Cowley Manor Hotel,** near Cheltenham, cowleymanor.com
- **Hare And Hounds Hotel,** Westonbirt, cotswold-inns-hotels.co.uk
- **The Lords of the Manor,** Upper Slaughter, lordsofthemanor.com
- **The Lygon Arms,** Broadway, lygonarms.co.uk
- **St Anne's B&B,** Painswick, st-annes-painswick.co.uk
- **The Wild Thyme,** Chipping Norton, wildthymerestaurant.co.uk
- **Wyck Hill House Hotel,** Stow-on-the-Wold, wyckhillhousehotel.co.uk

Snooty Fox Hotel

snooty-fox.co.uk
Market Place, Tetbury, GL8 8DD
01666 502436

Occupying a prime spot in the heart of Tetbury, this 16th-century coaching inn and hotel retains many of its original features. Sit in a leather armchair in front of the log fire with a pint of Wadworth 6X and order from the extensive bar menu. Alternatively, head for the restaurant.

PLACES NEARBY

Chavenage (see page 86), just over a mile to the northwest of Tetbury, is a delightful and possibly very haunted manor with a fine collection of furniture and 17th-century tapestries. The chapel, with its early Norman font, is close by. The gardens of **Highgrove**, the Prince of Wales' home, can be visited on a prebooked tour. Three miles southwest of Tetbury is the magnificent Westonbirt Arboretum (see page 220), managed by the Forestry Commission.

Tewkesbury MAP REF 260 C4

Tewkesbury is one of those Cotswolds names that just rolls pleasurably off the tongue. It's a proper old Saxon name – fitting for a town with such history behind it.

Tewkesbury has inspired more than its fair share of writers as well, but its larger historical significance is largely governed by its location on the banks of the rivers Severn and Avon, which were instrumental in the 16th-century cloth and mustard trades, and the later flour trade. Its importance depended, too, on its medieval Benedictine monastery, of which only the magnificent church remains. Robert Fitzhamon, one of William the Conqueror's most powerful barons, built the monastery between 1102 and 1121. He used the Severn to import stone from Normandy for its construction. After his death, the 'Honour of Tewkesbury', as the patronage came to be known, passed to an illegitimate son of Henry I, and then to the de Clare family. The abbey became one of the most powerful in the kingdom, building many fine tithe barns in the process – some of these survive, for example at Stanway (see page 193). The abbey used these to store the fluffy booty from its large ranges of sheep grazing land.

▼ Tewkesbury Abbey

Other Norman lords and their dynasties were connected with the abbey, and many of those lords are buried here. The 14th century brought two major changes to the Norman structure. First, vaulted roofs were inserted. Second, Lady Eleanor le Despenser, widow of one of England's most influential lords, transformed sections of the building. In part she worked to create a shrine to her husband and her family – like a really expensive and permanent Late Medieval scrapbook. Her ancestor Robert Fitzhamon, her husband Hugh le Despenser and her son and his wife are buried in the chapels around the choir. Many other hugely important participants in the wars, feuds and general politics of the Middle Ages are buried here. Among these is Edward of Westminster, Prince of Wales. He was the only son of Henry VI, and only heir apparent to the English throne to ever die in battle (right here in Tewkesbury). Some of the finest medieval stained glass in England glitters down on all this. Much of it dates from Eleanor's time.

The abbey was dissolved in 1539, but Tewkesbury's citizens bought the church for a total of £453. Because of its location – close to two rivers that tend to flood, and with the abbey lands at its back – the town, unable to expand, folded in on itself. Throughout the 17th and 18th centuries the townspeople built densely around narrow alleyways off the main streets. Surviving alleys such as Machine Court, Fish Alley and Fryzier Alley run off main streets like Barton Street, Church Street and High Street. Tewkesbury's collection of half-timbered and brick houses presents one of the finest historical ensembles in the country.

The heritage and tourist information centre, Out of the Hat, is an ideal place to start a visit to the city. The Abbey Church of St Mary dominates the town with its great 148-foot-high Norman tower. One of the most striking interior features is the set of 14 Norman pillars that support the 14th-century roof. The choir is illuminated by 14th-century stained-glass windows, while chapels containing monuments to the wealthy families that have influenced both the church and the town radiate around it. The west front exterior is notable for its dramatic Norman arch.

There is a lot to enjoy in the town. In dry weather a circular walk should include a stroll across the Ham to the river. The Ham is not a vast porky plane, but an enormous meadow that separates the Mill Avon from the Severn. Perhaps skip it if you're visiting in winter – the Ham invariably floods. The handsome Bell Hotel is opposite the church. From here Mill Street leads you down to the abbey mill. It's called Abel

Fletcher's Mill because it is thought to have played a role in Dinah Craik's 1856 novel, *John Halifax, Gentleman*. Much of the novel is set in the fictional town of Norton Bury, which is modelled on Tewkesbury. From here you can either walk along St Mary's Road, with its attractive timbered cottages, or cross the Avon and strike out across the Severn Ham. Every year the grass of the Ham, which is owned by the town, is cut and auctioned off according to a centuries-old tradition.

At the Severn, turn right to walk along the weir, and then return across the meadow this side of the flour mills. You can cross the old mill bridge and then walk along the Avon. At King John's Bridge, recross the river. Then turn right into the High Street and walk to The Cross, a war memorial built on the site of the medieval High Cross that the Puritans razed in 1650. On your left, Barton Street will take you to the fascinating Tewkesbury Museum. Located in a 17th-century building, the museum features a model of the 1471 Battle of Tewkesbury (see page 39, *The Cotswolds at War*). Many of the Lancastrian troops defeated in the battle sought sanctuary in the church, but they were slain nonetheless. That happens so often you almost wonder why they bothered trying it. 'Bloody Meadow', as the battlefield came to be known, is south of the church, off Lincoln Green Lane. The 'Battlefield Trail' will get you there and show you around.

▾ River Avon

Church Street, to your right, takes you past the distinctive Royal Hop Pole Hotel, which featured in Charles Dickens' *Pickwick Papers*. Beyond the hotel is a row of restored 15th-century cottages, built by medieval merchants. One, the Merchant's House, is presented as it would have looked in its heyday. Another, the John Moore Museum, takes its name from the local writer. Moore's stories were based on Tewkesbury and the countryside and villages to the northeast, around nearby Bredon. On the right, an alleyway leads down to the Old Baptist Chapel and Court. Although the building dates back to the 15th century, it became a chapel only in the 17th century.

Tewkesbury has a number of old and interesting inns: the previously mentioned Royal Hop; the Tudor House in the High Street, built in 1540 by the Pilgrim Fathers; Ye Olde Black Bear, near the junction with Mythe Road and High Street, which possibly dates back to 1308; and The Ancient Grudge, which takes its name from the Wars of the Roses.

Tewkesbury has yet more literary associations. Barbara Cartland (1901–2000) had links with the town, and the family monument is in the churchyard. The poet John Milton played the organ now in the abbey church when it was at Hampton Court. Daniel Defoe's observations on the town are recorded in his *A Tour Through the Whole Island of Great Britain*. He called Tewkesbury 'a large and very populous town situated upon the River Avon', famous 'for a great manufacture of stockings'. Seventy years later the essayist William Hazlitt, walking from Shropshire to Somerset, recorded how he spent a night in a Tewkesbury inn reading Saint Pierre's *Paul and Virginia*.

▾ Cottages in Mill Street

TAKE IN SOME HISTORY

Tewkesbury Abbey
tewkesburyabbey.org.uk
Church Street, the A38
Gloucester road, GL20 5RZ
01684 850959 | Open Mon–Tue, Thu, Sat 8.30–5.30, Wed, Fri 7.30–5.30, Sun 7.30–6

With its imposing central tower, Tewkesbury Abbey is a Norman church built on a cathedral scale. The sheer size of the building is further emphasised by the huge arch that entirely makes up the west end, which rises to the full height of the nave. The look and feel of grandeur is continued inside, where giant pillars soar up to the roof.

VISIT THE MUSEUMS

The John Moore Museum
johnmooremuseum.org
41 Church Street, GL20 5SN
01684 297174 | Open Apr–Oct Tue–Sat 10–1 and 2–5; open most Sat rest of year

Established in 1980 in memory of writer and naturalist John Moore, the museum is located in a cottage in a row of historic timber-framed buildings. It's home to an extensive natural history collection that features specimens of the mammals and birds native to the surrounding countryside, woodlands and wetlands of the Cotswolds.

The Merchant's House
johnmooremuseum.org
45 Church Street | 01684 297174
Open Apr–Oct Tue–Sat 10–1 and 2–5; open most Sat rest of year

Just a few doors down from the John Moore Museum is the Merchant's House, a two-storey building which has been beautifully restored by the same owners and furnished to show the construction of a 15th-century shop and dwelling. Audio guides with 'Living Voices' tell tales from the past – some hilarious, some poignant. Insightful stuff.

Out of the Hat
outofthehat.org.uk
Church Street, GL20 5AB
01684 855040 | Open Mon–Sat 10–4

This meticulously restored 17th-century building was once a hat shop. Nowadays it's a heritage centre. A wander around this charming building with interactive and portable guides will let you slip back in time and take you through Tewkesbury's history, from its initial settlement to the Wars of the Roses, the Civil War, the Industrial Revolution and on to the present day.

Tewkesbury Museum
tewkesburymuseum.org
64 Barton Street, GL20 5PX
01684 292901 | Open Apr–Aug Tue–Fri 1–4, Sat 11–4, Sep–Dec Tue–Fri 12–3, Sat 11–3, Jan–Mar Sat 11–3

Owned by a charitable trust, the Museum displays historical objects that illustrate the history of Tewkesbury and surrounding villages from pre-history to the present day. There are examples of stone masonry, metalwork, pottery, tiles and coins from the neolithic, medieval and Roman periods, and exhibits on the 1471 Battle of Tewkesbury, a particularly fine model fairground (with over 100 figures) and on Tewkesbury's very own Polar explorer, Raymond Priestley, who travelled to the Antarctic with both Ernest Shackleton and Robert Scott.

GET ON THE WATER

Croft Farm Waterpark
croftfarmleisure.co.uk
Bredons Hardwick, Tewkesbury, GL20 7EE | 01684 772321
Croft Farm is a windsurfing and sailing centre. Kayaking, canoeing and even husky sled rides are also available, where you can have the full 'hands-on mushing' experience.

GO TO THE THEATRE

Roses Theatre
rosestheatre.org
Sun Street, GL20 5NX
01684 295074
This busy arts centre offers an eclectic programme of live events, films, dance, exhibitions and festivals.

GO SHOPPING

Toff Milway
toffmilway.co.uk
Conderton, near Tewkesbury, GL20 7PP | 01386 725387
A wide range of homemade functional and artistic pottery, all made by the curiously named, but obviously prolific and hard-working, Toff.

PLAY A ROUND

Hilton Puckrup Hall
puckruphallgolfclub.co.uk
Puckrup, GL20 6EL | 01684 271591
Open daily all year
Set in 140 acres of undulating parkland, Puckrup Hall is one of the county's finest courses. Strong and testing with relatively modest yardage, it demands excellent course management and accurate striking, with a layout that manages to entertain golfers of all abilities.

EAT AND DRINK

Corse Lawn House Hotel
corselawn.com
Corse Lawn, GL19 4LZ
01452 780771
The red-brick house dates from the Queen Anne period of the early 18th century and stands on the village green in front of a large pond that once had the job of cleaning up both coach and horses. It's a lovely spot. The hotel has been run by the Hine family since 1978 and continues to be operated with old-school charm. There's a traditionally decorated bistro and a smart restaurant, with the latter serving up a classic modern British menu that makes good use of trusted local supply lines.

PLACES NEARBY

Deerhurst (see page 115), to the south, has a fine Saxon parish church. Classy Cheltenham (see page 88) would be the other obvious next port of call.

Thornbury MAP REF 256 B4

Thornbury, an attractive market town just north of Bristol, is known for its Tudor castle. The castle was built in 1510 by the extravagantly titled Edward Stafford, 3rd Duke of Buckingham and Lord High Constable of England. After the Duke was executed on charges of treason, Henry VIII appropriated Thornbury Castle. In 1535 he stayed here with Anne Boleyn. Queen Mary I also spent time here during her teens. She returned the castle to the Staffords, but after the Civil War it fell to ruin. It remained disused until 1824, when it became the residence of the Howard family. Now a luxury hotel, it is particularly noted for its handsome brick double chimney and the fine tracery of its oriel windows.

The Church of St Mary the Virgin, mainly built in the Perpendicular style, has a fine medieval tower. Inside the church is an unusual medieval stone pulpit. A cottage on Chapel Street houses the Thornbury and District Museum, which has exhibits on local life and heritage. The museum hosts events and organises guided walks. A way-marked heritage trail starts at the town hall in the High Street.

PLAY A ROUND

Thornbury Golf Centre
thornburygc.co.uk
Bristol Road, BS35 3XL
01454 281144

These two 18-hole pay-and-play courses, designed by Hawtree, are set in undulating terrain with views towards the Severn estuary. The Low 18 is a par 3 with holes ranging from 80 to 207 yards, and is ideal for beginners. The High course puts the more experienced golfer to the test.

EAT AND DRINK

Thornbury Castle @@
thornburycastle.co.uk
Castle Street, BS35 1HH
01454 281182

Construction work on the castle was well under way in the early 16th century when its intended occupant, Edward Stafford, became one of the many Tudor notables to find himself parting company with his head on the orders of Henry VIII. And then, cheekily, Henry spent part of his honeymoon here, with Anne Boleyn. This is the only English Tudor castle now run as a hotel. Thornbury isn't quite the full medieval fortress, more a castellated country house, but is not a whit less grandiose for that, and the hexagonal Tower dining room with its arrow-slits feels secure against the marauding hordes. The kitchen takes a contemporary, country-house view. Supplied in part from Thornbury's own gardens (and vineyard), the menu is in the vein of modern British pastoral, with invention and heritage running side by side. Small parties can dine in the dungeon – if they dare.

Ronnie's of Thornbury ◎◎
ronnies-restaurant.co.uk
11 St Mary Street, BS35 2AB
01454 411137
Hidden away in an unlikely location in the town's shopping precinct, Ronnie's is popular with locals. The vibe is easygoing whether you pop in for brunch or dinner. The modern European cooking style keeps things local, seasonal and to the point. Ronnie Faulkner's team will send you away happy if you turn up to kick-start the day with coffee and eggs Benedict, or round it off with an intelligent, precisely cooked dinner. The 17th-century building wears its contemporary look well. Paintings and photos by West Country artists perk up the classic stone walls, beamed ceilings, wooden floors and neutral hues.

PLACES NEARBY

Thornbury finds itself a bit cut off from its Cotswolds play-friends by the pesky M5, but the Sodburys (see page 189), to the southeast, aren't really all that far off, nor are Berkeley (see page 63) and Dursley (see page 117), both to the north. Bristol's to the south, but is too far away to be a base for the Cotswolds.

The Anchor Inn
anchor-inn-oldbury.co.uk
Church Road, Oldbury-on-Severn, BS35 1QA | 01454 413331
Set beside a tree-lined pill (stream) that meanders down to the nearby Severn Estuary, this family-friendly pub is on the Severn Way footpath and is a popular stopping place for ramblers. Parts of the stone-built inn are nearly 500 years old, and an olde-worlde welcome is assured for travellers to this charming, out-of-the-way village. Reliable real ales include guests like Severn Sins, plus there's a good range of bottled cider and perry.

Uley MAP REF 256 C3

Uley is a large and pretty village that became prosperous due to the wool dyeing trade. There is still a functioning brewery, and a fine pub – the Old Crown. Uley's 18th-century houses scuttle down the hillside into a deep valley. The long, flat-topped hill of Uley Bury overlooks the town. This 32-acre plateau, surrounded by steep drop-offs of nearly 330 feet (100m), made a spectacular site for a hill fort, and Iron Age Cotswoldians took advantage of it. The bury is worth a visit. It offers magnificent views down the escarpment, out across the Severn Vale and over the perky outlier hills of Cam Long Down (which local legend has it were built by the Devil) and Downham Hill (known locally as 'Smallpox Hill', because it was once the site of an isolation facility for disease victims). The boundaries of Uley Bury's 30-acre, multi-vallate fort are easy to detect, and date from around 300 BC. The site has never been excavated, though visitors have found Roman coins here.

North of Uley, towards Frocester Hill, you'll find Hetty Pegler's Tump. The unusual name comes from the 17th-century landowner's wife. This 120-foot neolithic barrow, surrounded by a stone wall, has a long central chamber. This can be entered, albeit with some discomfort; it may be wise to take a torch.

Nearby, slightly to the north, is Coaley Peak. This ideal picnic site has more cracking views across the Vale and down the escarpment. The Nympsfield Long Barrow is also on Coaley Peak. This chambered tomb dates to the neolithic period, around 2500 BC. An excavation here in 1862 uncovered the remains of at least 13 bodies, including the skeleton of a child, in a stone cist or coffin, as well as flint arrowheads and pottery. The internal chambers were constructed out of oolitic limestone that was probably quarried nearby. The long barrow has long been associated with legends and stories, including a rumour that it once served as a refuge for lepers.

East of Uley, within striking distance by foot, is Owlpen Manor. This beautifully situated and very picturesque 15th-century manor house was restored in the 1920s, and now displays a good collection of Arts and Crafts furniture. Close by are an 18th-century church and mill. About a mile east of Owlpen is Matara, a tranquil garden at Kingscote. Eastern and Western ideas of garden design blend here, producing a very restful result.

▼ Hetty Pegler's Tump

TAKE IN SOME HISTORY

Owlpen Manor

owlpen.com

Uley, GL11 5BZ | 01453 860261

This Tudor manor house (1450–1616) stands in a formal garden of magnificent yews. It feels deliciously hidden-away in Owlpen, a hamlet of Cotswold cottages surrounded by and secluded in a dramatic, curvy landscape. The house itself, which was left relatively undisturbed for hundreds of years until the Arts and Crafts Movements started careful restoration, is strikingly handsome. Some of Owlpen's cottages are holiday homes, available for rent.

GO ROUND THE GARDENS

Matara Gardens of Wellbeing

matara.co.uk

Kingscote Park, Kingscote, GL8 8YA
01453 861050 | Open May–Sep Mon–Thu 1–5 (may be closed for private events)

In 28 acres of glorious Cotswolds parkland, Matara Gardens of Wellbeing is built on earth-friendly principles. There are hundreds of trees, including oaks, beeches, apple trees, rowans and groves of magnolias. Land is set aside for wildlife, and the planting choices encourage butterflies and bees. The cafe's food is fresh, seasonal, local, organic, from sustainable sources and free from animal cruelty whenever possible.

GO BACK IN TIME

Uley Long Barrow (Hetty Pegler's Tump)

english-heritage.org.uk

0370 3331181 | Open at any reasonable time (torch required for interior)

This 120-foot-long neolithic long barrow is popularly known as Hetty Pegler's Tump, which sounds very *Carry On*. Actually this was the name of its 17th-century owner. The mound, surrounded by a wall, is about 85 feet wide. It contains a stone central passage and three burial chambers. The tump contained between 15 and 20 skeletons.

Whittington Court MAP REF 261 D5

hha.org.uk

Whittington, GL54 4HF | 01242 820556 | Contact for opening times

Whittington Court stands on the western edge of the Cotswolds, east of Cheltenham. The moat that surrounded the property still runs along two sides of the south garden. Whittington Church, probably once the court's private chapel, stands close by. It contains family memorials, including a brass to Richard Cotton (d.1556), for whom the house was built.

The original plan was E-shaped, but during the court's history the porch was moved to the eastern end of the great hall. The present cross wing was rebuilt in the 17th century.

Although Whittington Court seems to be a house built in the 16th and 17th centuries, its origins are much earlier. Probably named Witetune in Anglo-Saxon times, the manor of Whittington belonged to the de Crupe family in the Middle Ages. The tombs of three members of the family lie in the 12th-century church. Later the Despenser family, who were Earls of Gloucester, owned Whittington. After the death of the great Earl of Warwick, his widow, Anne, was persuaded to transfer Whittington to King Henry VII.

In 1545 the manor came into the hands of the Cotton family. John Cotton entertained Queen Elizabeth at Whittington in 1592. Records state that she 'dyned at Mr Coton's at Whytinton'. The manor later passed to Ann Cotton, who was married to Sir John Denham, a courtier, poet and dilettante architect who, at the Restoration, was given the post of Surveyor-General of the King's Works. It is likely that Denham brought his taste to bear in that period, adding some of the classical features to the house. The Grand Staircase has an original 17th-century dog gate on the first half-landing. This prevented dogs from going into the bedrooms.

PLACES NEARBY

The historic spa town of Cheltenham (see page 88) lies to the northwest, and the little village of **Andoversford** is to the southeast.

Winchcombe MAP REF 261 D4

Winchcombe was once the capital of the Anglo-Saxon kingdom of Mercia, but nowadays it has an equally prestigious, if unofficial, title: capital of walking in the Cotswolds. The Cotswold, Warden's, Windrush and Gloucestershire Ways all call into town, as does the newer, 42-mile Winchcombe Way. Needless to say there are also lots of excellent short walks available in the hills and valleys nearby.

Winchcombe is a town with a whole lot of history. As well as being a Saxon capital, it's near an ancient Salt Way trading route. Nearby Salter's Lane and Salter's Hill reflect this. Winchcombe was also home to an important abbey during the Middle Ages. The abbey was popular with pilgrims, who came to worship at the burial place of the martyred Prince Kenelm. Dissolved in 1539, all that remains of the complex is one side of the wall of the abbey terrace and the abbey church, now Winchcombe parish church. The handsome church, built between 1465 and 1470, owes its present form to wealthy local woolmen. The 40 or so gargoyles on the exterior, the Winchcombe Worthies, are said to represent really unpopular monks. They served as a contemporary sign of dissatisfaction with the abbey, and many are still very amusing today. The stone coffin inside the church is said to have once contained St Kenelm's body. The church also possesses a piece of embroidery that is attributed, in part, to Catherine of Aragon.

Around the west end of the church, towards the west tower door, you'll see what look like pockmarks in the north aisle wall. These holes were made by Parliamentary musket balls during the Civil War. Nearby Sudeley was held by Royalist sympathisers, and when Roundhead troops took the town in 1643, they brought the Royalist soldiers here and executed them by firing squad.

The main street has an assortment of interesting buildings, including the fine Jacobean old school on Abbey Terrace, as well as a small museum. The Winchcombe Folk & Police Museum in the town hall, next to the Tourist Information Centre, features finds from the Belas Knap neolithic barrow (see page 239). The old village stocks can be found outside the museum.

▾ Winchcombe from afar

Gloucestershire has relatively few castles, but romantic Sudeley Castle (see page 217) near Winchcombe is superb, as are its spectacular gardens. Visitors can enter the Castle via Vineyard Street.

A number of other places worth visiting are close to Winchcombe. These include Belas Knap, Cleeve Common and Toddington. At Toddington, you can board a restored steam train and ride a scenic stretch of the Gloucestershire Warwickshire Railway. You can also take the railway to Cheltenham Racecourse. The remains of Hailes Abbey, just off the Stow road, evoke the romance of the Middle Ages. Nearby Hailes parish church is also of great interest, with its medieval wall paintings, stained glass, 15th-century rood screen and attractive woodwork.

The slopes around Winchcombe were put to a number of uses apart from their obvious role in providing food for sheep. The monks from the abbey made wine here. Tobacco was an important crop for some decades after the Dissolution of the Monasteries by Henry VIII, until the government decided that the competition hampered the new colony of Virginia and proscribed the domestic cultivation of tobacco.

TAKE IN SOME HISTORY

Hailes Abbey

english-heritage.org.uk
Near Winchcombe, GL54 5PB
01242 602398 | Open Jul–Aug daily 10–6, otherwise 10–5; closed Nov–Mar

Richard, Earl of Cornwall, brother of King Henry III, founded Hailes Abbey in 1246 in thanks for surviving a shipwreck. It housed the Holy Blood of Hailes, claimed to be a phial of Christ's blood, and became a pilgrimage site. After the Dissolution in 1539, when many religious institutions in England were closed or destroyed, the abbey declined precipitously. King Henry VIII's commissioners even claimed that the Holy Blood of Hailes was actually just duck's blood, and it's difficult to venerate the holy martyrdom of a duck. Now only a few of the cloister arches and foundations remain, though one Cistercian drain still works, 750 years after its installation. They just don't make 'em like that anymore.

VISIT THE MUSEUMS

Winchcombe Folk & Police Museum

winchcombemuseum.org.uk
Town Hall, GL54 5LJ | 07708 798202 | Open Apr–Oct Mon–Sat 10–4

This fun folk and local history collection illustrates the lives of the people of ancient Winchcombe. The police collection includes British and international uniforms and equipment from down the years. There are activity sheets for children and a small shop.

GO BACK IN TIME

Cleeve Common

cleevecommon.org.uk

Neolithic man first cleared the trees from Cleeve Common, the highest point in the Cotswolds, around 6,000 years ago. There's evidence of prehistoric and Roman settlement here. Along with nearby Leckhampton Hill, Cleeve Common has the thickest sections of exposed Jurassic rocks in the country, and is a Site of Special Scientific Interest. The remains of an Iron Age hill fort, dating from around 500 BC, take up three acres of the common. These remains are arranged in a rough quarter-circle in the northwestern corner of the Common, above the settlement of Nutterswood. There's a cross dyke too, which probably served as a territorial boundary in the Bronze Age.

You may find examples of several species of orchids, including musk orchids, on the common. You might also see slow-worms, roe and muntjac deer, stoats, weasels and hares. Birds including meadow pipits, finches, linnets, yellowhammers, fieldfares, jackdaws, buzzards, kestrels, ring ouzels, stonechats, wheatears and great grey shrikes all call the common home. Cleeve Common is also one of the few locations where the Duke of Burgundy butterfly can still be found.

The views, which extend all the way to the Malverns, can be pretty sensational.

▾ Cleeve Common

SEE SOME LOCAL CHURCHES

Hailes Church

Off Salter's Lane, opposite Hailes Abbey, GL54 5PB

This tiny church is just down the road from its well-known neighbour, Hailes Abbey. It dates from the 12th century, but was given a thorough overhaul in the 13th century because of its close relationship with the then-new abbey. It remained relatively unaltered until the 17th century, when the church was reorganised to reflect changes in religious thinking; those physical alterations have been swept away in their turn. The stained glass in the east window is 15th-century, and originally came from the nearby abbey. During the 13th century the interior of the church was covered with wall paintings. Many of these survive, albeit in a somewhat faded and fragmentary state. They include a rendition of the popular *St Christopher Carrying the Christ Child* theme, as well as mythical creatures.

St Peter's Church, Winchcombe

Gloucester Street, GL54 5LU

This beautiful town church was built in the first half of the 15th century. It is the only church of its era in Gloucestershire to have a nave arcade of eight bays, and the only church of its era in the county without a chancel arch. These features give the church a wonderful light and airy feeling. They also draw the eye straight down to the east window and the bright masterpiece in stained glass therein. The window depicts Jesus walking on the water, with a faltering St Peter, who is beginning to sink. John Hardman Powell made the window in the late 1800s. A gallery of gurning stone figures array the church exterior, each one different from its fellows.

TAKE A TRAIN RIDE

Gloucestershire Warwickshire Railway

gwsr.com

Toddington Station, GL54 5DT

01242 621405

This railway line was built between 1900 and 1906 to improve through-services from Birmingham to Bristol and the West Country. It also carried fruit from the farming areas in the Cotswolds and Vale of Evesham to the rest of the nation. It closed in the 1960s, reopening as a heritage line in 1984. Nowadays visitors can enjoy views of classic Cotswolds countryside and the novelty of riding on a steam train on the 25-mile round trip between Laverton and Cheltenham Racecourse.

WATCH THE HILL CLIMB

Prescott Speed Hill Climb

prescott-hillclimb.com

GL52 9RD | 01242 673136

Prescott, 2 miles west of Winchcombe, hosts classic car and bike weekends on its steep, hilly course. It is also the home of the Bugatti Owners' Club.

GO WALKING

winchcombewelcomeswalkers.com

Take a walk from Winchcombe up to the Jurassic grasslands of Cleeve Common, the highest point in the Cotswolds. The common offers suitably vast views. Moving on from there to the enigmatic long barrow of Belas Knap makes for perhaps the best half-day walk in the whole region. Hailes Abbey is also within walking distance.

EAT AND DRINK

Lady Jane Tearoom

theladyjanetearoom.co.uk

7 Hailes Street, GL54 5HU

01242 603578

This inviting family-run tearoom serves up home-cooked breakfasts, light bites, lunches and afternoon cream teas. Eat indoors or in the garden. Traditional roasts available on a Sunday. Closed Thursdays and Fridays. The freshly made cakes and other treats are first class.

The Lion Inn

thelionwinchcombe.co.uk

37 North Street, GL54 5PS

01242 603300

This attractive watering hole is buzzy and welcoming. With 15th-century origins, care has been taken over the years to make sure the building's quirky charms remain. Lovers of wine and real ale are spoilt for choice in the spacious and relaxed bar – a pint of Brakspear Oxford Gold or a Prescott ale might be just the thing. The kitchen serves seasonal locally sourced modern British dishes.

Wesley House ®®

wesleyhouse.co.uk

High Street, GL54 5LJ

01242 602366

This half-timbered 15th-century merchant's house gets its name from the famous Methodist preacher, who stayed here in the 18th century. Period features like beamed ceilings, an inglenook fireplace and bare stone walls all feature in the traditional main dining room, and there's also a modern and stylish conservatory with rural views. Good-quality produce is the key to the kitchen's success as it works around an exciting modern European repertory.

Wesley House Wine Bar & Grill ®

wesleyhouse.co.uk

High Street, GL54 5LJ

01242 602366

Historic Wesley House – built for a merchant back in the 15th century – has a few tricks up its sleeve these days. Not the least of these is its Wine Bar & Grill, which is a delightful 21st-century interloper amid all this antiquity. It's a laid-back place, with a welcoming atmosphere, and a bistro feel to the downstairs area. The menu is built on bistro-lines too, with a Mediterranean focus. Sip on a cocktail and tuck into some excellent food.

PLACES NEARBY

Nowhere nearby has as many attractions as Winchcombe. Sudeley Castle (see page 217) is practically part of

Winchcombe, and then there's Cleeve Common and Belas Knap. The Guitings (see page 133), to the southeast, aren't that far off. Cheltenham (see page 88) is to the west. Or take to the saddle at Cotswolds Riding, in nearby Stanton.

Belas Knap Long Barrow
english-heritage.org.uk
Cleeve Hill | 0370 333 1181
Open any reasonable time
Dating from approximately 3800 BC, the remains of 31 bodies were found in Belas Knap Long Barrow when it was excavated in the 19th century, along with some Roman pottery. Particularly notable for its elaborate 'false entrance', the burial chambers are entered from the side of the barrow. The four-chambered burial cairn has been restored several times.

Cotswolds Riding
cotswoldsriding.co.uk
Washpool Equestrian Centre, Stanton, WR12 7NE | 01386 584250
Cotswolds Riding offers group hacks for riders of all ages from beginners right through to advanced ability. They also have pub rides with a stop along the way for lunch.

Windrush Valley MAP REF 258 B3

The Windrush rises near Taddington, south of Snowshill. It wanders through several villages, widening beyond Bourton and continuing north to join the Thames. The Windrush Way, a pleasant walking path, goes from Winchcombe to Bourton-on-the-Water.

Sherborne, on a tributary of the Windrush, has been part of the Sherborne estate for centuries. Before that, the Abbots of Winchcombe owned the land, and their sheep were sheared on the banks of the river every summer. A cottage at the eastern end of the village of Sherborne boasts a complete Norman doorway, which was presumably removed from an earlier incarnation of the local church. John 'Crump' Dutton, Royalist hunchback and former owner of Sherborne House, allegedly still haunts the local manor. The house was rebuilt in the 19th century. Occupied by the military during World War II, it then became a boarding school. It now belongs to the National Trust. Although it is not open to the public, there are waymarked walks through the nearby woods and parkland. Lodge Park, an elaborate grandstand built in the 17th century for deer-coursing, is open to the public.

The next village to the east of Sherborne is **Windrush**. Windrush's church is topped with a fine Perpendicular tower. Its magnificent Norman south doorway is surrounded by beakheads, bird-like grotesques with mysterious origins. Then come the Barringtons, first Little, then Great. The Barringtons

▲ Burford

were once renowned for their stone quarries, and for the Kempsters and the Strongs, the local families of masons who worked them. No evidence remains of these old subterranean quarries. **Little Barrington** is a quiet village, with cottages prettily clustered about its village green. The nearby Fox Inn is next to a bridge that crosses the river. It was built by local master mason Thomas Strong, the principal contractor of St Paul's. Christopher Wren regarded Strong as the leading builder of his day. **Great Barrington**, to the north, has a Norman church with some fine monuments by 18th-century sculptor Joseph Nollekens. To the east of the church you'll find the country house and landscaped gardens of Barrington Park.

East of Great Barrington lies **Taynton**, another village that once supplied London and Oxford with its famous prime building stone. Taken from open-cast quarries, the stone was transported overland to Lechlade, and thence by barge to London. Beyond Taynton is **Burford**, and then **Widford church**. The 13th-century church is all that remains of a once-thriving village that simply disappeared, probably as a result of the plague. Built on the site of a Roman villa, the church stands small and solitary on a raised mound overlooking the river. Its box pews and wall paintings, which date from the 14th century, are worth a look.

A short way from Widford, you'll find **Swinbrook**. The village is associated with the Mitford family, and the Mitford family's share in the public consciousness now pretty much begins and ends with Lord Redesdale's five daughters: Nancy, Diana, Unity, Jessica and Deborah. Unity became a close friend of Adolf Hitler; Diana married Sir Oswald Moseley, leader of the British Union of Fascists; Deborah became the Duchess of Devonshire; and Nancy and Jessica (the communist) became well-known writers. There was also a sixth daughter, who the Times called 'Pamela the unobtrusive poultry connoisseur', but for some reason people tend to forget about poor Pamela. Nancy, Pamela, Diana and Unity are buried in the graveyard of the church, which also contains the wonderful triple-decker monument to the Fettiplace family, who once owned a mansion here. Across the river to the southeast is **Asthall**, a charming village with a fine Elizabethan manor. Exhibitions of stone sculpture are held in the gardens for a short period every other summer.

TAKE IN SOME HISTORY

Asthall Manor

asthallmanor.com
Burford, OX18 4HW
01993 824319

The Mitford sisters, brother Tom and parents Lord and Lady Redesdale lived here between 1919 and 1926, and Asthall Manor turns up as Alconleigh in Nancy's *The Pursuit of Love*. The manor house is private, 'but the people who live here like to share parts of it from time to time,' says the website, via specific entertainments such as the sculpture displays. Check their website for events and open days.

GET OUTDOORS

Lodge Park and Sherborne Estate

nationaltrust.org.uk
Lodge Park, Aldsworth, GL54 3PP
01451 844130 | Open Mar–early Nov Fri–Sun 11–4, but occasionally closed for weddings; Sherborne Estate open dawn till dusk

National Trust-owned Sherborne Park is a working estate. It has an abundance of wildlife, from fallow and roe deer to badgers and foxes. The 18th-century water meadows are home to otters and water voles. Around the Pleasure Ground, there are child-friendly orienteering and sculpture trails, which start at Ewe Pen Barn. Parking is available at the Lodge and in the park. If you and yours enjoyed the sculpture trail, there's another children's quiz/trail at nearby Lodge Park, England's only surviving 17th-century grandstand, which once overlooked a one-mile stretch where deer-coursing took place and the gentry gambled on the outcome. It is also owned by the National Trust and offers picnic facilities and refreshments.

SEE A LOCAL CHURCH

St Mary's Church

Pebble Court, west side of Swinbrook village, Windrush Valley, OX18 4DY

Land mines, eh? Pesky things. St Mary's church has a curious 19th-century tower and an enormous east window, which was blown out by an exploding land mine in 1940. St Mary's is set in an attractive landscape, but nothing about the church's unassuming exterior hints at the extraordinary richness of the 17th-century monuments inside. These monuments depict six members of the Fettiplace family, who were one of the great families of Oxfordshire until they died out in the late 18th century. The highly stylised marble effigies are laid out on shelves. Each reclines rather raffishly on one elbow. There are also brasses commemorating other Fettiplaces.

The only Mitford son, Tom, who was killed in Burma in 1945, has a memorial inside the church.

Witney MAP REF 259 D3

Another Windrush town, Witney remains famous for its blankets. This mini-industry somehow managed to survive the collapse of the Cotswold woollen industry after the Industrial Revolution. The Market Square is the centre of the town. It contains an unusual Butter Cross, refurbished in the 19th century, and a 17th-century Town Hall. Beyond, near a green, you'll find the 13th-century church, complete with its massive tower. The green is also near a fine collection of houses that date from the 17th and 18th centuries. The town's museum is in Gloucester Court Mews, on the High Street. On the High Street you'll also see the Blanket Hall. The Witney Blanket Weavers Company, a group of prosperous weavers who were granted their charter in 1711, built it in 1721.

The Cogges Manor Farm Museum is just southeast of Witney, and is well-signposted from the A40. The museum reflects farming life in Victorian times. Among the machinery and livestock, you will find a working kitchen and dairy.

VISIT THE MUSEUM

Witney and District Museum

witney.net

Gloucester Court Mews, High Street, Witney, OX28 6JF | 01993 775915

Open Apr–Oct Wed–Sat 10–4 Sun (phone for information)

This large ground-floor gallery details the history of Witney over the last 1,000 years, including the history of local industries such as Witney blanket manufacture, glove making and brewing. Exhibits include the town's old stocks. The Museum is housed in a traditional Cotswold stone building. It was once the home of Malachi Bartlett, the proprietor of a well-known local building firm. The west end of the building was once used as a smithy.

ENTERTAIN THE FAMILY

Cogges Manor Farm
cogges.org.uk
Church Lane, Cogges, OX28 3LA
01993 772602 | Open Tue–Sun 10.30–5 (manor house only open weekends & BH)

Cogges is a manor house dating from the 13th century. Today it has a walled garden, a moat and islands to explore, a castle-style adventure playground, a zip wire, and a cafe. There are also farmyard animals, including Shetland ponies, pygmy goats, pigs, rabbits, ducks and Cotswold sheep. The manor house itself is only open on weekends and bank holidays.

PLAY A ROUND

Witney Lakes Golf Course
witney-lakes.co.uk
Downs Road, OX29 0SY
01993 893011
Open daily all year

Five large lakes come into play on eight holes. This excellent test of golf will have you using every club in the bag.

EAT AND DRINK

The Fleece
fleecewitney.co.uk
11 Church Green, Witney, OX28 4AZ | 01993 892270

Overlooking the village's beautiful church green in the heart of picturesque Witney, this fine Georgian building was once the home of Clinch's brewery. Dylan Thomas enjoyed a drink when he was living nearby. Nowadays, it serves food and drink from lunch through to dinner. Its well-kept ales are a big draw.

The Restaurant at Witney Lakes Resort ❁
witney-lakes.co.uk
Downs Road, Witney, OX29 0SY
01993 893012

This sprawling modern resort caters for iron-pumpers, niblick-swingers and the nuptial trade, as well as

▼ The Blanket Hall clock

offering contemporary brasserie cooking in a destination restaurant that has acquired a dedicated local following. Regular champagne evenings and gourmet Thursdays are all part of the drill, and there are tables on a lakeside terrace in the sunnier months, but the core attraction is a menu of consistently dependable modern classic dishes.

PLACES NEARBY

Witney's halfway between Oxford (see page 161) and Burford (see page 78), which likes to call itself the 'gateway to the Cotswolds'. Cute Minster Lovell (see page 149) is also in between these two. There's a church just on its outskirts that's worth visiting. **North Leigh** is about 3 miles northeast and has a fine Roman villa and church and **Crawley**, to the northwest, has a good pub.

The Lamb Inn

lambcrawley.co.uk
Steep Hill, Crawley, OX29 9TW
01993 708792

A white-washed Georgian inn not far from Witney, The Lamb has been given a strong makeover for the present day and retains the comforting country-pub ambience in the bar, but has nudged the supplementary dining area into modernity. There is an air of warm conviviality throughout, and the contemporary-style cooking is smartly presented with much flair and thought.

North Leigh Roman Villa

english-heritage.org.uk
2 miles north of North Leigh, off A4095 | 0370 333 1181
Open any reasonable daylight hours

The remains of this Roman villa are located by a loop of the River Evenlode. This was a courtyard-style villa, with a range of buildings on the three sides of a rectangle and a corridor and gatehouse on the fourth side. The villa dates to the 1st or early 2nd century, but finds of Iron Age pottery suggest earlier occupation on the site. Historians think that the majority of homes like this were built for leading members of the strata of the native population that had been co-opted into the empire, rather than having been constructed as residences for Roman officials. Nothing says 'I side with Rome rather than my own people, and also keep up with the Marcus Aurelius Joneses' quite like this impressive mosaic floor. The villa was abandoned when the Romans withdrew from Britain in the 5th century.

St Mary's Church

Church Road, North Leigh, OX29 6TX

The tall Saxon tower of St Mary's was not always at the west end of the church. The original nave, to the west of a central tower, was dismantled in the late Norman period. The Norman chancel became the nave, and a new chancel was added in the late 13th century.

The interior of the church has many fascinating features. A dramatic, highly coloured Doom painting over the chancel arch has survived from the 15th century. Below it is an unusual and rather heavy Victorian stone screen. The Perrott aisle, on the north wall, is an Italianate memorial chapel from about 1700. Don't overlook the tiny Wilcote chantry chapel, a superb example of mid-15th-century Perpendicular Gothic design, with fan vaulting, a beautiful east window with original glass, and fine alabaster effigies. It is among the treasures of Oxfordshire.

St Kenelm's Church

Old Minster, OX29 0RR

Beautifully sited on the River Windrush, St Kenelm's stands next to the dramatic ruined manor house of the Lovells, who rebuilt the original priory church (or minster) in the mid-15th century. Soon afterwards, this great family made its exit from history. Francis Lovell, the ninth Baron, henchman and lifelong friend of Richard III, disappeared in 1487. The crown seized the Lovell lands, and he was never heard of again.

The cruciform church has scarcely been altered since it was built. The central tower rests on four great pillars. A fan vault spans the crossing. A well-preserved Lovell tomb with a fine alabaster effigy and colourful heraldic symbols occupies the south transept.

10 mansions and manor houses

- **Blenheim Palace (below)** page 250
- **Chastleton House** page 154
- **Chavenage House** page 86
- **Kelmscott Manor** page 144
- **Owlpen Manor** page 232
- **Rodmarton Manor** page 111
- **Snowshill Manor** page 187
- **Stanway House** page 193
- **Sudeley Castle** page 217
- **Woodchester Mansion** page 214

Woodstock & Blenheim Palace MAP REF 259 D3

Woodstock is a small town of some charm just to the north of Oxford, not to be confused with the town in upstate New York that hosted the legendary 1969 music festival. Oxfordshire's Woodstock is home to one of the greatest palaces in England, World Heritage-listed Blenheim, which is most famous as the ancestral home of the Churchill family.

Woodstock has enjoyed royal patronage since Henry I built a park and hunting lodge here in the 12th century. His grandson, Henry II, preferred to use it to entertain his mistress, the fair Rosamund. The lodge became a palace, and the town grew around it. Geoffrey Chaucer, the medieval author of *The Canterbury Tales and Troilus And Criseyde* (which, be honest, you haven't read), may have lived in Woodstock for some years. In later centuries the town was noted for its glove-making.

▼ Blenheim Palace seen across the lake

The story of Blenheim Palace began when John Churchill married the future Queen Anne's lady-in-waiting and confidante, Sarah Jennings. As soon as Anne became queen in 1702, she gave Churchill the title of Duke of Marlborough. His career was a triumph, with a string of spectacular victories in the War of Spanish Succession. The first victory saw England defeat France and Bavaria in the Battle of Blenheim in 1704. In recognition of the nation's gratitude, Anne gave him the manor of Woodstock and the money to build a grand house there.

John Vanbrugh, the architect, designed a main block surmounted by four towers. Two wings projected off the main block, which earned it the nickname 'Blenheim Castle'. Its Baroque extravagance was brilliantly humanised by the beauty of the 2,000-acre park, which was landscaped by the ubiquitous 'Capability' Brown.

Blenheim's facade is a magnificent sight. From the central block, curved walls lead to the east and west wings. As you enter through the east gateway, look out for the carvings of the English lion strangling the French cockerel. Inside, there is another reference to the Battle of Blenheim on the 67-foot-high ceiling of the marbled Great Hall, in the oval painting by Sir James Thornhill. In 1874, in a small, plain bedroom, American expat Jennie Churchill gave birth to a son, Winston. Winston's father, Lord Randolph Spencer-Churchill, briefly became Chancellor of the Exchequer, but his son was to achieve far greater fame through his dogged leadership of Britain during World War II. A nearby exhibition about Winston includes a set of his young curls and a maroon velvet boiler suit that he wore during the war, together with some of his oil paintings. Winston Churchill was premature (which may well be tactful for 'born less than eight months after his parents' marriage'), and born at Blenheim by chance. He nevertheless maintained a great affection for the place, and is buried at nearby Bladon churchyard.

A prodigious display of ill feeling, in keeping with the magnitude of the undertaking, sadly accompanied the construction of Blenheim Palace. The design is the work of Sir John Vanbrugh, who also built Castle Howard in Yorkshire. With Sarah Jennings, the wife of the Duke of Marlborough, Vanbrugh found himself in the hands of a demanding employer. Her capricious nature finally led him to resign the commission in 1716, fortunately after most of the work had been accomplished. Although Nicholas Hawksmoor oversaw the final stages of construction, it was largely the tenacity of the Duchess that ensured the completion of the building after the death of her husband. Not only did she find the money when Queen Anne's government failed to stump up all the promised funds, she was also responsible for much of the interior design.

Today the palace is full of gilt and grandeur, with carvings by Grinling Gibbons, Flemish tapestries illustrating the martial valour of the duke, and a fine collection of paintings. In the Great Hall you'll find a magnificent ceiling painted by Sir James Thornhill, while the Long Library is one of the longest single rooms in Britain. The first duke and duchess are buried in the chapel, which was built by Hawksmoor in 1731. The room where Sir Winston Churchill was born is the focal point of an exhibition devoted to his life.

The beauty of the relationship between the palace and its grounds can best be appreciated by walking from the town and entering the park through Nicholas Hawksmoor's Triumphal Arch. The arch surmounts what is also known as the Woodstock Gate, just off Park Street. Walk around the palace, cross the Grand Bridge and admire the views of the Great Lake as you walk to the Column of Victory, then enjoy the rose garden and the world's largest symbolic hedge maze, designed to mimic the architecture of the palace itself. There's also a butterfly house and a children's playground. The park also serves as a venue for events such as craft fairs, horse trials and even jousting throughout the year.

The town of Woodstock itself is worthy of exploration, too. The streets that cluster around the 18th-century Town Hall are lined with a fine assortment of houses and inns from the 17th and 18th centuries. The most famous is the ivy-clad Bear Hotel, which dates back to the 13th century. St Mary Magdalen Church is set in a charming churchyard, and is surmounted by a classical tower which was built in 1784. The original Norman south doorway is a particularly fine survivor from the orginal church.

Opposite the church, in Park Street, is Fletcher's House. Originally built for an 18th-century merchant, it now houses the Oxfordshire Museum. Its galleries and exhibitions about the history and traditions of Oxfordshire cover three floors. The museum has a convenient small cafe and gift shop, and if you're looking for something to do with fussy children, the town stocks are preserved at the museum entrance. (These stocks lock both feet of a seated captive so that they can be scorned by people passing by. Unusually, the Woodstock version has five holes rather than the usual even number.) This elegant townhouse also has pleasant gardens.

TAKE IN SOME HISTORY

Blenheim Palace
see highlight panel overleaf

VISIT THE MUSEUM

Oxfordshire Museum
oxfordshire.gov.uk
Fletcher's House, Park Street, OX20 1SN | 01993 811456
Open all year Tue–Sat 10–5, Sun 2–5, open BH Mon, please check for opening hours

Situated in the heart of Woodstock and set in attractive gardens, Fletcher's House provides a home for the county museum. The museum is the product of an award-winning redevelopment. It celebrates Oxfordshire, and features collections on local history, art, archaeology, landscape and wildlife, as well as a gallery exploring the county's innovative industries, from nuclear power to nanotechnology. Interactive exhibits offer new learning experiences for visitors of all ages. The museum's purpose-built Garden Gallery houses a variety of touring exhibitions of regional and national interest. A display of dinosaur footprints from Ardley Quarry and a replica megalosaurus are located in the walled garden.

EAT AND DRINK

The Feathers Hotel ®®
feathers.co.uk
Market Street, OX20 1SX
01993 812291

A feature in Woodstock since the 17th century, The Feathers carries itself in a thoroughly modish manner these days. This is boutique hotel territory, and The Feathers blends the indisputable traditional charms of the old building it occupies with a stylish contemporary sheen. Get a load of those eye-popping colours: rooms turned out in appetising collisions of lime and cherry, a dining room with raspberry-red banquettes and a mixture of bold graphic and abstract artworks. A copiously stocked

Blenheim Palace MAP REF 259 D3

blenheimpalace.com
Woodstock, OX20 1PP | 0800 849 6500 | Open daily; Palace & Gardens mid-Feb to mid-Dec 10.30–5.30 (last admission 4.45); Park daily all year 9–6 (last admission 4.45 or dusk)

Home of the Dukes of Marlborough and birthplace of Sir Winston Churchill, Blenheim Palace is an English Baroque masterpiece. Fine furniture, sculpture, paintings and tapestries are set in magnificent gilded staterooms that overlook sweeping lawns and formal gardens. 'Capability' Brown landscaped the 2,000-acre park, which is open to visitors and offers pleasant walks and beautiful views. A permanent exhibit called 'Blenheim Palace: The Untold Story' explores the lives of those who have lived here through the eyes of the servants. Check ahead for details of the full event programme throughout the year. It might include a Jousting Tournament and the Battle Proms.

gin bar is in the record-books for having the most varieties on offer. Thoroughly modern British cooking is the order of the day, with organic and local produce among the menu ingredients, as well as seafood from the distant coasts.

Hampers
hampersfoodandwine.co.uk
30–31 Oxford Street, OX20 1TH
01993 811535
Enjoy fine dining in this small cafe with a buzzy atmosphere, which serves up tasty meals from the menu using ingredients from the range of goodies available in the attached deli. This is not your average cafe so expect to find platters with a Middle Eastern or Greek theme alongside the traditional cream tea. In a hurry? Just grab a takeaway baguette or ciabatta from the deli. Or start the day by treating yourself to a full English breakfast – a favourite with the locals, and that is always a good recommendation.

The Kings Arms Hotel
kings-hotel-woodstock.co.uk
19 Market Street, OX20 1SU
01993 813636
The white-painted, Georgian Kings Arms fits in perfectly in well-to-do Woodstock, with its air of distinction and its handsome country décor. It's only a short stroll from the splendour of Blenheim Palace, after all. The comfortable bar area with stripped wooden floors, a log-burning stove and marble-topped counters, is where regulars Brakspear Bitter, North Cotswold Brewery Cotswold Best and Loose Cannon Gunners Gold are on offer. The all-day bar menu lists sandwiches, sharing boards and cream teas. For rather more stylish surroundings, go to the Atrium Restaurant with its black-and-white tiled flooring and high-backed leather chairs.

Macdonald Bear Hotel ◎◎
macdonaldhotels.co.uk/bear
Park Street, OX20 1SZ
01993 811124
Woodstock is certainly not without attractive old buildings, and this creeper-covered hotel is one of them. Inside, the great age of the property can be seen in the oak beams, stone walls and open fireplaces of the traditional-looking dining rooms. The kitchen clearly has its fingers on the pulse of today's tastes with its modern cooking.

▶ PLACES NEARBY

As far as the Cotswolds are concerned, Woodstock is stuck out on a bit of a limb. But Witney's (see page 242) keeping a friendly eye on it from the southwest, and if Woodstock really gets lonely, Oxford (see page 161) is only 8 miles to the south, and Chipping Norton (see page 101) 11 miles to the northwest. Woodstock is a good base from which to visit any of these places.

Wotton-under-Edge MAP REF 256 C4

Wotton-under-Edge is one of the most interesting small towns in the Cotswolds. Tucked comfortably under the escarpment (there's a clue in the name), it feels pleasingly unblemished by the passage of time. However, the old market town hall was very much blemished in the 13th century, when King John, enemy of the Berkeley family, burnt it to the ground. Rude.

In the Middle Ages, Wotton was an important wool town, with much of the work carried out from cottage homes, and it did well in the cloth trade of the 17th and 18th centuries. Because transportation to other textile industry centres, such as Stroud and Dursley, was easier, Wotton didn't become over-industrialised. This means that its town centre has more or less survived untouched since the early Victorian period. A number of Wotton's late medieval, Jacobean and Regency houses are still in use today. Much-loved 20th- and-21st-century poet Ursula Askham Fanthorpe lived in the town, and wrote such poems as 'Wotton Walks' and 'Tyndale in Darkness'.

In the Middle Ages, markets and fairs were held at the Chipping, part of which is now a car park. The old fire station in the Chipping is now an interesting heritage centre, which shows the history of the town and the surrounding area. From the Chipping, Market Street leads to a junction with High Street and Long Street, past the Star Inn and the Town Hall.

On the corner of Market Street and High Street you'll find the smart, red-brick Tolsey House. It was granted to the town in 1595 by the Countess of Warwick to serve as a market court. The old police station overlooks the High Street from the other side of Haw Street.

Long Street, the main shopping thoroughfare, is lined with buildings in an array of architectural styles. A stroll along Orchard Street on the right will bring you to the school where Isaac Pitman, inventor of shorthand, taught. At the end of Long Street, turn left into Church Street, opposite the 17th-century Falcon Inn. On the right you'll see a row of delightful almshouses, which were built in 1638. If you like, go into the courtyard and visit the little chapel, lit by a pair of depictive stained-glass windows.

Church Street then crosses over Old Town to Culverhay. This brings you to the 18th-century Church Hall, former home to the Blue Coat Church of England School. The Church Hall is also the entrance to the parish church, which was consecrated in 1283. Most of the church, however, dates from the 15th century. Beyond the churchyard is Potters Pond. There you'll find the Ram Inn. Dating from before 1145, the Ram is thought to be both the oldest surviving building in the area and *very* haunted.

The surrounding area is excellent for walking in. The Cotswold Edge, especially the Tyndale Monument (see page 118 and page 254), provide epic views. Just over a mile to the east at Ozleworth stands Newark Park. This unusual 16th-century house was built as a hunting lodge, and offers magnificent views across the countryside.

TAKE IN SOME HISTORY

Newark Park
nationaltrust.org.uk
Ozleworth, Wotton-under-Edge, GL12 7PZ | 01793 817666
Open Mar–Oct Wed–Sun 11–5; mid- to end Feb Wed–Sun 11–4; early to mid-Dec Sat–Sun only

This corner of Gloucestershire can feel surprisingly remote. Sometimes barely a sign of modern life is visible amid the overgrown valleys and tumbling combes. Newark Park looks down into the Ozleworth valley and out onto Somerset's Mendips.

Founded by an influential courtier to Henry VIII, Newark Park is a place of architectural intrigue, quaint gardens and sprawling parkland. The estate's prosperity wasn't permanent, and some time later it almost collapsed into financial ruin. Fortunately, it was dramatically rescued by Robert Parsons, a Texan architect, who became the Trust's first tenant in 1970.

VISIT THE HERITAGE CENTRE

Wotton-under-Edge Heritage Centre
wottonheritage.com
The Chipping, Wotton-under-Edge, GL12 7AD | 01453 521541
Open Tue, Thu–Fri 10.30–12.30 and 2–4, Sat 10–1, Apr–Oct Sun 2.30–5

The Centre holds three to four exhibitions a year, which display interesting items from local and sometimes national history. There's a small library and archive and the centre also arranges lectures throughout the year.

PLAY A ROUND

Cotswold Edge Golf Club
cotswoldedgegolfclub.org.uk
Upper Rushmire, GL12 7PT
01453 844167

This meadowland course is situated in a quiet Cotswold valley, which offers magnificent views. The course's first half is flat and open, while its second half is more varied.

EAT AND DRINK

Tortworth Court Four Pillars Hotel ®
four-pillars.co.uk
Tortworth, GL12 8HH
01454 263000

This impressive, listed Victorian mansion was built in the middle of the 19th century for the 2nd Earl of Ducie and is a fine example of Victorian architecture, with vast gables and soaring chimneys: ideal material, then, for the country-house hotel treatment. With 30 acres of lovely gardens, including its own arboretum, spa facilities and a range of restaurants and bars, there's plenty to admire here. The house is magnificent inside, and splendidly proportioned. Moreton's, the main dining room, with its original oak panelling, ornately carved panels and huge mullioned windows, was originally the library. The kitchen takes a something-for-everyone approach, an appealing mix of upmarket brasserie-type fare.

PLACES NEARBY

North Nibley

Notable for the 111-foot Tyndale Monument up on the limestone edge above the village and some big views across the vale from the same spot. Local man William Tyndale translated the Bible into English, which challenged the hegemony of the Roman Catholic Church and English Laws. Predictably, in retrospect, he was convicted of heresy, executed, then burnt at the stake in 1536. The last battle between private armies fought on English soil .was at Nibley Green in 1469–70 between William, Lord Berkeley, and Thomas, Lord Lisle. The village is the site of an annual music festival (July). Intriguing Newark Park (see page 253) is to the east.

▼ North Nibley

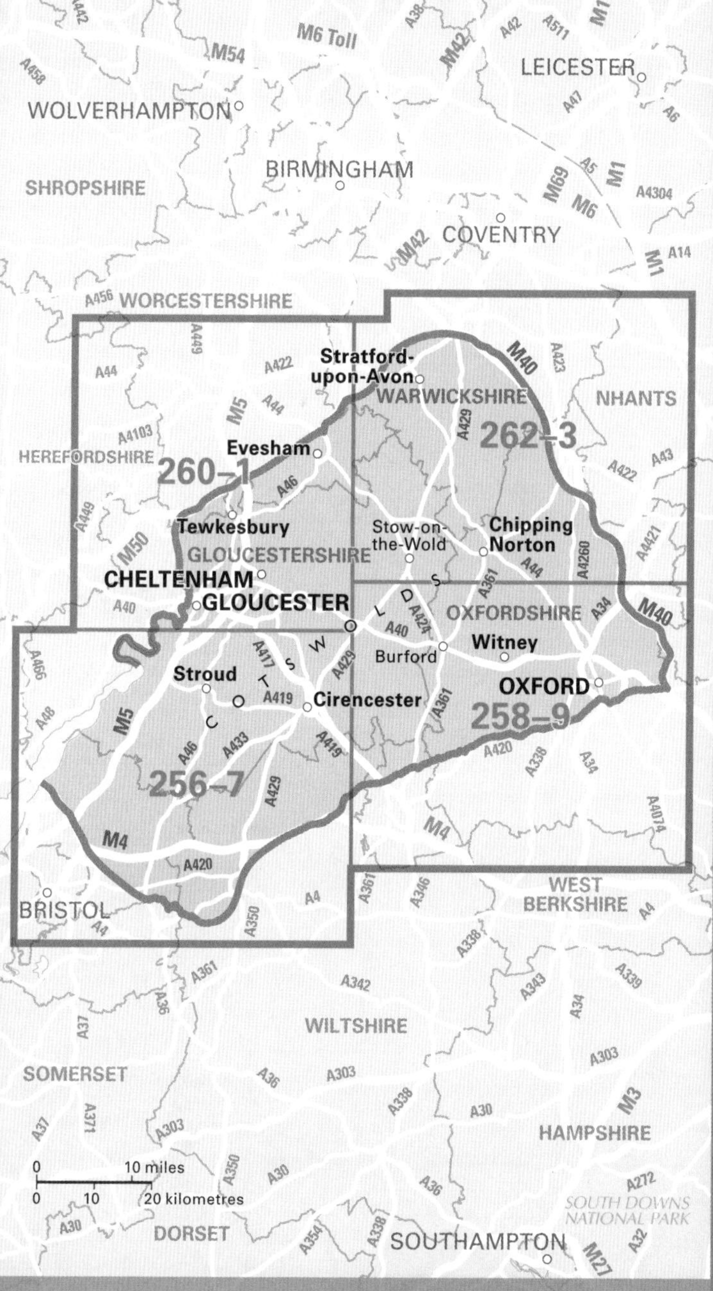

ATLAS

★ A-Z places listed

• Places Nearby

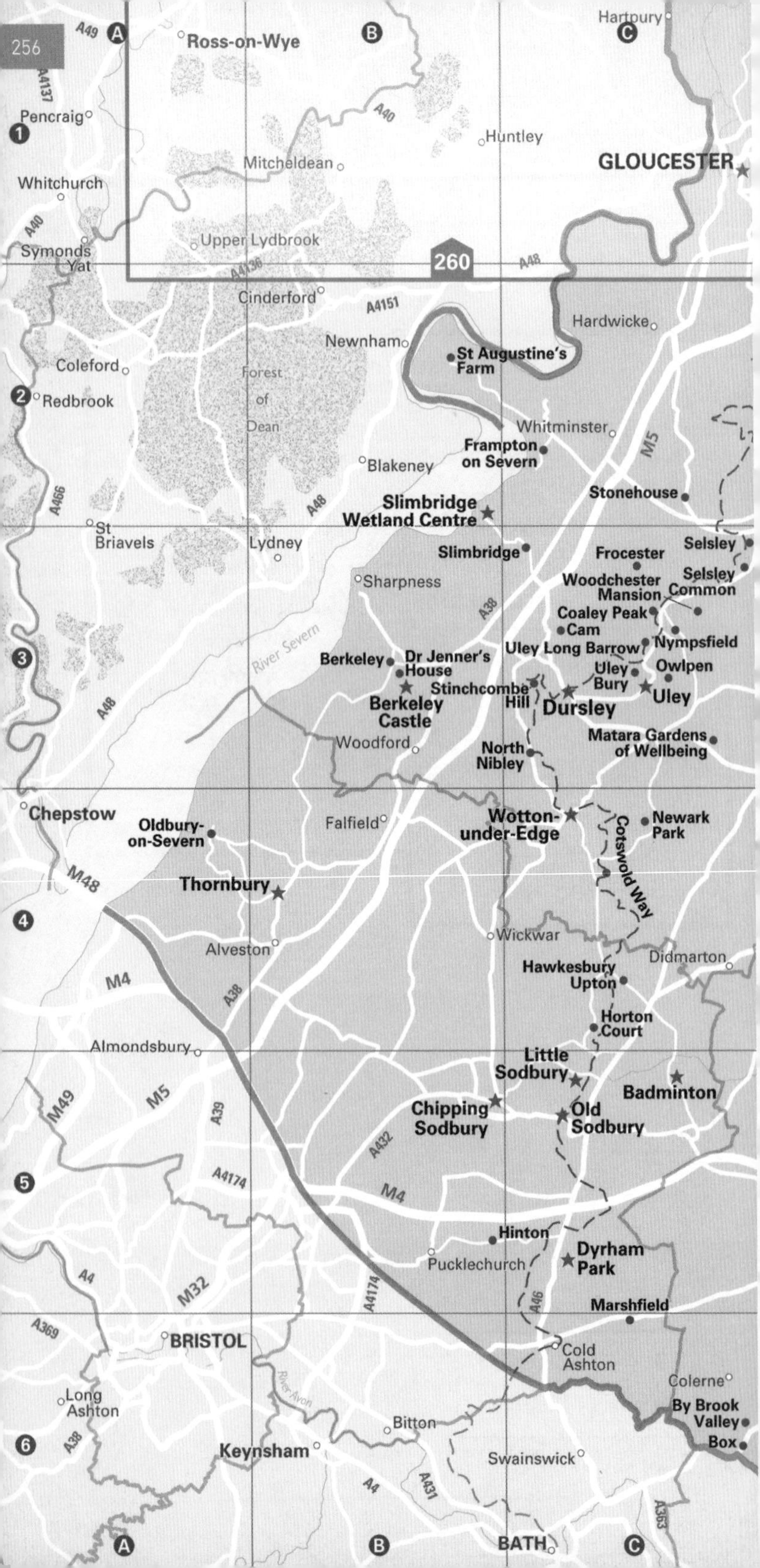

A
B
C
1
2
3
4
5
6
Ross-on-Wye
Hartpury
A49
A4137
Pencraig
A40
Huntley
GLOUCESTER
Mitcheldean
Whitchurch
A40
Symonds Yat
Upper Lydbrook
A4136
260
A48
Cinderford
A4151
Hardwicke
Newnham
St Augustine's Farm
Coleford
Forest of Dean
Redbrook
Whitminster
Frampton on Severn
M5
Blakeney
A466
Stonehouse
A48
Slimbridge Wetland Centre
St Briavels
Lydney
Slimbridge
Frocester
Selsley
Sharpness
Woodchester Mansion
Selsley Common
A38
Coaley Peak
Cam
River Severn
Uley Long Barrow
Nympsfield
Berkeley
Dr Jenner's House
Uley Bury
Owlpen
Stinchcombe Hill
Uley
Berkeley Castle
Dursley
A48
Matara Gardens of Wellbeing
Woodford
North Nibley
Chepstow
Oldbury-on-Severn
Falfield
Wotton-under-Edge
Newark Park
Cotswold Way
M48
Thornbury
Wickwar
Alveston
Didmarton
M4
Hawkesbury Upton
A38
Horton Court
Almondsbury
Little Sodbury
Badminton
M49
M5
A39
Chipping Sodbury
Old Sodbury
A432
A4174
M4
Hinton
Dyrham Park
Pucklechurch
A4
M32
A4174
A46
Marshfield
A369
BRISTOL
Cold Ashton
River Avon
Colerne
Long Ashton
By Brook Valley
Bitton
A38
Box
Keynsham
Swainswick
A4
A431
A363
BATH

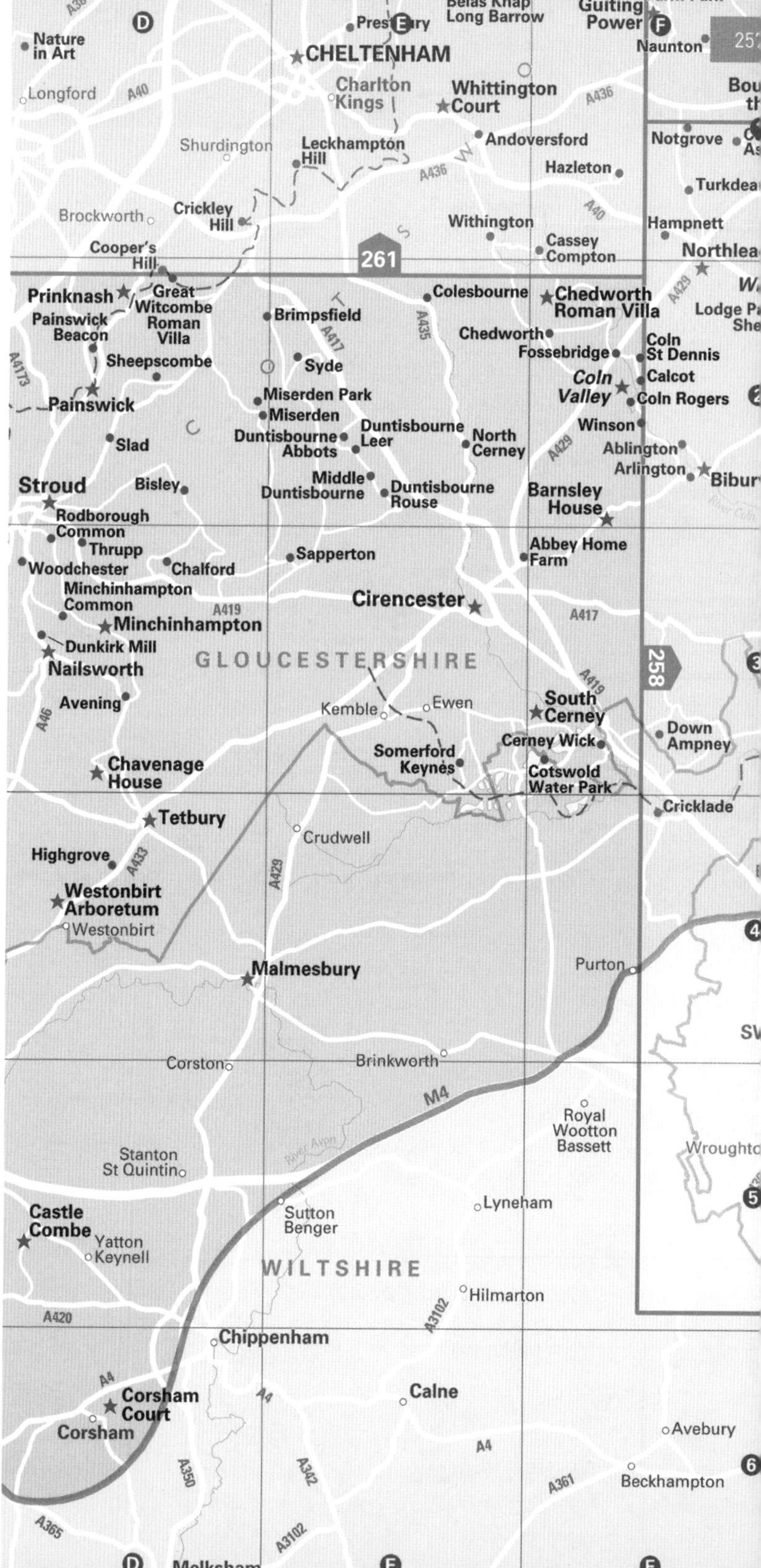

Nature in Art
Prestbury
Belas Knap Long Barrow
Guiting Power
Farm Park
Naunton
CHELTENHAM
Longford
Charlton Kings
Whittington Court
Bourton-on-the-Water
Shurdington
Leckhampton Hill
Andoversford
Notgrove
Hazleton
Turkdean
Brockworth
Crickley Hill
Withington
Hampnett
Cooper's Hill
Cassey Compton
Northleach
261
Prinknash
Great Witcombe Roman Villa
Colesbourne
Chedworth Roman Villa
Lodge Park Sherborne
Painswick Beacon
Brimpsfield
Chedworth
Fossebridge
Coln St Dennis
Sheepscombe
Syde
Coln Valley
Calcot
Painswick
Miserden Park
Coln Rogers
Miserden
Winson
Slad
Duntisbourne Abbots
Duntisbourne Leer
North Cerney
Ablington
Arlington
Bibury
Stroud
Bisley
Middle Duntisbourne
Duntisbourne Rouse
Barnsley House
Rodborough Common
Thrupp
Woodchester
Chalford
Sapperton
Abbey Home Farm
Minchinhampton Common
Cirencester
Minchinhampton
Dunkirk Mill
Nailsworth
GLOUCESTERSHIRE
258
Avening
Kemble
Ewen
South Cerney
Down Ampney
Cerney Wick
Somerford Keynes
Chavenage House
Cotswold Water Park
Cricklade
Tetbury
Crudwell
Highgrove
Westonbirt Arboretum
Westonbirt
Malmesbury
Purton
Corston
Brinkworth
M4
Royal Wootton Bassett
Stanton St Quintin
River Avon
Wroughton
Lyneham
Castle Combe
Sutton Benger
Yatton Keynell
WILTSHIRE
Hilmarton
Chippenham
Corsham Court
Calne
Corsham
Avebury
Beckhampton
Melksham

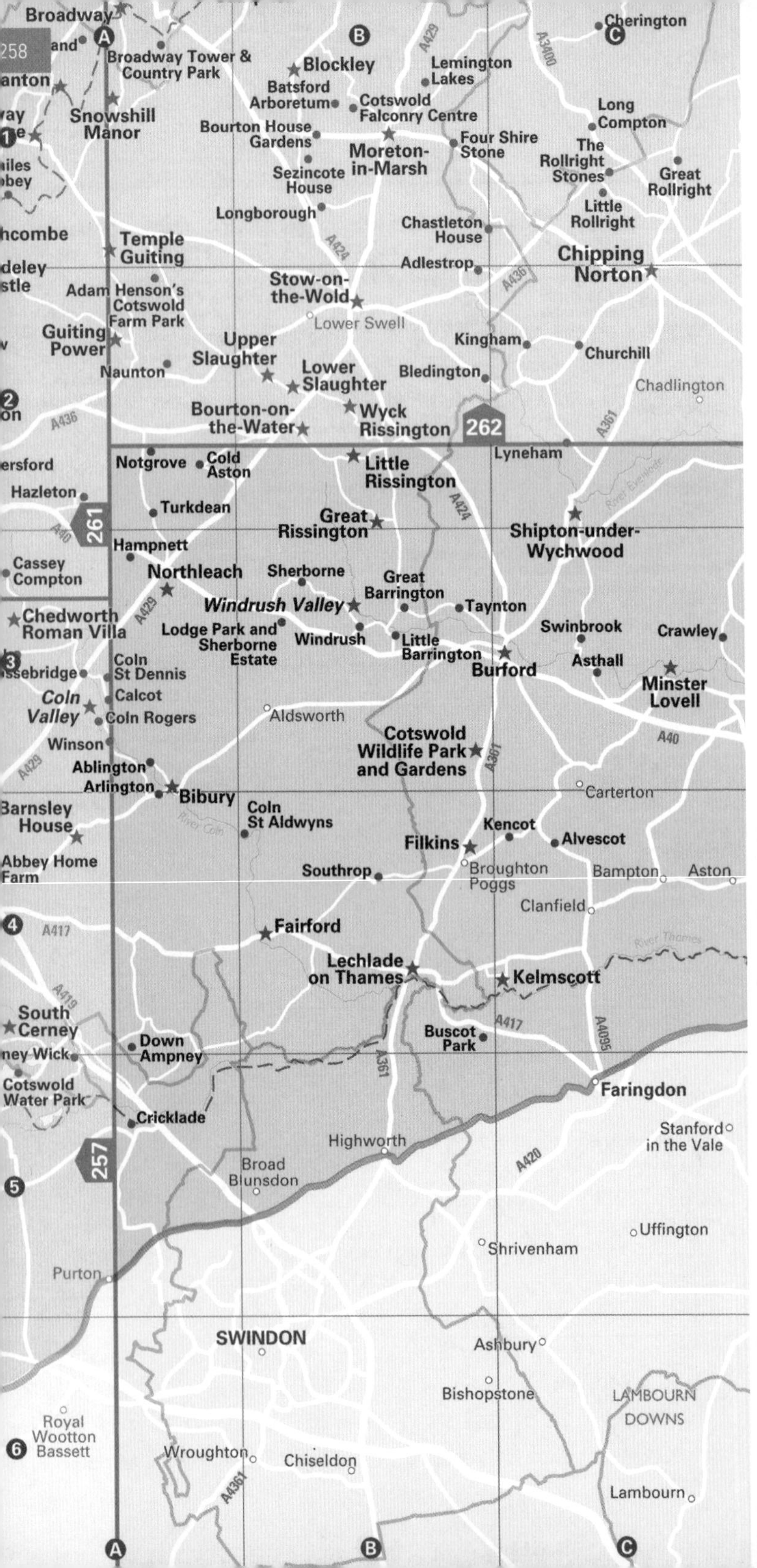
Broadway
Broadway Tower & Country Park
Snowshill Manor
Blockley
Batsford Arboretum
Cotswold Falconry Centre
Lemington Lakes
Cherington
Long Compton
Bourton House Gardens
Moreton-in-Marsh
Four Shire Stone
The Rollright Stones
Great Rollright
Sezincote House
Little Rollright
Longborough
Chastleton House
Temple Guiting
Adlestrop
Chipping Norton
Adam Henson's Cotswold Farm Park
Stow-on-the-Wold
Lower Swell
Guiting Power
Upper Slaughter
Kingham
Churchill
Naunton
Lower Slaughter
Bledington
Chadlington
Bourton-on-the-Water
Wyck Rissington
262
Notgrove
Cold Aston
Little Rissington
Lyneham
Hazleton
Turkdean
261
Great Rissington
Shipton-under-Wychwood
Hampnett
Cassey Compton
Northleach
Sherborne
Great Barrington
Chedworth Roman Villa
Windrush Valley
Taynton
Lodge Park and Sherborne Estate
Windrush
Little Barrington
Swinbrook
Crawley
Burford
Asthall
Minster Lovell
Coln St Dennis
Calcot
Coln Valley
Coln Rogers
Aldsworth
Winson
Cotswold Wildlife Park and Gardens
A40
Ablington
Arlington
Bibury
Carterton
Barnsley House
Coln St Aldwyns
Kencot
Alvescot
Filkins
Abbey Home Farm
Broughton Poggs
Southrop
Bampton
Aston
Clanfield
Fairford
Lechlade on Thames
Kelmscott
River Thames
South Cerney
Buscot Park
Down Ampney
Cotswold Water Park
Faringdon
Cricklade
Stanford in the Vale
257
Highworth
Broad Blunsdon
Uffington
Shrivenham
Purton
SWINDON
Ashbury
Bishopstone
LAMBOURN DOWNS
Royal Wootton Bassett
Wroughton
Chiseldon
Lambourn
A
B
C

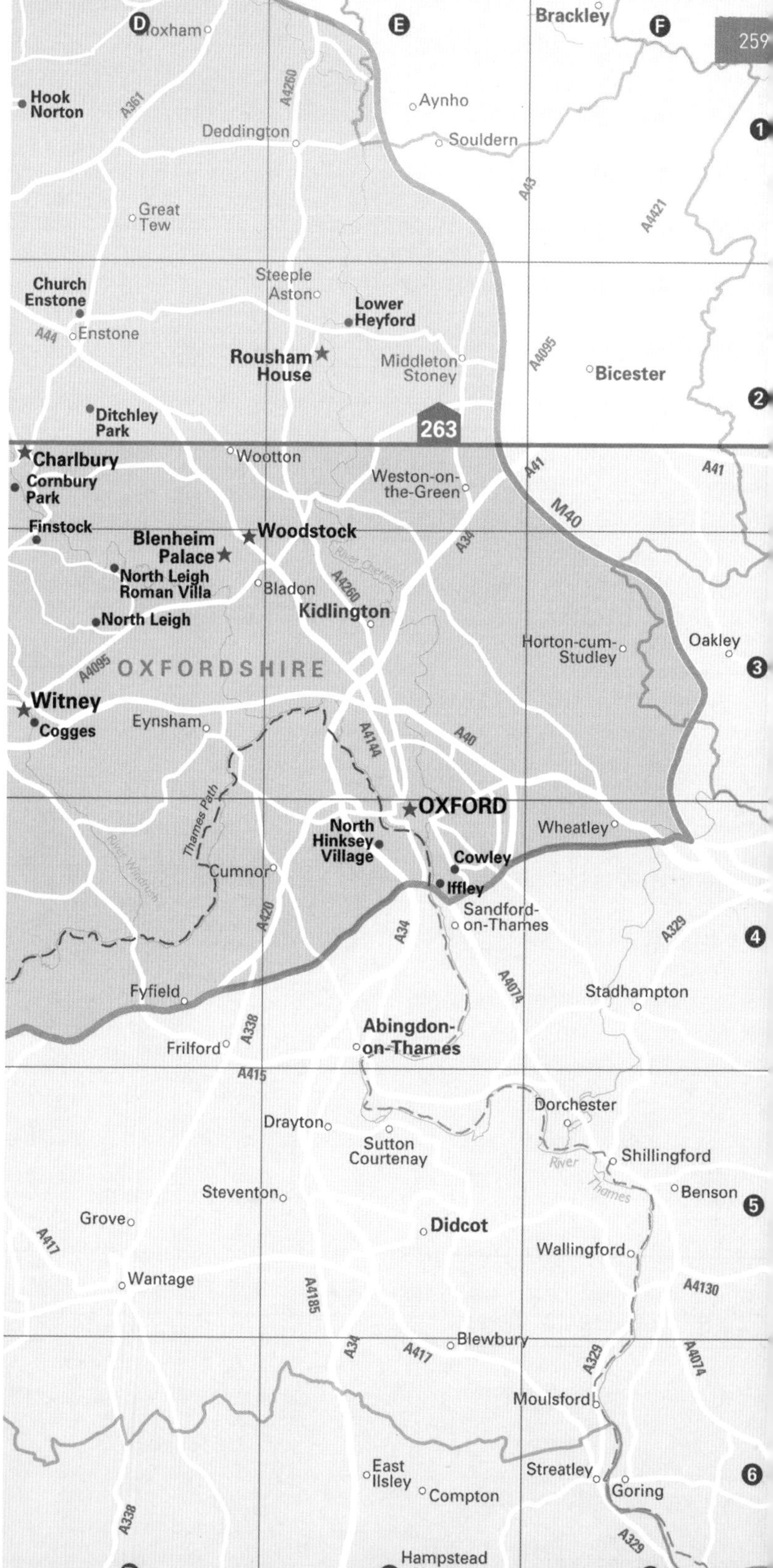
D
E
F
1
2
3
4
5
6
Bloxham
Brackley
Hook Norton
A361
A4260
Aynho
Deddington
Souldern
A43
A4421
Great Tew
Church Enstone
Steeple Aston
Lower Heyford
A44
Enstone
Rousham House
Middleton Stoney
A4095
Bicester
Ditchley Park
263
Charlbury
Wootton
Weston-on-the-Green
A41
A41
Cornbury Park
M40
Finstock
Blenheim Palace
Woodstock
A34
River Cherwell
North Leigh Roman Villa
Bladon
A4260
Kidlington
North Leigh
Horton-cum-Studley
Oakley
A4095
OXFORDSHIRE
Witney
Cogges
Eynsham
A4144
A40
Thames Path
OXFORD
River Windrush
North Hinksey Village
Wheatley
Cumnor
Cowley
Iffley
Sandford-on-Thames
A420
A34
A329
A4074
Fyfield
Stadhampton
A338
Abingdon-on-Thames
Frilford
A415
Dorchester
Drayton
Sutton Courtenay
Shillingford
River Thames
Steventon
Benson
Grove
Didcot
A417
Wallingford
Wantage
A4185
A4130
Blewbury
A34
A417
A329
A4074
Moulsford
East Ilsley
Streatley
Compton
Goring
A338
A329
Hampstead Norreys
Pangbourne

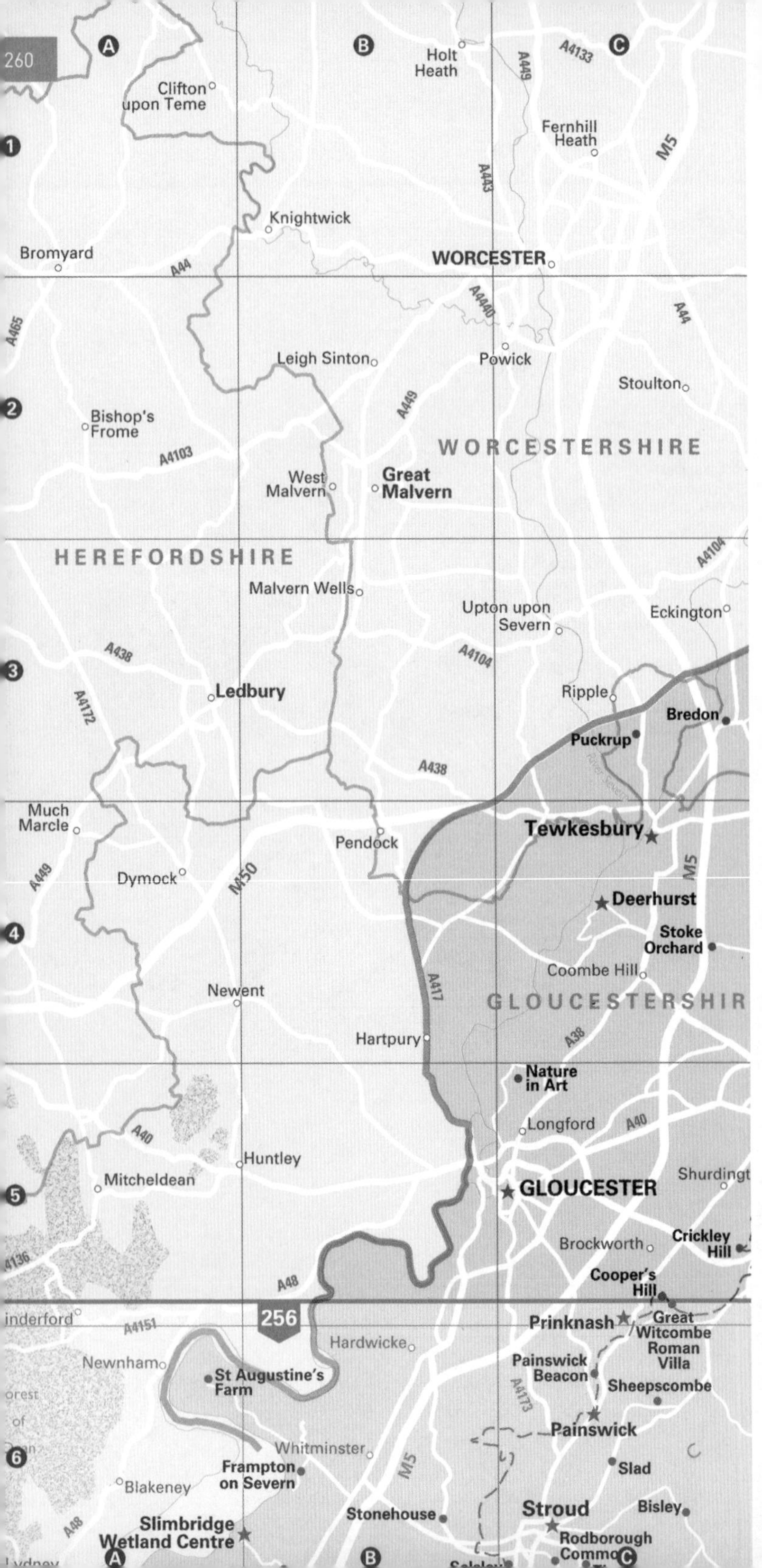

A
B
C
1
2
3
4
5
6
Clifton upon Teme
Holt Heath
Fernhill Heath
Knightwick
Bromyard
WORCESTER
Leigh Sinton
Powick
Stoulton
Bishop's Frome
WORCESTERSHIRE
West Malvern
Great Malvern
HEREFORDSHIRE
Malvern Wells
Upton upon Severn
Eckington
Ledbury
Ripple
Bredon
Puckrup
Much Marcle
Pendock
Tewkesbury
Dymock
Deerhurst
Stoke Orchard
Coombe Hill
GLOUCESTERSHIR
Newent
Hartpury
Nature in Art
Longford
Huntley
Mitcheldean
GLOUCESTER
Shurdingt
Brockworth
Crickley Hill
Cooper's Hill
256
Prinknash
Great Witcombe Roman Villa
Hardwicke
Newnham
St Augustine's Farm
Painswick Beacon
Sheepscombe
Painswick
Whitminster
Frampton on Severn
Slad
Blakeney
Stonehouse
Stroud
Bisley
Slimbridge Wetland Centre
Rodborough Common
A4133
A449
A443
M5
A44
A4440
A465
A4103
A4104
A438
A4172
M50
A417
A38
A40
A4136
A48
A4151
A4173

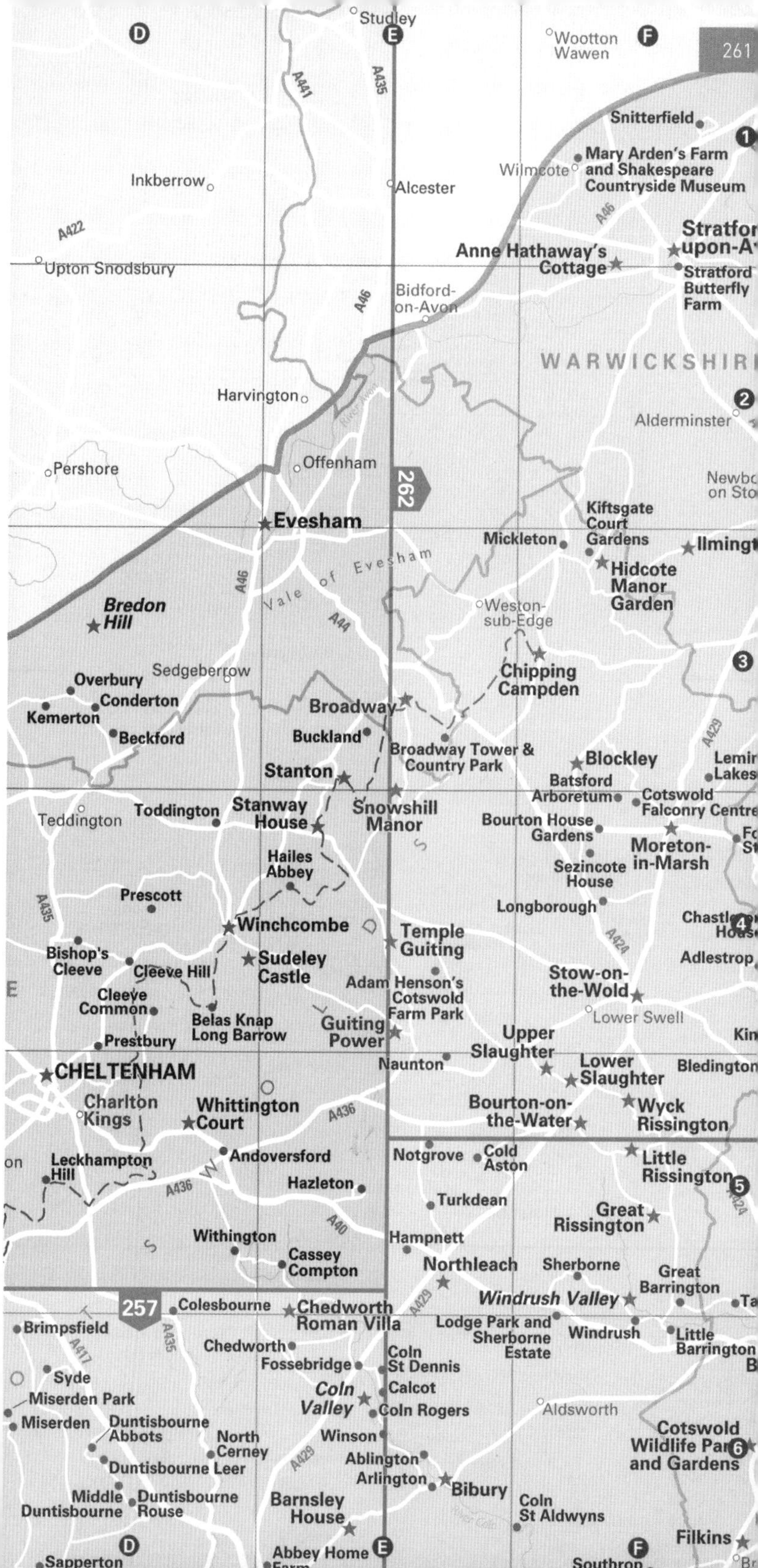

Studley
Wootton Wawen
Snitterfield
Mary Arden's Farm and Shakespeare Countryside Museum
Wilmcote
Inkberrow
Alcester
A422
A441
A435
A46
Upton Snodsbury
Anne Hathaway's Cottage
Stratford Butterfly Farm
Bidford-on-Avon
WARWICKSHIR
Harvington
Alderminster
River Avon
Offenham
Pershore
262
Evesham
Kiftsgate Court Gardens
Mickleton
Hidcote Manor Garden
Vale of Evesham
Bredon Hill
Weston-sub-Edge
A44
Chipping Campden
Sedgeberrow
Overbury
Conderton
Kemerton
Beckford
Broadway
Buckland
Broadway Tower & Country Park
Blockley
A429
Stanton
Batsford Arboretum
Cotswold Falconry Centre
Teddington
Toddington
Stanway House
Snowshill Manor
Bourton House Gardens
Moreton-in-Marsh
Hailes Abbey
Sezincote House
Prescott
Longborough
A435
Winchcombe
Temple Guiting
Bishop's Cleeve
Cleeve Hill
Sudeley Castle
A424
Adlestrop
Cleeve Common
Adam Henson's Cotswold Farm Park
Stow-on-the-Wold
Lower Swell
Belas Knap Long Barrow
Prestbury
Guiting Power
Upper Slaughter
Naunton
CHELTENHAM
Lower Slaughter
Bledington
Charlton Kings
Whittington Court
A436
Bourton-on-the-Water
Wyck Rissington
Leckhampton Hill
Andoversford
Notgrove
Cold Aston
Little Rissington
Hazleton
Turkdean
A436
A40
Great Rissington
Withington
Hampnett
Cassey Compton
Northleach
Sherborne
Great Barrington
Windrush Valley
257
Colesbourne
Chedworth Roman Villa
A429
Lodge Park and Sherborne Estate
Windrush
Little Barrington
Brimpsfield
A417
A435
Chedworth
Fossebridge
Coln St Dennis
Syde
Calcot
Coln Valley
Miserden Park
Coln Rogers
Aldsworth
Miserden
Duntisbourne Abbots
North Cerney
Winson
Cotswold Wildlife Park and Gardens
A429
Duntisbourne Leer
Ablington
Arlington
Bibury
Middle Duntisbourne
Duntisbourne Rouse
Barnsley House
Coln St Aldwyns
River Coln
Filkins
Sapperton
Abbey Home Farm
Southrop

TCH
Ullenhall
Henley-in-Arden
M40
Haseley
A46
ROYAL LEAMINGTON SPA
Warwick
A4189
Claverdon
A425
Studley
Wootton Wawen
A452
A441
A435
Barford
Snitterfield
A439
Mary Arden's Farm and Shakespeare Countryside Museum
Wilmcote
Alcester
Charlecote
A46
Stratford-upon-Avon
Wellesbourne
Anne Hathaway's Cottage
Stratford Butterfly Farm
Bidford-on-Avon
A46
Loxley
WARWICKSHIRE
A422
Kineton
Ettington
Alderminster
A3400
Pillerton Priors
Offenham
261
Newbold on Stour
Oxhill
Whatcote
Evesham
Kiftsgate Court Gardens
Mickleton
Ilmington
Tredington
Honington
Hidcote Manor Garden
Vale of Evesham
Weston-sub-Edge
Shipston-on-Stour
A44
Chipping Campden
Broadway
Cherington
Buckland
A429
A3400
Broadway Tower & Country Park
Blockley
Lemington Lakes
Stanton
Batsford Arboretum
Cotswold Falconry Centre
Snowshill Manor
Long Compton
Bourton House Gardens
Moreton-in-Marsh
Four Shire Stone
The Rollright Stones
Hailes Abbey
Sezincote House
Great Rollright
Little Rollright
Longborough
Chastleton House
Temple Guiting
A424
Chipping Norton
Adlestrop
Stow-on-the-Wold
A436
Adam Henson's Cotswold Farm Park
Lower Swell
Guiting Power
Upper Slaughter
Kingham
Churchill
Naunton
Lower Slaughter
Bledington
Chadlington
Bourton-on-the-Water
Wyck Rissington
A436
A361
Notgrove
Cold Aston
Little Rissington
258
Lyneham
Hazleton
A424
River Evenlode
Turkdean
Great Rissington
Shipton-under-Wychwood
A40
Hampnett
Cassey Compton
Northleach
Sherborne
Great Barrington
Windrush Valley
Taynton
Chedworth Roman Villa
A429
Lodge Park and Sherborne Estate
Windrush
Swinbrook
Crawley
Little Barrington
Burford
Asthall
Minster Lovell
Fossebridge
Coln St Dennis
Calcot
Coln Valley
Coln Rogers
Aldsworth
Winson
Cotswold Wildlife Park
A361
A40

D
E
F
A426
A45
Long Itchington
Welton
M1
1
A425
Southam
Daventry
Staverton
A45
Flore
Weedon
A5
A361
A423
Preston
Capes
Gaydon
Fenny
Compton
2
M40
Blakesley
Chipping
Warden
Warmington
Cropredy
NORTHAMPTONSHIRE
A422
3
A43
Wroxton
Middleton Cheney
Syresham
Banbury
A422
Swalcliffe
Brackley
A422
Bloxham
A4260
Hook
Norton
A361
Aynho
4
Deddington
Souldern
A43
A4421
Great
Tew
Church
Enstone
Steeple
Aston
Lower
Heyford
A44
Enstone
Rousham
House
Middleton
Stoney
A4095
Bicester
5
Ditchley
Park
Charlbury
Wootton
259
Weston-on-
the-Green
A41
A41
Cornbury
Park
M40
Finstock
Blenheim
Palace
Woodstock
A34
River Cherwell
North Leigh
Roman Villa
A4260
Bladon
North Leigh
Kidlington
Horton-cum-
Studley
Oakley
6
A4095
OXFORDSHIRE
Witney
Cogges
Eynsham
A4144
A40
D
E
F

Index, themed

Page numbers in **bold** refer to main text entries

ABBEYS
Hailes Abbey 235
Prinknash 178–9
Tewkesbury Abbey 223–4, 227

ANCIENT ARCHAEOLOGY
Belas Knap 16, 33, 140, 235, 239
Bredon Hill 26, 33, 39, 48, **76**, 209
Cleeve Common 236
Crickley Hill 17, 33, 39, 48, 140
Hetty Pegler's Tump 231, 232
Kimsbury Camp 178
Longborough 151
Nympsfield Long Barrow 16, 33, 231
Rollright Stones 17, 28–9, 33, 55, 103–4
Shenberrow Hill 192
Uley Bury 17, 23, 33, 230–1

ARBORETUMS
Batsford Arboretum 154
Westonbirt Arboretum 15, 55, **220**

ARTS CENTRES
Cirencester 106, 109
Gloucester 130
Nailsworth 156
Stanton 192–3

BOATING
Oxford 171
Bodleian Library, Oxford 162, 165

CANALS
Stratford-upon-Avon Canal 205
Stroudwater Canal 213
Thames and Severn Canal 190

CASTLES
Berkeley Castle 43, **63–5**
Sudeley Castle 15, 43, 48, 63, **217–18**, 235
Thornbury Castle 229
see also historic houses

CHURCHES
Church of St Mary de Crypt, Gloucester 127
Gloucester Cathedral 48, 125, 127, 128
Hailes Church, Winchcombe 237
Holy Trinity Church, Stratford-upon-Avon 199, 205–6
North Cerney All Saints, Cirencester 109
Odda's Chapel, Deerhurst 116
The Old Quaker Meeting House, Ettington 210
Oxford Oratory Church of St Aloysius Gonzaga 169
St Andrew's, Castle Combe 84
St James the Great, Snitterfield 210
St James the Great, Stoke Orchard 94, 116
St John the Baptist, Cirencester 106, 108–9
St Kenelm, Minster Lovell 149
St Kenelm, Witney 245
St Lawrence, Oxhill 181
St Lawrence's, Bourton-on-the-Water 70
St Mary Magdalen, Oxford 169–70
St Mary the Virgin, Charlbury 85
St Mary the Virgin, Iffley 175
St Mary the Virgin, Tetbury 219
St Mary the Virgin, Thornbury 229
St Mary's, Bibury 66–7
St Mary's, Shipton-under-Wychwood 183
St Mary's, Swinbrook 242
St Mary's, Tewkesbury 224
St Mary's, Witney 244–5
St Mary's Priory Church, Deerhurst 115, 116
St Michael and All Angels, Bishop's Cleeve 95
St Michael and All Angels, Stanton 192
St Michael at the North Gate, Oxford 170
St Michael's, Duntisbourne Rouse 111
St Nicholas', Loxley 210
St Peter and St Paul, Northleach 159, 160
St Peter's, Winchcombe 237
University Church of St Mary the Virgin, Oxford 164, 169
Wesley Memorial Church, Oxford 170
Whatcote St Peter 182
Widford church 240
see also wool churches

CINEMAS
Oxford 170–1
Stratford-upon-Avon 206

COUNTRY PARKS
Broadway Tower & Country Park 77–8
Cornbury Park 85
Lodge Park 241
Newark Park 253
Robinswood Hill Country Park 128
Sherborne Estate 241

CRAFTS
Cotswold Woollen Weavers, Filkins 123, 124
Lechlade 145

CYCLING
Bibury 67
Bourton-on-the-Water 75
Burford 82
Cheltenham 92
Oxford 171
South Cerney 191
Stratford-upon-Avon 206

EAT AND DRINK
Barnsley 62
Berkeley Castle 65
Bibury 67, 68
Bourton-on-the-Water 75
Broadway 78
Burford 82
Castle Combe 84
Charlbury 85
Cheltenham 93–4, 95
Chipping Campden 98–100
Chipping Norton 102–3
Cirencester 109–10
Corsham Court 114, 115
Dursley 117
Dyrham Park 120
Gloucester 131–2
The Guitings 134
Hook Norton Brewery 105
Ilmington 141–2
Lechlade 145–6
Minchinhampton 148
Minster Lovell 150–1
Moreton-in-Marsh 152–3
Nailsworth 156–8
Northleach 160
Oxford 172–5
Painswick 178
Shipston-on-Stour 182
Shipton-under-Wychwood 183–4
The Slaughters 185
Stow-on-the-Wold 196–7
Stratford-upon-Avon 206, 208–9
Stroud and Five Valleys 214–15
Tetbury 55, 219, 221–2
Tewkesbury 228
Thornbury 229–30
Winchcombe 238–9
Witney 243–4
Woodstock 249, 251
Wotton-under-Edge 253–4

FARMERS' MARKETS
Stow-on-the-Wold 196

FESTIVALS AND EVENTS
Artburst, Painswick 55
arts festivals **95**
Banbury Hobby Horse Festival 55
Boxing Day Duck Race, Bibury 55

Cheese-rolling, Cooper's Hill 54
Cotswold Olimpick Games, Chipping Campden 54
Football in the River, Bourton-on-the-Water 55, 71
Leveller's Day, Burford 54
Loghborough Festival Opera 55
Marshfield Paperboys 55
Morris dancing 54, 141
Painswick Ancient Clypping Ceremony 55
Ramsden Fete 54–5
Randwick Wap & Spring Time Cheese-rolling Ceremony 54
Shakespeare's Birthday Celebrations 206
Summer Solstice, Rollright Stones 55
Tetbury Food and Drink Festival 55
Tetbury Woolsack Races 54
Three Choirs Festival, Gloucester 130
Treefest, Westonbirt Arboretum 55

FISHING
Bibury 67
Chipping Norton 101
Lechlade 145
Moreton-in-Marsh 152

FOOTBALL GROUND
Gloucester 130

FOOTPATHS AND TRAILS
Cotswold Way 32, 96
Dursley Sculpture and Play Trail 117
Jurassic Way 105
Ridgeway National Trail 172

GARDENS
Athelstan Manor Gardens, Malmesbury 147
Barnsley House 60–2
Bourton House Gardens 151, 152
Cotswold Wildlife Park and Gardens, Burford 13, 52, 81
Dragonfly Maze, Bourton-on-the-Water 72
Dyrham Park 119–20
Ernest Wilson Memorial Garden, Chipping Campden 96
Hidcote Manor Garden 13, **135–9**
Ilmington Manor 142–3
Kiftsgate Court Gardens 139
Matara Gardens of Wellbeing, Kingscote 231, 232
Mill Dene Garden, Blockley 69
Misarden Park Gardens 95
Oxford Botanic Garden 169
Painswick Rococo Garden 178
Rousham House 180–1
Sezincote House 151, 152
Snowshill 26, 47, **187–9**

GEOGRAPHIC FEATURES
Cam Long Down 23, 118
Cam Peak 118
Cotswold Edge 22, 23, 33, 39, 211
see also ancient archaeology; hills and commons

GLIDING
Nailsworth 156

GOLF
Castle Combe 84
Cheltenham 93
Chipping Norton 102
Cirencester 109
Gloucester 131
Minchinhampton 148
Stinchcombe 118
Stratford-upon-Avon 206, 209
Tewkesbury 228
Thornbury 229
Witney 243
Wotton-under-Edge 253

HERITAGE CENTRES
Evesham 121
Minster Lovell 150
Out of the Hat, Tewkesbury 227
Tetbury Heritage Centre 219
Wotton-under-Edge 253

HILLS AND COMMONS
Bredon Hill 39, 48, **76**
Cleeve Common 33, 140, 236
Cleeve Hill 50, 140
Coaley Peak 231
Cooper's Hill 33, 54, 140
Crickley Hill 17, 33, 39, 48, 140
Dover's Hill 96
Haresfield Beacon 17
Haresfield Common 33
Leckhampton Hill 33, 140
Minchinhampton Common 33, 110, 147, 148–9, 160
Painswick Beacon 17, 33, 43
Rodborough Common 26, 28, 33, 46, 213
Selsley Common 33, 212
Shenberrow Hill 192
Stinchcombe Hill 118

HISTORIC HOUSES
Anne Hathaway's Cottage, Stratford-upon-Avon 12, 199, **204**
Arlington Row 66
Asthall Manor 241
Badminton 60
Barnsley House 60–2
Blenheim Palace 14, 21, 47, **247–8, 250**
Bliss Tweed Mill 101
Buscot Park 144, 145
Cassey Compton 111
Chastleton House 154
Chavenage House 49, **86–7**, 222
Corsham Court 113–15
Ditchley Park 85
Dyrham Park 60, **119–20**
Hall's Croft, Stratford-upon-Avon 200, 202
Harvard House, Stratford-upon-Avon 202
Horton 190
Keble House 122
Kelmscott Manor 21, 144
Mary Arden's Farm, Stratford-upon-Avon 205
Merchant's House, Tewkesbury 227
Minster Lovell Hall and Dovecote 150
Nash's House, Stratford-upon-Avon 202
New Place, Stratford-upon-Avon 202
Owlpen Manor 49, 231, 232
Rodmarton Manor 111
Sezincote House 151, 152
Shakespeare's Birthplace, Stratford-upon-Avon 12, **203**
Snowshill Manor 47, **187–9**
Stanway House 48, **193–4**
Whittington Court 232–3
Woodchester Mansion, Nympsfield 213, 214
see also castles

HORSE RACING
Cheltenham Racecourse 91

HORSE RIDING
Bourton-on-the-Water 75
Cheltenham 92, 95
Cirencester 109
Moreton-in-Marsh 152
Nailsworth 156
Painswick 178
South Cerney 191
Stanton 193, 239

HOT AIR BALLOONING
Bourton-on-the-Water 72
Cheltenham 92
Cirencester 109
South Cerney 191
Tetbury 219

INDUSTRIAL ARCHAEOLOGY
Dunkirk Mill Centre, Nailsworth 156
Gloucester Docks 130
The Model Village, Bourton-on-the-Water 72

MONUMENTS
Four Shire Stone 154
Somerset (Hawkesbury) Monument 190

Tyndale Monument 118, 190, 253, 254

MOTOR SPORTS
Castle Combe 84
Winchcombe 237

MUSEUMS AND GALLERIES
Almonry Museum and Heritage Centre, Evesham 121
Ashmolean Museum of Art & Archaeology, Oxford 14, 162, **167**
Athelstan Museum, Malmesbury 147
Bourton Model Railway Exhibition 72
Cassey Compton 111
Chipping Norton Museum 101
Corinium Museum, Cirencester 106, 108
Cotswold Motoring Museum and Toy Collection, Bourton-on-the-Water 15, **73**
Cotswold Woollen Weavers, Filkins 123, 124
Court Barn Museum, Chipping Campden 96–7
Dr Jenner's House, Berkeley Castle 65
Gloucester City Museum & Art Gallery 128–9
Gloucester Folk Museum 129
Gloucester Waterways Museum, Gloucester 129
Gordon Russell Museum, Broadway 77
Holst Birthplace Museum, Cheltenham 90–1
John Moore Museum, Tewkesbury 226, 227
Mechanical Music Museum, Northleach 160
Modern Art Oxford 166
Museum in the Park, Stroud 212, 214
Museum of Oxford 166
Museum of the History of Science, Oxford 162, 166
Nature in Art, Gloucester 132
Old Mill Museum, Lower Slaughter 185
Oxford Castle Unlocked 165
Oxford University Museum of Natural History 165–6
Oxfordshire Museum, Woodstock 248, 249
Pitt Rivers Museum, Oxford 13, 162, **168**
Pittville Pump Room, Cheltenham 91
Shakespeare Countryside Museum, Stratford-upon-Avon 200, 205
Soldiers of Gloucestershire Museum, Gloucester 127, 128
Tewkesbury Museum 225, 227–8
Thornbury and District Museum 229
Wellington Aviation Museum, Moreton-in-Marsh 151
The Wilson, Cheltenham 90
Winchcombe Folk & Police Museum 234, 235
Witney and District Museum 242–3

PERFUMERY
Cotswold Perfumery, Bourton-on-the-Water 72

PETTING FARMS
Cogges, Witney 243
Cotswold Farm Park 18, 52, 133, 197
St Augustine's Farm, Arlingham 216
see also wildlife attractions

RAILWAY ATTRACTIONS
Bourton Model Railway Exhibition 72
Gloucestershire Warwickshire Railway 51, 52, 235, 237

RIVERS
River Cherwell 166, 169
River Thames 166, 169

ROMAN SITES
Chedworth Roman Villa 17, **87–8**, 110
Fosse Way 17
Great Witcombe Roman Villa 17, 140, 179
North Leigh Roman Villa 244
Roman Amphitheatre, Cirencester 107–8
Woodchester 213

SHOPS, HISTORIC
Alice's Shop, Oxford 171
House of the Tailor of Gloucester, Gloucester 130

SPORTS AND ACTIVITIES CENTRES
Gloucester 131
South Cerney 191
see also waterparks

THEATRES
Cheltenham 91
Gloucester 130
Royal Shakespeare Company, Stratford-upon-Avon 12, 200–1, **207**
Sheldonian Theatre, Oxford 162, 165
Tewkesbury 228

TITHE BARN
Frocester Tithe Barn 212

UNIVERSITY COLLEGES
Oxford 48, 164–5

VALLEYS
By Brook Valley 114, 115
Coln Valley 111–13
Five Valleys 19, 23, **211–16**
Slad Valley 33, 35, 38
The Windrush Valley 239–42

WATERPARKS
Cotswold Water Park 52, 110, 123, 190, 191
Croft Farm Waterpark, Tewkesbury 228

WILDLIFE ATTRACTIONS
Batsford Park 69, 153, 154
Bird and Deer Park, Prinknash 179
Birdland, Bourton-on-the-Water 14, 52, **74**
Cotswold Falconry Centre, Batsford 154
Cotswold Wildlife Park and Gardens, Burford 13, 52, **81**
Slimbridge Wetland Centre 52, 65, **185–7**
Stratford Butterfly Farm 205
The Bird and Deer Park, Prinknash 179
see also petting farms

WOOL CHURCHES
Church of St John the Baptist, Burford 80, 82
Church of St Peter and St Paul, Northleach 159, 160
St James wool church, Chipping Campden 96, 97
St Mary's, Fairford 121–2

Index, places

Page numbers in **bold** refer to main entries; page numbers in *italics* refer to maps

A

Abbey House Gardens, Malmesbury 147
Ablington 68
Adam Henson's Cotswold Farm Park, Guiting Power 18, 52, 133, 197
Adlestrop 197
Alice's Shop, Oxford 171
Almonry Museum and Heritage Centre, Evesham 121
Alvescot 124
the Ampneys 192
Andoversford 233
Anne Hathaway's Cottage, Stratford-upon-Avon 12, 199, **204**
Arlington Row 66
Ashmolean Museum of Art & Archaeology, Oxford 14, 162, **167**
Asthall 241
Asthall Manor 241
Avening 160

B

Badminton 60
Bampton 49
Banbury 51, 55
Barnsley and Barnsley House 60–2, *68*
The Barringtons 239–40
Bath 17, 32
Batsford 69, 153, 154
Batsford Arboretum 52, 153, 154
Batsford Park 69, 154
Beckford 76
Belas Knap 16, 33, 140, 235, 239
Berkeley Castle 43, **63–5**
Dr Jenner's House 65
Betty's Grave 30
Bibury 19, 51, 55, **66–8**
Arlington Row 66
St Mary's Church 66–7
The Bird and Deer Park, Prinknash 179
Birdland, Bourton-on-the-Water 14, 52, **74**
Bishop's Cleeve 95
Bisley 26, 51, 215
Bladon 47
Blenheim Palace 14, 21, 47, **247–8, 250**
Bliss Tweed Mill, Chipping Norton 101
Blockley 52, **68–9**
Mill Dene Garden 69
Bodleian Library, Oxford 162, 165
Bourton House Gardens 151, 152
Bourton-on-the-Hill 151
Bourton-on-the-Water 34, 47, 48, 51, 53, 55, **70–2**, *71*, 185
Birdland 14, 52, **74**
Bourton Model Railway Exhibition 72
Cotswold Motoring Museum and Toy Collection 15, **73**
Cotswold Perfumery 72
Dragonfly Maze 72
The Model Village 72
St Lawrence's Church 70
Box 114–15
Bredon Hill 26, 33, 39, 48, **76**, 209
Brimpsfield 94
Broadway 25, 43, 47, 51, **77–8**
Broadway Tower & Country Park 77–8
Gordon Russell Museum 77
Broadwell 195
Brockworth 54
Buckland 78
Buckland Manor 78
Burford 18, 51, 54, **78–83**, 240
Church of St John the Baptist 80, 82
Cotswold Wildlife Park and Gardens 13, 52, **81**
Buscot Park 145
By Brook Valley 114, 115

C

Calcot 112
Cam 118
Cam Long Down 23, 118
Cam Peak 118
campsites 56–7
Cassey Compton 111
Castle Combe 83–4
Chalford 110, 212–13
Charlbury 84–5
Church of St Mary the Virgin 85
Chastleton House 154
Chavenage House 49, **86–7**, 222
Chedworth 88
Chedworth Roman Villa 17, **87–8, 110**
Cheltenham 10, 33, 46, 51, **88–95**, *89*
Cheltenham Racecourse 91
Holst Birthplace Museum 90–1
Pittville Pump Room 91
The Wilson 90
Cherington 181
Chipping Campden 18, 19, 20, 21, 23, 32, 33, 51, 53, 54, **96–100**
Court Barn Museum 96–7
Dover's Hill 96
Ernest Wilson Memorial Garden 96
Grevel House 96
St James wool church 96, 97
Chipping Norton 45, 53, **101–5**
Bliss Tweed Mill 101
Chipping Norton Museum 101
Chipping Sodbury 60, 189
Christ Church College, Oxford 48, 164
Churchill 104–5
Cirencester 10, 17, 18, 43, 45, 47, 53, **105–11**
Brewery Arts Centre 106
Church of St John the Baptist 108–9
Cirencester Park 106, 107
Corinium Museum 106, 108
Corn Hall 106
North Cerney All Saints 109
Roman Amphitheatre 107–8
St Thomas's Hospital 106
Cleeve Common 33, 140, 236
Cleeve Hill 50, 140
Coaley Peak 231
Cogges Manor Farm, Witney 243
Cold Aston 75
Coln Rogers 112
Coln St Aldwyns 112–13
Coln St Dennis 112
Coln Valley 111–13
Cooper's Hill 33, 140
Corinium Museum, Cirencester 106, 108
Cornbury Park 85
Corsham 114
Corsham Court 113–15
Cotswold Edge 9, 22, 23, 33, 39, 211
Cotswold Falconry Centre, Batsford 154

Cotswold Motoring Museum and Toy Collection, Bourton-on-the-Water 15, **73**
Cotswold Perfumery, Bourton-on-the-Water 72
Cotswold Water Park, South Cerney 52, 110, 190, 191
Cotswold Way 32, 96
Cotswold Wildlife Park and Gardens, Burford 13, 52, **81**
Cotswold Woollen Weavers, Filkins 123, 124
Court Barn Museum, Chipping Campden 96–7
Covered Market, Oxford 171
Crawley 151
Cricklade 192
Crickley Hill 17, 33, 39, 48, 140
Croft Farm Waterpark, Tewkesbury 228

D
Deddington 45
Deerhurst 115–16
  Odda's Chapel 116
  St Mary's Priory Church 115, 116
Ditchley Park 85
Dover's Hill 96
Down Ampney 192
Dr Jenner's House, Berkeley Castle 65
Dragonfly Maze, Bourton-on-the-Water 72
Dunkirk Mill Centre, Nailsworth 156
Duntisbourne Abbots 111
Duntisbourne Leer 111
Duntisbourne Rouse 111
Dursley 23, 34, 65, **117–18**
  Dursley Sculpture and Play Trail 117
Dyrham Park 60, **119–20**

E
Eastleach Martin 122
Eastleach Turville 122
Ernest Wilson Memorial Garden, Chipping Campden 96
Evesham 121
  Almonry Museum and Heritage Centre 121

F
Fairford 121–3
  Church of St Mary 121–2
  Keble House 122
Filkins 123–4
  Cotswold Woollen Weavers 123, 124
Finstock 85
Five Valleys 19, 23, **211–16**
Fosse Way 17
Fossebridge 111–12
Four Shire Stone 154
Frampton Court Estate 216
Frampton on Severn 187, 216
Frocester 118
Frocester Tithe Barn 212
Frome 19

G
Gloucester 17, 43, 49, **124–32**, *125*
  Blackfriars 127
  Church of St Mary de Crypt 127
  Gloucester Cathedral 48, 125, 127, 128
  Gloucester City Museum & Art Gallery 128–9
  Gloucester Docks 130
  Gloucester Folk Museum 129
  Gloucester Waterways Museum 129
  House of the Tailor of Gloucester 130
  Nature in Art 132
  Soldiers of Gloucestershire Museum 127, 128
Gloucestershire Warwickshire Railway 51, 52, 235, 237
Golden Valley 19, 110
Gordon Russell Museum, Broadway 77
Great Barrington 240
Great Rissington 179
Great Rollright 104
Great Witcombe Roman Villa 17, 140, 179
Guitings 133–4
  Adam Henson's Cotswold Farm Park 18, 52, 133, 197

H
Hailes Abbey, Winchcombe 235
Hailes Church, Winchcombe 237
Hall's Croft, Stratford-upon-Avon 200, 202
Hampnett 160
Haresfield Beacon 17
Haresfield Common 33
Harvard House, Stratford-upon-Avon 202
Hawkesbury Upton 190
Hazleton 75
Hetty Pegler's Tump 231, 232
Hidcote Manor Garden 13, **135–9**
Highgrove gardens 222
Holst Birthplace Museum, Cheltenham 90–1
Holy Trinity Church, Stratford-upon-Avon 199, 205–6
Honington 181
Hook Norton 105
Hook Norton Brewery 105
Horton 28, 190
House of the Tailor of Gloucester, Gloucester 130

I
Ilmington 140–2, 181
Ilmington Manor 142–3

J
John Moore Museum, Tewkesbury 226, 227
Jurassic Way 105

K
Kelmscott 21, **143–4**
  Kelmscott Manor 21, 144
Kemerton 76
Kencot 124
Kiftsgate Court Gardens 139
Kimsbury Camp 178

L
Lechlade on Thames 144–6
  Buscot Park 145
Leckhampton Hill 33, 140
Little Barrington 240
Little Rissington 179
Little Rollright 28, 104
Little Sodbury 60, 189–90
Lodge Park 241
Long Compton 28, 105
Longstone 27, 29
Lower Heyford 181
Lower Slaughter 34, 47, 184
Lower Swell 196

M
Malmesbury 43, **146–7**
Marshfield 55, 190
Mary Arden's Farm, Stratford-upon-Avon 205
Matara Gardens of Wellbeing, Kingscote 231, 232

Mechanical Music Museum, Northleach 156
Merchant's House, Tewkesbury 227
Mickleton 139
Middle Duntisbourne 111
Mill Dene Garden, Blockley 69
Minchinhampton 33, 51, **147–9**
Minchinhampton Common 33, 110, 147, 148–9, 160
Minster Lovell 149–51
Church of St Kenelm 149
Minster Lovell Hall and Dovecote 150
Minster Lovell Heritage Centre 149, 150
Misarden Park Gardens 95
Miserden 33, 95
The Model Village, Bourton-on-the-Water 72
Modern Art Oxford 166
Money Tump 27
Moreton-in-Marsh 43, 51, 53, 55, **151–4**
Bourton House Gardens 151, 152
Sezincote House 151, 152
Wellington Aviation Museum 151
Museum in the Park, Stroud 212, 214
Museum of the History of Science, Oxford 166

N

Nailsworth 19, 34, 52, 103, 118, **155–8**
Dunkirk Mill Centre 156
Ruskin Mill College Gallery 156
Nash's House, Stratford-upon-Avon 202
Nature in Art, Gloucester 132
Naunton 34, 75, 185
New Place, Stratford-upon-Avon 202
Newark Park 253
Nibley Knoll 118
North Cerney All Saints, Cirencester 109
North Leigh Roman Villa 244
North Nibley 186, 254
Northleach 18, 46, 134, **158–60**
Church of St Peter and St Paul 159, 160
Mechanical Music Museum 160
Notgrove 75
Nympsfield Long Barrow 16, 33, 231

O

Odda's Chapel, Deerhurst 116
Old Mill Museum, Lower Slaughter 185
The Old Quaker Meeting House, Ettington 210
Old Sodbury 60, 189
Overbury 76
Owlpen Manor 49, 231, 232
Oxford 10, 45, 46, 49, 51, **161–75**, *162–3*
Alice's Shop 171
Ashmolean Museum of Art & Archaeology 14, 162, **167**
Bodleian Library 162, 165
Christ Church 48, 164
colleges 164–5
Covered Market 171
Modern Art Oxford 166
Museum of Oxford 166
Museum of the History of Science 166
Oxford Botanic Garden 169
Oxford Castle Unlocked 165
Oxford Oratory Church of St Aloysius Gonzaga 169
Oxford University Museum of Natural History 165–6
Pitt Rivers Museum 13, 162, **168**
Radcliffe Camera 165
Rivers Thames and Cherwell 166, 169
St Edmund Hall 164
St Mary Magdalen 169–70
St Martin's Church 164
St Michael at the North Gate 170
Sheldonian Theatre 162, 165
University Church of St Mary the Virgin 164, 169
Wesley Memorial Church 170
Oxfordshire Museum, Woodstock 248, 249
Oxhill 181

P

Painswick 19, 21, 25, 30, 43, 52, 55, **176–8**
Painswick Rococo Garden 178
Painswick Beacon 17, 33, 43
Pitt Rivers Museum, Oxford 13, **168**
Pittville Pump Room, Cheltenham 91
Prestbury 30, 94
Prinknash 178–9
The Bird and Deer Park 179

R

Ramsden 54–5
Randwick 54
Ridgeway National Trail 172
The Rissingtons 179–80
River Cherwell 166, 169
River Thames 166, 169
Robinswood Hill Country Park 128
Rodborough Common 26, 28, 33, 46, 213
Rodborough Fort 213
Rodmarton Manor 111
Rollright Stones 17, 28–9, 33, 55, 103–4
Roman Amphitheatre, Cirencester 107–8
Rousham House 180–1
Royal Shakespeare Company, Stratford-upon-Avon 12, 200–1, **207**
Ruskin Mill College Gallery, Nailsworth 156

S

St Augustine's Farm, Arlingham 216
St Edmund Hall, Oxford 164
St James the Great Church, Snitterfield 210
St James the Great Church, Stoke Orchard 94, 116
St James wool church, Chipping Campden 96, 97
St John the Baptist Church, Burford 80, 82
St John the Baptist Church, Cirencester 106, 108–9
St Kenelm's Church, Minster Lovell 149
St Kenelm's Church, Witney 245
St Lawrence's Church, Bourton-on-the-Water 70
St Lawrence's Church, Oxhill 181
St Mary de Crypt Church, Gloucester 127
St Mary Magdalen Church, Oxford 169–70
St Mary the Virgin Church, Charlbury 85
St Mary the Virgin Church, Tetbury 219
St Mary the Virgin Church, Thornbury 229
St Mary the Virgin, Iffley 175
St Mary's Church, Bibury 66–7
St Mary's Church, Fairford 121–2
St Mary's Church, Shipton-under-Wychwood 183
St Mary's Church, Swinbrook 242
St Mary's Church, Tewkesbury 224
St Mary's Church, Witney 244–5
St Mary's Priory Church, Deerhurst 115, 116
St Michael and All Angels Church, Bishop's Cleeve 95
St Michael and All Angels Church, Stanton 192

St Michael at the North Gate, Oxford 170
St Michael's Church, Duntisbourne Rouse 111
St Nicholas' Church, Loxley 210
St Peter and St Paul Church, Northleach 159, 160
St Peter's Church, Winchcombe 237
Sapperton 21, 33, 110, 213
Selsley Common 33, 212
Sezincote House 151
Shakespeare Countryside Museum, Stratford-upon-Avon 200, 205
Shakespeare's Birthplace, Stratford-upon-Avon 12, **203**
Sheepscombe 26, 178, 216
Sheldonian Theatre, Oxford 162, 165
Shenberrow Hill 192
Sherborne 239
Sherborne Estate 241
Shipston-on-Stour 181–2
Shipton-under-Wychwood 182–4
  St Mary's Church 183
Slad 19, 35, 36, 38, 178, 215–16
Slad Valley 33, 35, 38, 214
The Slaughters 184–5
  Old Mill Museum 185
Slimbridge Wetland Centre 52, 65, **185–7**
Snowshill 26, 34, 48, 189
Snowshill Manor and Garden 47, **187–9**
The Sodburys 189–90
Soldiers of Gloucestershire Museum, Gloucester 127, 128
South Cerney 110, **190–2**
  Cotswold Water Park 52, 110, 190, 191
Stanton 34, 189, **192–3**, 194
  St Michael & All Angels 192
  Shenberrow Hill 192
Stanway 34, 189, 193
Stanway House 48, **193–4**
Stinchcombe Hill 118
Stoke Orchard 94, 116
Stow-on-the-Wold 42, 43, 45, 53, **195–7**
Stratford-upon-Avon 10, 45, 51, **198–210**, *199*
  Anne Hathaway's Cottage 12, 199, **204**
  Hall's Croft 200, 202
  Harvard House 200, 202
  Holy Trinity Church 199, 205–6
  Mary Arden's Farm 205
  Nash's House 202
  New Place 202
  Royal Shakespeare Company 12, 201, **207**
  Shakespeare Countryside Museum 200, 205
  Shakespeare's Birthplace 12, **203**
  Stratford Butterfly Farm 205
Stroud 19, 21, 23, 33, 35, 45, 46, 51, 52, **211–16**
  Museum in the Park 212, 214
  Woodchester Mansion 213, 214
Stroudwater Canal 213
Sudeley Castle 15, 43, 48, 63, **217–18**, 235
Swinbrook 241
Syde 94

T

Taynton 240
Temple Guiting 19, 133–4
Tetbury 44, 46, 52, 53, 54, 55, **219–22**
  St Mary the Virgin Church 219
  Tetbury Police Museum & Courtroom 219
  Westonbirt Arboretum 15, 55, **220**
Tewkesbury 223–8
  Church of St Mary 224
  Croft Farm Waterpark 228
  John Moore Museum 226, 227
  Merchant's House 227
  Out of the Hat Heritage Centre 227
  Tewkesbury Abbey 223–4, 227
  Tewkesbury Museum 225, 227–8
Thames and Severn Canal 190
Thornbury 229–30
  Church of St Mary the Virgin 229
  Thornbury and District Museum 229
  Thornbury Castle 229
Toadsmoor 19, 33
Toddington 235
Tredington 181
Turkdean 75
Tyndale Monument 118, 190, 253, 254

U

Uley 230–2
  Hetty Pegler's Tump 231, 232
  Matara Gardens of Wellbeing 231, 232
  Owlpen Manor 49, 231, 232
  Uley Bury 17, 23, 33, 230–1
University Church of St Mary the Virgin, Oxford 164, 169
Upper Rissington 48
Upper Slaughter 34, 47, 184–5
Upper Swell 196

W

Wellington Aviation Museum, Moreton-in-Marsh 151
Wesley Memorial Church, Oxford 170
Westonbirt Arboretum 15, 55, **220**
Whatcote St Peter 182
Whittington Court 232–3
Widford church 240
The Wilson, Cheltenham 90
Winchcombe 17, 18, 34, 43, 47, 51, **233–9**
  Belas Knap 16, 33, 140, 235, 239
  Cleeve Common 33, 140, 235, 236
  Gloucestershire Warwickshire Railway 51, 52, 237
  Hailes Abbey 235
  Hailes Church 237
  St Peter's Church 237
  Winchcombe Folk & Police Museum 234, 235
Windrush 239
The Windrush Valley 239–42
Winson 112
Withington 111
Witney 242–5
  Cogges 243
  North Leigh Roman Villa 244
  St Kenelm's Church 245
  St Mary's Church 244–5
  Witney and District Museum 242–3
Woodchester 28, 37, 213
Woodchester Mansion 213, 214
Woodstock 42, 47, **246–51**
  Blenheim Palace 14, 21, 47, **247–8, 250**
  Oxfordshire Museum 248, 249
Wotton-under-Edge 26, 28, 33, 65, **252–4**
  Newark Park 253
  Wotton-under-Edge Heritage Centre 253
Wyck Rissington 180
Wychwood Forest 26

The Automobile Association wishes to thank the following photographers and organisations for their assistance in the preparation of this book.

Abbreviations for the picture credits are as follows – (t) top; (m) middle; (b) bottom; (l) left; (r) right; (c) centre; (AA) AA World Travel Library.

4tl AA/S Day; 4tr AA/H Palmer; 4b AA/J Tims; 5r AA/D Hall; 5bl AA/J Tims; 8–9 AA/S Day; 11 AA/H Palmer; 12t AA/H Palmer; 12b Matthew Barnes/Alamy; 13bl Courtesy of Pitt Rivers Museum, University of Oxford; 13tl The National Trust Photolibrary/Alamy; 13mr Courtesy of Cotswold Wildlife Park; 14t AA/C Jones; 14m Courtesy of Birdland; 14b AA/J Tims; 15t AA/M Moody; 15m Courtesy of Cotswold Motoring Museum & Toy Collection; 15b AA/K Doran; 16 AA/D Hall; 18 AA/S Day; 19 AA/H Palmer; 20 AA/S Day; 21 AA/C Jones; 22 AA/D Hall; 23 AA/D Hall; 24 AA/S Day; 24–5 AA/T Souter; 27 AA/S Day; 29 AA/S Day; 31 AA/F Stephenson; 32 AA/P Baker; 35 AA/K Doran; 36 Martin Beddall/Alamy; 36–7 Colin Underhill/Alamy; 39 AA/R Rainford; 40 Tim Gainey/Alamy; 41 AA/K Doran; 42 AA/D Hall; 43 AA/S Day; 44 Simon Reddy/Alamy; 45 Stephen Shepherd/Alamy; 47 AA/J Tims; 50 AA/S Day; 53 AA/F Stephenson; 54 AA/S Day; 56 AA/A Burton; 58–9 AA/M Moody; 61 Homer Sykes/Alamy; 64 AA/D Hall; 66 AA/D Hall; 69 AA/D Hall; 70 AA/D Hall; 73 Courtesy of Cotswold Motoring Museum & Toy Collection; 74 Courtesy of Birdland; 79 AA/S Day; 81 Courtesy of Cotswold Wildlife Park; 86 dk/Alamy; 91 AA/R Duke; 92 AA/R Duke; 98 AA/S Day; 104 AA/T Souter; 107 AA/R Duke; 112 AA/S Day; 116 AA/S Day; 119 AA/S Day; 126 AA/H Palmer; 131 AA/H Palmer; 134 AA/C Sawyer; 135 AA/S Day; 136 AA/S Day; 139 AA/D Hall; 141 AA/D Hall; 145 AA/K Doran; 149 AA/S Day; 155 SFL Travel/Alamy Stock Photo; 9 AA/S Day; 161 AA/J Tims; 165 AA/J Tims; 167 AA/J Tims; 168 Courtesy of Pitt Rivers Museum, University of Oxford; 171 AA/J Tims; 172 AA/J Tims; 176 AA/S Day; 183 AA/K Doran; 186 AA/R Duke; 194 AA/A Lawson; 198 AA/M Moody; 201 AA/H Palmer; 203 AA/H Palmer; 204 AA/J Wyand; 207 Matthew Barnes/Alamy; 209 AA/M Moody; 211 AA/D Hall; 212 AA/K Doran; 217 AA/F Stephenson; 220 AA/M Moody; 223 AA/D Hall; 225 AA/F Stephenson; 226 AA/D Hall; 231 AA/S Day; 234 AA/D Hall; 236 AA/D Hall; 240travellinglight/Alamy Stock Photo; 243 AA/S Day; 245 AA/M Birkitt; 246 AA/C Jones; 249 AA/H Palmer; 250 AA/C Jones; 254–5 Cotswolds Photo Library/Alamy

Every effort has been made to trace the copyright holders, and we apologise in advance for any unintentional omissions or errors. We would be pleased to apply any corrections in any following edition of this publication.

Series editor: Rebecca Needes
Author: Damian Hall
Updater: Anita Sach
Project editor: Karen Kemp
Proofreader: Dominique Shead
Designer: Kat Mead
Digital imaging & repro: Ian Little
Art director: James Tims

Additional writing by other AA contributors. *Lore of the Land* feature by Ruth Binney. Some content may appear in other AA books and publications.

Has something changed? Email us at travelguides@theaa.com.

YOUR TRUSTED GUIDE

The AA was founded in 1905 as a body initially intended to help motorists avoid police speed traps. As motoring became more popular, so did we, and our activities have continued to expand into a great variety of areas.

The first edition of the AA Members' Handbook appeared in 1908. Due to the difficulty many motorists were having finding reasonable meals and accommodation while on the road, the AA introduced a new scheme to include listings for 'about one thousand of the leading hotels' in the second edition in 1909. As a result the AA has been recommending and assessing establishments for over a century, and each year our professional inspectors anonymously visit and rate thousands of hotels, restaurants, guest accommodations and campsites. We are relied upon for our trustworthy and objective Star, Rosette and Pennant ratings systems, which you will see used in this guide to denote AA-inspected restaurants and campsites.

In 1912 we published our first handwritten routes and our atlas of town plans, and in 1925 our classic touring guide, *The AA Road Book of England and Wales,* appeared. Together, our accurate mapping and in-depth knowledge of places to visit were to set the benchmark for British travel publishing.

Since the 1990s we have dramatically expanded our publishing activities, producing high quality atlases, maps, walking and travel guides for the UK and the rest of the world. In this new series of regional travel guides we are drawing on more than a hundred years of experience to bring you the very best of Britain.